A NEW LOOK AT KABIR

A NEW LOOK AT KABIR

Krishna P. Bahadur

Ess Ess Publications

4837/24, ANSARI ROAD, DARYA GANJ
NEW DELHI-110002
PH.: 3260807

First Published 1997

ISBN : 81-7000-205-2

Rs. 495/-

Published by
Ess Ess Publications
4837/24, Ansari Road, Darya Ganj
New Delhi-110 002 Ph. 3260807

Composed by
Classic Computer Services
RZ 128/6K Lane No. 9 East Sagar Pur,
New Delhi-110 046 Ph. 5529455

Printed at: Mehra Offset Press

FOR MY WIFE

FIFTY YEARS' COMPANIONSHIP
4 MAY 1946 TO 4 MAY 1996

गृम्णामि ते सौभागत्वाय हस्तं मया पत्या जरदष्टिः यथा असः
भगः अर्यमा सविता पुरधिः मह्यम् त्वा अदुः गहपत्याय देवाः
ऋग्वेद १०.८५.३६

('For the sake of happiness, I take you by your right hand:
That you may reach old age along with me.
By God's grace and my good fortune.
Aryamā, Sāvitra and Purundhi have given you to me
So that we may run our home together in prosperity'.)

— WHAT THE BRIDEGROOM SAYS TO HIS BRIDE AT THE HINDU WEDDING CEREMONY

A NOTE ON THE PRONUNCIATION OF VERNACULAR WORDS

The letter 'o' (which bears no diacritical mark) is pronounced as *o* in 'm*o*re' (not as in 'lion'). The *m* nasalizes and lengthens the preceding vowel as *n* in bo*n* (French). The *ch* sound is also not to be found in English. It is pronounced with the tip of the tongue placed higher against the upper palate than in uttering the *c* sound.

The cerebrals (*t*, *th*, *d*, *dh*, *n*) are pronounced with the tongue retroflected. The dentals (*t*, *th*, *d*, *dh*, *n*) are pronounced with the tongue against the back of the upper front teeth.

Other marks are explained as follows:-

a as *u* in c*u*t

a as *a* in f*a*ther

i as *i* in f*i*t

i as *i* in mach*i*ne

u as *u* in p*u*t

u as *u* in r*u*le

e as *ay* in m*ay*

n as *n* in wi*n*g

sh as *s* in *s*ugar

g as *g* in *g*oad

t as *t* in *t*ongue

t, *d*, *n* are dentals

d as *d* in *d*ent

c as *ch* in *ch*urch

Other letters may be pronounced as they are in English. The letter 'n' on which a curved mark is put--n is to be pronounced as n in Senor (Spanish).

PREFACE

tananā bunanā sabhu tajio hai kabīra
hari kā nāmu likhi līo sarīra

DISCOVERING KABĪR

Kabīr was a Moslem weaver living in Kashi (modern Varanasi) or in a village near it called Magahar. As in the case of many other saints and poets of India, we have very little authentic details about his life and times. Most probably he lived in the second half of the fifteenth century and died in the early part of the sixteenth, as Farquahar and Keay believe though according to some scholars it was much earlier. While it is certain he expressed himself in verse it is questionable how many ascribed to him are really his. Scholars like P.N. Tiwari, Dr Mata Prasad, S.S. Das and so forth, have tried to find out, but in the end despite all the researches, one can't be sure. The literary quality of the verses depicts a kind of seesaw between the crude and the sublime, and leaves a strong suspicion that they couldn't possibly be from the same pen. Kabīr had no education whatever. 'I never touched ink or paper' he says 'nor did I hold a pen'. His verses were, as he admitted 'by word of mouth'. Then, how have they come down to us in massive anthologies and recensions? The only way it could be possible is that devoted disciples noted them down. Some of these scripts were preserved (two of them have been reproduced in the illustratons in this book), but their genuineness is doubtful. Learning is not essential for inspired utterances, particularly poetry which as Keats says comes naturally as 'leaves to a tree'. The author once came across an ascetic in the district of Muzaffarnagar (U.P.) near Delhi, who could rattle off spiritual verses (couplets), most of them very striking, extempore. So all the evidence we have of the authenticity of Kabīr's verses are these handwritten script of doubtful origin. That's not much to go upon. But nonetheless we have to make do with what we have.

It is this uncertainty indeed which results in the numerous contradictions we find in what these verses depict, which makes the likelihood of their being compositions of different persons even more. Kabīr condemns idol-worship, yet his *Padas*, *Sākhīs* and *Ramainīs* have innumerable references to Hindu gods like Krishna, Rāma, Hari and Shiva. Mythological references concerning Hinduism abound. He is against avatars, yet sings their praises. Foreign writers believe the Indian scholars of Kabīr have unnecessarily tried to project Kabīr as a Hindu spiritualist. If the very fact of being born a Moslem debars one from expressing sentiments that are akin to Hinduism, these western writers are quite right. But if such proclivities cut across race, nationality and birth, then a human being may incline to any belief that appeals to him. Sister Nividetta, Rasakhan Abdur Rahim Khana-khana the Sūfī saints, and others, are testimony to this. The Sūfīs, despite being staunch Moslems, had much in common with Vaiṣṇavaism. It isn't the Indian scholars who have tried to Hinduize Kabīr as Charlotte Vaudeville puts it (*A Weaver Named Kabīr*)— 'the evident anxiety displayed by S.S. Das to "hinduize" Kabīr' which 'appears somewhat coloured by the rising Hindu patriotism of the time'. Apart from mixing religion with politics, such a view conceives religious belief—and religion includes philosophy too— as a kind of ancestral heritage, which it certainly is not, for we find such a great thinker as Schopenhauer saying about the *Upaniṣads* 'There is no study... so beneficial and as elevating as that of the *Upaniṣads*. They are the products of the highest wisdom. *They are destined sooner or later to become the faith of the people*'; and Paul Deussen. 'The *Upaniṣads* formulate philosophical conceptions unequalled in India *or perhaps anywhere in the world*'. It is not the Hindu scholars who have 'Hinduized' Kabīr, it is Kabīr who has 'Hinduized' himself. Or else he could never have said: 'I was on the *haj* pilgrimage bound for Kaabaa when *Ḳhudā* met me on the way and said sternly "Who ordered you to slaughter cows?" '(*Sākhī* 32- *Sakhīs From the Guru Grantha Sahib*);[1] or while quoting the sage Ravidāsa, that one who does not put his trust in Hari but worships other gods will go to hell (*Sākhī* 38 of the same section). He even goes to the extent of saying: 'That family is good in which there is a devotee of Hari. The family in which there is no such devotee is useless as a barren *ḍhāka* or *palasa* tree'.[2] Such observations are spread all over Kabīr's verses.

Though very much a householder, with two wives living, we find Kabīr lambasted women calling them hell's cesspool and even berated conjugal love [*Sākhīs* 2 and 3 (12) Lasviciousness], which is again another contradiction in him and may be due to his personal exasperation with one of his wives who was a flirt and a shrew. Nonetheless his bawl out in regard to women would infuriate the protagonists of the women's lib.

KABĪR'S RĀMA

Kabīr professed himself to be a believer in the one Formless *Brahman* (the Cosmic Absolute). This *Brahman* (or *Brahma*) envelopes the universe and yet is outsid it— *guna meṁ niraguna niraguna meṁ guna* and:

pyaṇḍa brahmāṇḍa kathai saba koī
vākai ādi aru anta na hoī
pyaṇḍa-brahmāṇḍa chāṁṛi je kahiye
kahai kabīra hari soī

This *Brahma*, Hari, or Rāma is in the soul of all creatures— *ghaṭi ghaṭi rahyau samāī*. This spirit is subtle not coarse or material— *thūla nahiṁ asthūla*. Kabīr is dead against the Hindu belief of avatar. Thus the gods he speaks of in his verses— Rāma, Govinda, Keshava (names of Krishna) Shiva, Hari and so forth— are meant in the sense of the Hindu Īśvara. Yet we find illusions to Hindu mythology and they presuppose an avatar. Unless we take these verses (they are among his *Padas*) to be spurious or later accretions, it seems the Kabīr's opposition to avatars was watered down by his references to them. And that would add to the contradictions in his thought. He positively believed that the formless Rāma he spoke of can be worshipped. The devotee can become one with him (*ekameka*). He (*Rāma*) can easily be attained by love because that Formless One is contained in all bodies and indeed in everything (*bhūta*) having form.[3]

The view is much the same as that in the *Bhagavadgītā* where after showing Arjuna his Cosmic Form (*virāṭa rūpa*)

Shrī Bhagavāna Says (11.54): 'I can be seen, Arjuna, by single-minded devotion. In this way I can indeed be known, seen and realized'.[4] While Kabīr emphasizes the formless *Brahman* believing it to be of the same nature as the *ātman*— a view akin to the Vedānta— he also conceives the Īśvara or Vāsudeva of the *Gītā*. He keeps wavering between monism and duality.

We also find the other elements of Hinduism in Kabīr, as for example maya, the Sāṁkhya doctrine of the *guṇas* and references to Tantra and the *kuṇḍalinī*. Maya, he says is God's power which hides the truth. People are deceived by it because though on the surface it appears attractive and sweet. (*kabīra māyā mohanī jaisī mīṭhi khānḍa*), it's a sort of La belle dame sans Merci. The only way cut of its snare is devotion to God. The concept is much the same as found in Hindu philosophy. So too with the *guṇas*. He only can go beyond them (*guṇātīta*) who puts his trust in the divine. Kabīr very often speaks of Tantra, particularly of the six *cakras* (centres) believed by it to be in the spinal column, from the lowermost *mūladhāra* near the umbilical cord and the topmost one, the *sahastrāra*; the awakening of the *kuṇḍalinī*, *śabda* and the *anahata* sound of *laya* yoga.

He denounced all religious rites and practices which he believed to be mere show, such as pilgrimages, fasts, austerities and so forth among Hindus and *rozā*, *namāz*, *azān* circumcision etc., on the part of Moslems. Mere reading of the scriptures was no good. The *Veda*, the *Purāṇas* and the Quran are all false, he said. What was necessary was to see the Lord in one's own heart and to be completely devoted to him. He was particularly censorious of the Śaktas as they were often drunk and debauched, and were suspected to practise abominable *tāntrik* rites. 'A pig' he said 'is better than a Śākta. It keeps the village clean at least.' In principle he was right, but at times his utterances could hurt the devout. Kabīr seemed to forget that religion is largely a matter of faith and belief and to inject rationality in it is of no avail. Nevertheless his emphasis on love and devotion is praiseworthy.

LOVE

For Kabīr love has two aspects, the divine and the ecstatic. One is the soul's search for God, 'the worship the heart gives above' of which Shelley speaks.[5] Love looks not with the eyes but with the mind',[6] so it can never be told. Kabīr, too saya:

akatha kahānī prema kī, kach kahī na jāī
gūṁge kerī sarakarā, baiṭhe musakaī

Love, says Kabīr is completely devoid of sensual pleasure. It isn't physical love which finds expression in sex. yet it is endless bliss *rāma rasāina prema rasa, pīvata adhika rasāla*. It is heady wine which makes the devotee so drunk that the intoxication of love never leaves him:

harirasa pīyā jāṇiye, je kabahūṁ na jāi khumāra
maimantā ghumata rahai, nāhiṁ tana kī sāra

This love of Hari is rejuvenating, indeed so much that it is like the touch of the *pārasa* stone which transforms iron into gold:

sabai rasāiṇa maiṁ kiyā, hari sā aura na koi
tila ika ghaṭa meṁ sancarai, tau saba taṇa kancana hoi

But before one can hope to please God with his love he must shed all egoism and arrogance. So long as a man keeps saying 'I' he cannot come near to Hari. When he says 'It is thou O Lord, not I' then only can his love draw God toward him. Kabīr says:

prema na khetauṁ ūpajai, prema na hāṭi bikāi
rājā parajā jisa rucai, sira de so le jāi

('Love is not like crop which springs up in fields nor like goods on sale in a bazaar. It can be acquired by everyone whether king or commoner, the only qualification being that the person seeking it eschews all arrogance and egotism').

Love requires complete surrender. When it comes, desires for all sensual pleasures and material things (*vāsānās*) are ended. The mind becomes pure and all arrogance and cravings die away. The rain of divine love falls like manna from the heavens: *kabīra bādala prema kā hama para barṣyā āi*. There is no place in the heart of God's devotee for anyone except God. Kabīr expresses this in a very apt and striking metaphor. He says:

kabīra kājara rekhahū aba to daī na jāya
nainani prītama rami rahā, dūjā kahāṁ samāya

['My lover (God) has sunk so fully in my eyes that there is no space in them for anything at all not even for their being anointed with lamp-black']. When this stage comes God himself keeps calling for his devotee: *pāche lage hari phiraiṁ, kahaiṁ kabīra kabīra* ['Hari then keeps himself pursuing me (says Kabīr) calling out "Kabīr, Kabīr"!'].

SEPARATION AND UNION

Hindi mystic poets often express the soul's longing for God in symbols markedly erotic, which may often leave Western readers balled-up and occasionally some Indian ones too who are nurtured on western traditions. for example a prominent writer and journalist obsessed with sex, mistaking Mīrā Bāī's spiritual love for Lord Krishna for lasviciousness, wackily wrote in one of his columns that she was an adulteress! The Vaiṣṇava *mādhurya* kind of God-devotion, which is considered to be of the highest type, conceives the relation between God and the devotee as that of the lover and the beloved. Kabīr often expressed his longing for Hari in this mode. He is like a girl awaiting her lover's coming. Her heart aches for him and her mind is restless:

bahuta dinana kī jovatī, baṭa tumhārī rāma
jiva tarasai tujha milana ko, mana nāhīṁ viśrāma

'I will make my body a lamp' says Kabīr, 'with my soul as its wick and my blood as the oil in it. Burning the lamp, I will await my Lover's coming, so that I may be able to see his face'.[7] 'I can't stand this separation from you day after day, any longer, O Beloved. Either come to me and end it or else give me death'.[8]

When Mahendra (M.) a disciple of Shri Ramakrishna asked the sage 'Under what conditions does one see God?' he answered 'Cry to the Lord with an intensely yearning heart and you will certainly see him. People shed a whole jug of tears for wife and children. They swim in tears for money. But who weeps for God? Cry to him with a real cry.... Longing is like the rosy dawn. After the dawn out comes the sun. Longing is followed by the vision of God'.[9] Like Mīrā and others, Kabīr wept for God. 'My eyes have become red because of continually weeping for my Beloved (Lord)' he says, 'but people wrongly think they are so because of disease'.[10] Much like what Shri Ramakrishna said, Kabīr says, 'Leave laughter aside, and instead, weep. Can you ever hope to meet the Beloved, (i.e., the Lord) without shedding tears for him?'[11] Much of this is true. It is not the merrymakers and pleasure. Seekers who find God, but those whom the sorrows of the world make them turn away from it. As Browning says:

'Poor vaunt of life indeed,
Were man but formed to feed
On joy, to solely seek and find and feast:
....
Then welcome each rebuff
That turns earth's smoothness rough,....
Be our joys three-parts pain.....'[12]

Despite their high spiritual contents, Kabīr's verses on parting and meeting do not have Mīrā's poetic charm. One reason for this could be that while Kabīr pursued Hari as the Impersonal Cosmic Absolute, Mīrā's love was concentrated on the personal Krishna and to her he was all in all. Just as the sun's heat when spread out can give only diffused warmth, but when brought to a point through a magnifying glass it becomes intense enough to burn, Mīra's love was centred on her Govinda while Kabīr's was dispersed. Mīrā had only the single-minded desire for union with Krishna while Kabīr's objective was Hari's grace (*anugraha*)- *barasyā bādala prema kā, bhīji gayā saba anga*/ Mīrā did not wish for union by such indirect means. She wanted to mingle herself completely with Krishna-*anga se anga* ('limb to limb'). And as Shakespear says:

'Love is not love
When it is mingled with regards that stand
Aloof from the entire point'.[13]

KABĪR'S LANGUAGE

As Kabīr lived for the most part of his life in or nearabout Benares, his language was the one spoken in those parts, i.e., *pūrabī* (*pūraba-* 'east') or *bhojpuri.* He himself wrote in one of his *Sākhīs* 'My language is of the east' (*bolī hamārī pūraba kī*'). But here again critics, not being satisfied by what he himself said, have drawn the issue of language too into controversy, and P.Chaturvedi even stretches 'east' to signify 'the ultimate spiritual stage which is the aim of the yogis'![14] This, along with the other aspects of Kabīr's thought, namely his view of God, love, separation and meeting and so forth, touched upon briefly here; will be spoken of more fully in the introduction which follows. It will suffice to say that since the genuineness of all the verses ascribed to him is itself doubtful— he is said to have written forty to eighty works, or even more— we can't be sure that the various dialects in which we find them are really his. His language was rather rough, and does not have the mellifluous flow of Tulsī or Mīrā, and at times is rather forced. For example in one of his *Sākhīs* (*ślokas*) in the Guru Grantha Sahib (no. 35 in the translated ones included in this book) writing about the land required for a grave he says— *sāḍhe tīne hātha* (three and a half yards). That would be quite self-explanatory, but he goes on to add— *ghanī ta paune cāri* ('or maybe three and three fourth yards')! which is quite unnecessary, and has obviously been added just to complete the verse and conform to the couplet's form. However occasionally his metaphors and similes are striking, and his rugged language is particularly suitable for his satirical verses.

ESTIMATE

Some scholars have written encomiums on Kabīr, while others have said he wasn't a poet at all. The truth perhaps lies midway and the matter is all the more confused because of the uncertainty about his writings. That he was a man of high ideals and a true devotee of God, is beyond dispute. It is in no way sure, however, that he achieved *Brahma* knowledge, as he often claimed.. No one save himself could really know. According to Shankaracharya the knower of the *ātmā* (or *Brahman*) defies classification. he says of the *Brahman*-knower: '.... he wanders in the world, sometimes like a madman, sometimes like a child, having no more care for neatness of appearance, having no other clothes on his person except the quarters, or sometimes wearing clothes, or perhaps barks at other times.... Sometimes a fool, sometimes a sage, sometimes possessed of regal splendour, sometimes wandering. Sometimes keeping aloof, sometimes bearing a benign expression; sometimes honoured, sometimes insulted, sometimes unknown— thus lives the man of realization, ever happy with supreme bliss. Though without riches, yet content, though helpless yet very powerful, though not enjoying the sense-objects, yet eternally satisfied, though without an example, yet looking upon all with an eye of equality'.[15]

Kabīr led a homely life. he was desirous of the company of sages and doubtless spent his spare time with them much to the chagrin of his wife, Loī, and his in-laws. He did, however have some of the qualities of a *Brahma*-knower mentioned by Shankara. And we know that he miraculously thwarted the designs of Sikandar Shah to do away with him. Thus he had the quality, of being 'very powerful, though helpless' that Shankara mentions as a mark of the knower of the *ātmā*.

Kabīr tried to reform both Hindus and Moslems by decrying empty rituals carried out for show and rapping shibboleths. But his observations, though very rational and sensible, failed to make any impact. The fanatics of religions stuck to their fanaticism. And it is they who by making themselves prominent, often with the assistance of political patronage, guide and keep inflaming to frenzy, the followers of the particular religion they belong to. The saints of today are not a patch on that abstemious weaver, Kabīr, of few wants and of simple habits. These modern saints live in palatial mansions and have sex with young girls whom they euphemistically call their 'secretaries'. Even VVIP's are their fall guys. So too, in different ways, is the case with the Moslem controllers of Islam. These fanatics make it impossible for the peaceful observance of religious rites which becomes much like weaving a rope of sand. Religion is something inborn as one's mother tongue or the love of one's own country. Normally it aims a providing solace to mankind. But when uncompromising fanatics and militants take a hand in it, it is no longer balm for troubled minds but a state of violent disorder.

That said, it must be admitted that Kabīr's devotion to God, his longing for the divine and for emancipation, his rational view of religious observances and his concept of humanity being one vast brotherhood despite the differences, and above all his contented and simple living; make him one of the most universally loved and revered of saint-poets.

It is hoped this brief study of his life and times and the translation of a few of his verses, will succeed in creating interest in this renowned sage and will prove to be a small contribution towards understanding the nature of his ideals. The author is aware that some repetitions might have occurred in this narrative which is purely for emphasizing some point.

The verses of Kabīr quoted in the introduction have been given in their translated form in order to avoid a disjointed narrative. Their transliterated version will be found in the notes at the end of the book.

The author is grateful to his publisher for bringing out this book in these hard times and in an excellent format.

NOTES

1. The references are to the text contained in this book.
2. *kabīra soī kula bhalī jā kula hari ko dāsu*
   jiha kula dāsu na ūpajai so kula ḍhaka palāsu
3. *kahyaṁ na upajai upajaṁ nahiṁ jāṇai bhāva abhāva bihunā*
   udai asta jahāṁ mati-budhi nāhīṁ sahaji rāma lyau līnā
4. *bhaktyā tv ananyayā śākya ahaṁ evaṁ-vidho 'rjuna*
   jñātuṁ draṣṭum ca tattvena praveṣṭum ca paraṃtapa
5. One Word is too often Profained.
6. Shakespeare. *The Merchant of Venice.*
7. *yahi tana kā divalā karauṁ, bātī melauṁ jīva*
   lohū sīṁcauṁ tela jyauṁ, kaba mukha dekhauṁ pīva
8. *kai virahina ko mīcu dai, kai āpa dikhalāya*
   āṭha pahara kā dājhanā, mo pai sahāna na jāya
9. *The Gospel of Sri Ramakrishna* by M.Trans. Swami Nikhilanand Madras: Sri Ramakrishna Math, 1964, p., 7.
10. *aṁkhaṅiyā prema kasāiyaṁ, loga jānai dukhaṅiyāṁ*
    sāiṁ apane kāraṇaiṁ, roi-roi rataṅiyāṁ
11. *kabīra haṁsanā dūra kara, kara rovana soṁ citta*
    bina roye kyoṁ pāie, prema piyārā mitta
12. Robert Browning. *Robbi Ben Ezra.*
13. Shakespeare. *King Lear.* Act 1, scene 1.
14. P. Chaturvedi. *kabīr sahitya kī parakh.* Prayaga. pp., 209-10. Quoted. C. Vaudeville. *A Weaver Named Kabīr.* Oxford, 1993, p., 119.
15. *Vivekachuḍāmaṇī.* Trans. Swami Madhvananda, 542-43.

CONTENTS

ACKNOWLEDGEMENTS

The author gratefully acknowledges the assistance of the following Hindi works in the compilation of the English translation of Kabīr's verses:

Gupta, Dr Mata Prasad. *Kabīr Granthāvalī*. Allahabad: Sahitya Bhawan Pvt. Ltd. 1985.

Singh, Dr Jagdeva and Dr Vāsudeva. *Kabīr Vāṇī Pīyūṣa*. Varanasi: Vishvavidyalaya Prakashan, 1976.

Varma, Ramakumar. *Sant Kabīr* Allahabad: Sahitya Bhawan Ltd. 1947.

-----------X----------

The author is also indebted to Vaudeville, C. *A Weaver Named Kabir* Delhi: OUP, 1991 for the compilation of the Bibliography in this book.

-----------X----------

jala mem kumbha, kumbha mem jala hai,
bāhira bhītara pānī
phūṭā kumbha, jala jalahi samāyā
yaha tataha samajaho jñānī

KABĪR

('There is water outside and inside the pot. When the pot breaks the water is one. So too the Soul becomes one with the Absolute')

ḥamāre rāma rahīma karīma keso,
alaha rāma sati soī
bisamila meṭi bisambhara ekai,
aura na dūjā koī

KABĪR

('The Formless Brahma goes by different names—Rāma, Rahīma, Govinda Keśava, Karīma, Allah')

INTRODUCTION

kabīra kāni rākhī nahīṁ varṇāśama ṣaṭ darasanī
bhakti vimukh jo dharama tahi adharama kari gāyav
joga jagya vrata dāna bhajan bina tuccha dikhāyau
hindū turaka pramāna ramainī sabhī sākhi
pacchapāta nahiṁ bacata sabati ke hita kī bhākhī
ārūṛha hasā vhai jagata par, mukha dekhī nahina bhanīṁ
kabīra kāni rākhī nahiṁ varṇāśma ṣaṭ darasanī

Bhaktamāla

(Kabīr did not acknowledge caste distinctions nor saw any truth in the Six Systems of Hindu philosophy, Nor did he accept the four divisions of life (*āśaramas*). To him religion shorn of devotion was useless and it was no use practising ascetism; fasting or giving alms without singing God's praises. He taught Hindu and Turk religion by his *Ramainīs*, *Śabdas* and *Sākhīs*. He did not distinguish between sects, but taught what was of benefit to all. He spoke forcefully, not caring for what men might say).

KABĪR THE REFORMER

Kabīr has been praised to the skies by writers and critics in honeyed phrases like 'one of the best-known and most revered names in Indian tradition,' 'the father of Hindi literature,' 'one of the greatest (poets) known in India and elsewhere'; and so forth. He has been likened to Tulīdāsa, the author of the *Rāmacaritamānasa* and even to Lord Buddha! and in his writings to the Gospel of St John! This is really laying it on too thick and the comparison to Buddha and St John is outlandish. Lord Buddha (whom Hindus have accepted as divine and in faet one of the incarnations of Viṣṇu) founded a faith that has become one of the world religions and Kabir can't compare with founders of religion. Although he composed verses which were later written down, he can't be called a conventional Hindi poet for he had neither style nor embellishment (*śailī* and *alankāra*). As poets, Tulsī (who was both a saint and a poet), Bihārī Keshavadāsa and many others, were by far superior.[1] Nonetheless Kabīr stands out among mystics of the Ramanand tradition, in line with others like Ravidāsa a cobbler, Dhanna, a peasant, and among the higher echelons, Mīrabāī and Pīpā. These mystics, except some, like Mīrā, were largely from the lower classes as distinguished from caste Hindus, particularly brahmins. Kabīr was, as he himself says in various verses, a weaver (julāhā).[2] He nowhere says whether he was a Hindu or a Moslem and so there could only be guesses about it. The general belief is that he was a Moslem or a convert to Islam, though this could at best be a surmise, for he calls himself a *korī* too at places.[3] *Korīs* were Hindus, though, like the *julāhās*, they too were relegated to the lower castes. The *julāhā* were concentrated in eastern Uttar Pradesh, particularly in the districts of Gorakhpur, Basti, Azamgarh and spreading out into the provinces of Bihar and and Bengal. Whatever might be Kabīr's religion, his own *think* was more akin to Hinduism than to Islam. He mentioned many Hindu terms such as maya, karma (or karam) *pūrab janam* (*purva janam,* i.e., 'past life') and so forth, as also many Hindu gods and sages such as Brahmā Viṣṇu and Maheśa (Śiva) the gods of the Hindu trinity, Krishna and Rāma, incarnations of Viṣṇu, and sages like Nārada, Sanaka, Yājñavalkya Dattrāteya, Vyāsa and Vasiṣṭha.

Many saints and reformers and a few politicians too, have tried to effect a synthesis of Hinduism and Islam and bridge the gap between them. There have been a few Moslems like Raskhan, Dara, the royal Moslem patron of Hindu culture, and the Sūfīs, who by their personal lives have tried to bring about a hook-up. These, however, are lone examples. Kabīr, too, was one of those who tried to do so, and that is considered to be his most significant achievement. There are two ways in which reformers try this tie-up. One is by persuading the two communities to come together and forget the differences, and the other to lambaste both. The first method was adopted by people like Gandhi and Swami Rama Tirtha, and the other—giving the rap—by saints like Swami Dayananda who tongue-lashed not only orthodox Hinduism and Islam, but also all other faiths. Kabīr's approach towards Hinduism and Islam was of the Dayananda variety. For example in one of his verses he blasts the Moslem belief in the observance of Ramzān and the sacret formula, the Kalimā 'Allah is God and Mohammed is his Prophet' and says Kaabaa, the most sacred place for a Moslem, is in one's own soul, not anywhere else[4] He condemns Hindus who keep chanting the Vedas and the sacred Gāyatrī *mantra*, yet sacrifice animals to the goddess Kali. He deprecates the practice of giving alms to brahmins during an eclipse (to ward off its evil effect), the *mundan* ceremony (in which a child's head is shaved), *brahmacarya* (continence), the Vedantic belief that the Cosmic Absolute (*Brahman*) and the soul (*atman*) are of the same nature, the god Śiva's praise of Rāma (calling yogis who meditate, pundits who read the Purāṇas ascetics and sannyasis and even Śiva, mad). He dismisses the Veda and Quran as false and says that the pandits who read their holy books go to hell. He castigates the Shāktas, gives the go-over to the image-worshipper, *jaws* the muezzin who goes up the minaret of the mosque to call the *azān* and gives short shrift to the Moslem rite of circumcision by the simplimism that this implies Moslem women are not Moslems!

KABĪR'S RĀMA

Kabīr appears to confuse mythology and ritual with philosophy. Religion comprises both, and though rituals and mythology are a sizable part of it, they aren't its crux. The aspects of Hinduism and Islam which Kabīr denounces (*mundan*, circumcision and so forth) are their rituals. Having had no systematic education in Sanskrit, (the script of Hindu scriptures like the *Gītā*, *Upanisads* and the *Brahmasūtras*) which he contemptuously dismisses as 'the stagnant water in a well', or of Arabic, the language of the Holy Quran, to ridicule or pan out on what one is ignorant of, can't be called commendable criticism. Kabīr rejects both the Quran and the Veda as well as the Six Systems of Hindu philosophy including Pātanjali's Yoga, and the Vedānta, without even knowing what they were about! As regards rituals, they are based more on superstition and blind faith than on reason, and so it is easy to criticize and condemn them. While philosophy is the meeting ground of religions, rituals and mythology keep them apart so that 'The religion of one seems madness unto another'.[5] Having pulled ritualism to pieces and driven out the gods from temples and the muezzins from minarets, what has Kabir to offer in their place? We find the word 'Rāma' scattered throughout his utterances, but this does not imply Tulsī's Rāma, the incarnation of Lord Viṣṇu, for it is clear beyond doubt that he never believed in God incarnating himself as Krishṇa says in the *Gītā* (4.7-8). In his verses Kabīr says: 'When neither the earth nor the sky were in existence, then tell me, folk, from where did Nanda (believed to be Krishna's foster father) come? Saints sing the praises of That which is neither born nor dies, which is beyond all sorrows, and is never destroyed. This Nanda has gone through eighty-four lakh births! (so how can he be an incarnation's foster father)[6].... O Lord, people call you the lifter of the mount Goverdhan, when really all mountains are the dust of your feet and the seven seas are as though lamp-black for your eyes'.[7] Nor is Kabir a *saguna-bhakta*, i.e., a worshipper of God with form (Ishvara or Vāsudeva), even though he does not altogether reject such devotion, as is evident from some of his verses, quoting only one of them:

> *jākai nābhi padam a sum udita brahmā, carana ganga taranga re*
> *kahai kabīra hari bhagati bāmchūm, jagata gura gobyanda re*

(Govinda is in truth the Master of the universe. Kabīr says I sing the praises of that Hari (Viṣṇu) from whose navel Brahmā (the Creator) issued and from whose feet the waters of the river Ganga flowed).[8]

While it must be admitted that there are only a few stray verses denoting dualism, it does show that Kabīr had flexibility in his attitude towards religion, for no Mohammedan would express veneration for Viṣṇu, and the other Hindu gods and sages we come across in his verses. Besides it does involve some confusion of thought, for he says he does not recognize avatars, and yet speaks of Viṣṇu, and in one verse of Narasimga (the Man-Lion incarnation of the god) also. Nonetheless in general he is a monotheist, and one should not forget that there is considerable difference of opinion about the verses which are genuinely his, so that the few which depict a dualist attitude might not be his at all. But then the question arises what exactly is this monism, this One Unseen whom he calls Rāma, beyond destruction and change, birth and death? Critics distinguish Kabīr's concept of this qualitiless (*nirguṇa*) Rāma from the *Brahman* (Cosmic Absolute) of the *Upanṣhads*. According to them his Rāma is outside the universe, yet completely pervades it. In one of his verses he says:

'O sages do not be misled. There are qualities in the qualitiless and in the qualitiless there are qualities (*guṇa meṁ nirguṇa, nirguṇa meṁ guṇa*). He (my Hari, or Rāma) has no relation with anyone, no form or shape (*nāti-svarūpa,varaṇa nahim jāke*). He is everywhere and all space is filled by him (*ghaṭi ghaṭi rahau samai*). He is without beginning or end, both outside the universe as well as in it'. Since Rāma is in everyone he can easily be known by love. This concept is substantially not any different from that of the Vedānta, and the critics seem to be pussyfooting when they think the two to be at variance. The Vedānta equates the soul with *Brahman* in expressions like *aham brahmāsmi, joham soham*, and so say the very thing Kabīr points out in his verses:

seī tumha seī hama ekai kahiyat, jab āpā par nahīṁ jāṃnāṁ
jyūṁ jala maiṁ jala paisi na nikasai, kahai kabīra mana māṁnāṁ

['There is no difference between you and me, (i.e., between the soul and Rāma) just as water when mixed with water are the same— so says Kabīr']. The same thought is expressed in another verse of his also:

maiṁ taiṁ taiṁ dvai nāṁhīṁ
āpai akala sakla ghaṭa māṁhīṁ
ātamalīna akhaṇḍita rāṁāṁ
kahai kabīra hari māṁhi samāṁāṁ.

('There remained no difference between "You" and "me" and the soul mingled with the World Soul. Thus the *ātmān* became one with the infinite Rāma'.) The Vedānta says the same in the Vedāntic expression *aham brahmāsmi*, i.e., *ātmān* (the soul) is the same as *Brahman*.

DEVOTION AND LOVE

How is this Rāma Kabīr conceives, to be realized? Obviously some bond has to be established between this *nirguṇa* Rāma and the devotee otherwise he would remain only a concept of the mind. This realization is by means of love and devotion; and in this we approach the view of the Vaiṣṇavas and also of the Vedanta (as interpreted by the dvaitists). The chanting of Rāma's name is advocated by Kabīr in many of his verses. By repeating Rāma's name one achieves not merely nearness to him, he becomes in truth one with Rāma:

merā mana sumirai rāma kūṁ, merā mana rāmahiāhi

ib mana rāmahi hvai rahyā, sīsa navāvaum̐ kāhi

('My mind remembers Rāma's name, nay, it is Rāma itself. When my mind has become Rāma, to whom am I to bow?')

He believes that if even the thought of Rāma enters the mind, all the countless ill-effects of karma are destroyed, otherwise no good can ever come to the man:

koṭi karama pelai palaka maim̐, je rancaka āvai nāmum̐
aneka juga je puri karai, nahim̐ rāma bina ṭhamum̐

The height of Vaiṣṇava devotion is *mādhurya bhāva* which is expressed as the love of a man and a woman, the bliss of complete union, of which John Donne sings:

'Take me to you, imprison me, for I
Except you enthrall me, never shall be free,
Nor ever chaste except you ravish me'.[9]

The symbolism of a lover embracing his beloved is much older than either Kabīr or the Vaiṣṇavas or the Sūfīs. In fact it goes back to about eight hundred years before the birth of Christ, when it was used to express the acme of spritual union: 'As a man clasping his wife limb to limb, is immersed completely in bliss and is unaware of everything else, the individual soul enfolded by the Supreme Soul (*prajña*) knows neither inside nor outside. It has fullfilled all desires and no longer craves for anything. It has transcended both desires and sorrows'.[10] Kabīr, addressing a *sakhi* (companion) in the pravalent poetic style, says 'O my friend. I have been blessed by my Lover's coming after a long time. It was my good fortune that I was able to meet him thus effortlessly. ....The place was suddenly full of light and I found myself asleep with my Lover on the bed. This is all due to you, my friend (that you united me with him. It was Rāma who by my good fortune thus deigned to come to me'[11] Kabīr has expressed his craving for Rāma in the usual manner of *śingāra-rasa* in terms of parting (*viraha*) and meeting (*milan*). In many ways he recalls Mīrā, who was also a saint-poet of north India, though of a high and ruling family of Mewāra. In the same vein as Kabīr, Mīrā wrote: 'Friend, I dreamt I married Krishna. There were five hundred and sixty million men in the marriage procession, with Krishna at its head. Festoons decked the gay pavilion. He took my hand in his making me his bride. Then the dream ended. it was only because of my good works friend, in my past lives that I could become his wife even in a dream'. In another verse Kabīr expresses a similar thought as in the one of his just quoted. He says: 'Listen O friend, Hari came to me when I was asleep and when he touched me I woke up. i was disappointed (because then I lost him). O friend, let us not delay, says Kabīr, hurry, for till there is life in this body, one should try to unite oneself with Jagannatha'.[12]

Mīrā, too, says much the same in one of her *padas* though she refers to Krishna, not to Jagannatha: 'When my eyes were closed (and I was dreaming), I found my Lover and when they opened, I lost him. Others miss lovemaking while sleeping, I miss it by waking!' For Kabīr, therefore, one approach to God is through devotion and love. This, includes the chanting of his name which brings one peace.

YOGA

The other approach to God is through yoga. Although he was against debased Tāntric practices even calling yogi's who practised concentration,'mad', he advocated Tantra-yoga as a means of realizing God. He recognizes the six *cakras* or centres. According to Tantra these are *mūlādhāra*, the region of the earth; *svadiṣṭhāna* which is just above that and is the region of water; *maṇipura* which is at the navel and represents fire; *anāhata* (air): *viśuddha* (ether)) at the base of the throat; and *ājñā* (psychic) between the eyebrows. By the piercing (*bheda*) of these six *cakras* the elements of which the body consists are purified, and thereby one reaches the Supreme. In one of his verses (*Padas*) he speaks of these six *cakras* as follows:

> *ṣaṭ cakra kaṁval bedhā, jāri ujārā kinhāṁ*
> *kāma krodha lobha moha, hāki syavaja dīnhāṁ.*

('I got rid of desire, anger, greed and attachment by removing darkness and seeing the light, when the six *cakras* were pierced').

Apart from these six centres that are believed to be in the body, there is one above called the *sahastrāra* or *śūryacakra* —Kabīr called this *gagan-maṇḍala* ('the region of the heavens)— which is above the head. it is also believed that there are very fine and subtle arteries called *nāḍis*, seventy-two thousand in number. According to Laya-yoga the *kuṇḍalinī* ('the Nature energy') is awakened by yogic practices, the main element of which is concentration, and thereafter this energy rises through the six *cakras* along the central artery of the subtle body, from the root at the base of the spinal cord to the thousand petalled lotus, the aforesaid *sahastrāra*, at the top of the head. When this is brought about, the aspirant is freed from all desires and attains peace. Another practice of Laya-yoga is to listen to the inner sound called *nāda* and see the soul's light. The yogi closes all the upper apertures of the body—ears, nose and mouth—with his fingers, and it is then that the *nāda* sound is heard. But Kabīr does not believe in doing so—*āṁkha na mūduṁ, kāna na rūdhuṁ, kāyā kaṣṭa na dhārūṁ*. ('I do not close my ears nor my eyes for I do not wish to torture my body in any way'). Coming back to Tantra-yoga, it believes that creation begins with sound (*nāda*), from *nāda* there is *bindu* and from *bindu, śabda* (the Word), from that the ethereal regions (*ākāśa*) and air, fire water and earth. The reversal of this process results in dissolution. It is easy to see how some writers have spoken of the influence of the Gospel of St John on Kabīr, for the Gospel begins by saying 'In the beginning was the Word, and the Word was with God, and the Word was God. The same was in the beginning with God. All things were made by him; and without him was not anything made that was made. In him was life; and the life was the light of men. And the light shineth in darkness; and the darkness comprehended it not'.[13] Kabir could not have any knowledge of *St John*, besides Tantra has a very ancient origin, and if one sees any similarity in language or thought it could only be accidental. in fact such similarities in great utterances are universal.

Kabīr doubtless conceived yoga as one of the ways

of reaching God, but he was against all outward show which the Hatha-yogis of his times indulged in like smearing the body with ashes, carrying all kinds of quaint iron rods (*cunṭīs*) and torturing the body by adopting intricate postures. He expressed his yoga as follows: 'O ascetic *avadhūta*, one does not become a yogi by adopting various postures or outward show. He should have devotion and love (for God). The *nāda* (sound) he hears is not that of the horn which is heard only till the horn is blown, but which is heard eternally. He remains absorbed in *Brahman* and savours the nectar of heavenly bliss. He experiences the *śūnya* and having awoken the *kuṇḍalinī* he never returns to worldliness. he wears old and torn clothes but his heart is clean and shines as a mirror. He does not sit and bathe at the confluence of the sacred rivers (the Ganga and Yamuna) but sits and directs his mind in the middle of the forehead between the eybrows. Kabīr says, such a man indeed is the king of yogis, (i.e., in truth a yogi) and his mind is always immersed in the *śūnya*'.[14]

Kabīr has been able to remove the dross from *Tantra-vidya*, and in doing so he has instinctively and in flashes of inspiration which only a saint-poet can be capable of, accomplished the task which took Sir John Woodroffe years to accomplish by studious research. Kabīr took the best out of both Tantra-yoga and Laya-yoga. But his yoga was more akin to Rāja-yoga which is the classical yoga of Pātanjali set forth in his *Yoga-sūtras* His quest was for Rāma (which is the infinite and the deathless *Brahman*) in all the three planes, the outer, the inner and the intermediary. Like the *Gītā*, however, Kabīr does not believe as Pātanjali did, that the aim of yoga is to destroy the mind-thought(*citta-vṛti mirodha*), but rather through meditation, to seek the Soul.

THE QUEST OF THE SOUL

Kabīr gives this quest the name *sahaja*, which is nothing else but the attainment of the knowledge of Rāma who resides in the hearts of all human beings. To know *sahaja* is not, however, easy. It is, as the *Upaniṣhad* says, 'hard to tread; much like walking on a blade sharp as a razor's edge'.[15]

'People keep on repeating "*sahaja*" "*sahaja*" again and again without understanding its import. It means, in truth, the abandonment of worldly pleasures and keeping all the five senses under control, having no attachment to sons, wife, wealth and sensual enjoyments. Kabīr, Rāma's slave has united himself with Rāma. *Sahaja* implies all those means by which one is able, to find Hari in this way, i.e., by becoming one with him'.[16]

Reverting to the yoga symbolism. Kabīr asserts that the state of union with Rāma which comes by *sahaja* is hearing the *nāda* (*ajapā apata suni abhi antara, yahu tata jānai soī*) and also by observing silence and realizing the soul within (*kahata kabīra soī jogesvar, sahaja suni lyauṁ lāgai*). Without God's grace it is difficult, nay impossible, to get rid of suffering. Giving an example Kabīr says that when there is a forest fire people rush with buckets of water to put it out, but what if the water itself emits fire? (*jalahiṁ māṁhi agani jau nikase*). In that case it is only Rāma who can extinguish the fire. Therefore, says Kabīr: 'You, O Govinda, are the redeemer as well as the means of redemption. I know no other. Kabīr says, I seek your refuge. I know no other gods'.[17] So much so, that in seeking Rāma one should be prepared to make the supreme sacrifice of laying down his life itself: 'The ambrosia of Rāma-love is very sweet indeed, but difficult to drink because he who drinks it must surrender his life. Many come to taste of it, but only he can do so who is ready to give up his life'.[18] Again he says 'O Kabīr, this house is of love; meant only for the mature (not children). Only he enters in it who can cut of his head from his body and make an offering of it'.[19] There are many such verses (*Sākhīs*) in the same strain, of which only one more may be mentioned because it contains the thought which is practically analogous to that of the *Kaṭha Upaniṣad* we have quoted before, about the path to knowledge of the soul being sharp as a razor's edge. Echoing the Upaniṣadic thought, Kabīr says:

> *kabīra bhagati duhelī rāma kī, jaisī khanḍa kī dhāra*
> *je ḍolai to kaṭi paṛai, nahīṁ to utarai pāra*

('Devotion for Rāma is not child's play. It's like the blade of a sword, and if one loses his balance even a little, he will be cut apart and fall. Only he who walks carefully will be able to make it').

Thus the quest of the soul is not at all easy. It implies sacrificing all joys and pleasures, and even life itself. The Holy Bible says 'For what shall it profit a man, if he shall gain the whole world, and lose his own soul?[20] Kabīr's *think* is much in the same vein. He also recalls Mīrā who is prepared to die for Krishna. Mīra's Krishnaism is much like Kabīr's Rāma-devotion, except that her Krishna was a deity whom she saw, loved and lived with, while Kabīr's stress was on the infinite *Brahman*. Kabīr believed that his Rāma was within himself—*bāhari khojata janama gammāyā unamanīṁ dhyāna ghaṭa bhītara pāyā* ('All my life I searched for him outside, but when I controlled my senses and meditated. I discovered he was inside me'), and so too Mīrā declared that her Lover (Krishṇa) was in her own heart, what need had she to go anywhere?— m*erā piyā mere hiya basata hai, na kahūm ātī jātī*. She is also ready to die for the Lord and even willing to reduce her body to ashes so that he may smear his body with them—*jala bala bhaī bhasma kī ḍherī, apane anga lagā jā*. Kabir's comparison of surrender of the body by reducing it to ashes must be taken in the same spirit, although he speaks of it as immolation of a widow on her husband's dead body. The comparison is only symbolic just as Mīrā's: 'Kabīr says, the sati, resolving to prove the vow of truth (*satya*), spread her bed on the faggots of wood. Taking her Lover in her lap she set it afire and burnt herself too with him'.[21] What this implies in not the barbarous rite of sati but that one ought to be prepared even to reduce his body to ashes for obtaining Rāma.

ARROGANCE

We have shown that according to Kabīr it is very difficult to taste the nectar of Rāma devotion, for this is not possible without keeping oneself aloof from the various sense-pleasure of living and the joys of existence. Yet to reach Rāma (which means for him to know the soul or

Brahman) one must forsake completely all such pleasures and also free himself from the pitfalls of devotion—kāma (desire) *krodha* (anger) *lobha* (greed) and *moha* (attachment). In the *Bhagavadgītā*, Krishṇa tells Arjuna what a hard pull is the withdrawing of the senses from their objects: 'Because, O Arjuna even if the person who is sincere about this task tries in all ways to control his senses, they are so powerful that they will prevail despite his efforts.'[22] So too Kabīr says that the wayward mind should be suppressed even if it means tearing it to pieces: 'Kabīr says, one should shatter the mind (which runs after the senses) to bits for if he plants the seeds of sense-pleasures there, it is his own ballywrack, for he will have to reap the harvest of sense-pleasures.'[23] But even after thus bringing the mind to blue ruin, Kabīr doubts if it will lose its appetite for sense-pleasures. He says 'I fear that even if the mind is destroyed it may again revive when fanned by the breeze of the senses. It's like a fish which even if cut to bits and put in the sling-net (*chīkā*), may retain some of its former nature'.[24] Thus recalls Śankarācārya 'The great *ahaṁkara* (egoism) even though apparently cut down to the roots, will if excited only for a moment by the mind, come to life again and cause a hundred distractions, just as during the rain, clouds are scattered about the storm'.[25] Still one should not despair, says Kabīr, for if one earnestly strives to control the mind it can yet be wrested from sense-pleasures. For then it becomes the Lord himself—*jemana rākhai jagat kari, tau āpaiṁ karatā soī*. In this again he appears to have drawn upon what Krishna says in the *Gītā*. Arjuna says that the mind is restless, obstinate and stubborn. It seems as difficult to curb as the wind'. Krishna says 'The mind is doubtless fickle and hard to subdue, O Arjuna, but it can be brought under control by sustained practice and dispassion'.[26]

VAIṢṆAVAISM IN KABĪR

Vaiṣṇavism, a the name implies, means the worship of Viṣṇu and following the *bhakti* cult. After the death of Rāmānuja, the Vaiṣṇava sage in 1137, the Vaiṣṇavas broke up into two sects, the Vaḍakalais who were Sanskritists and emphasized the *Vedas*, *Upaniṣads* and the *Gītā*, and th Tenkalais who were Tamilians in favour of the Tamil *Prabhandas*. Minor differences cropped up between them. The former enjoined self-effort. The Tenkalais however believed in the spontaneity of God's love and held that this comes without any effort. Also that God can, by his grace condone sins. A striking difference between the two was in their attitude towards the Sudras. The Tenkalais were more telerant in this, than the other school, and they believed that caste was no obstacls. Even low caste persons could recite the sacred *mantras* and be religious teachers (as for example, Raidas, Ravidās Kabīr and so forth).

The Sūfīs, too, were akin to Vaiṣṇavas, though it is a misnomer that the Vaiṣṇavas got their inspiration from the Sūfīs. In fact it is the other way around. Like the Vaiṣṇavas, Sūfīs extolled love. Ibn-El-Arabi said 'My religion is love'. According to Hazrat Inayat Khan 'Love is God, and it is sacrilege to speak of it repeatedly in vain. It is the divine spark within the heart. It implies universal love and the spirit of service'. The Sūfīs believed that those who love their fellow human beings, love God the most. Thus the Sūfīs' concept of love is much like the *bhakti* of the Vaiṣṇavas. They believe in the formless Cosmic Absolute as well as God as Self-revelation. There is one God, They say but he may have different names such as Allah, Khuda, Bhagavan, Īśvara and so forth. He exists in different forms, yet is beyond all forms. We can see the likeness of Kabīr's thought in these beliefs. In fact his Rāma is much like the Vedāntic *Brahman* and the Islamic Khuda. The Sūfīs looked on God as a Lover, much like the *mādhurya* concept of the Vaiṣṇavas. A verse of Rumi conveys almost identicaily what Kabīr himself staunchly believed:

'I found him not in church or temple,
Nor in a pagoda;
I found him not on the hill of Herat,
Nor in Kalandar or Kaf.
I searched in Kaabaa too, he was not there,
Nor could any holy man tell me the place:

Vain was my search, for his abode
Was nowhere but within my own heart'.

Ahmad, a native of Balkh (Afghanistan) said, 'God can be seen. Surely they are blind who cannot see him'. As Kabiṛ emphasized the giving up of all worldly pleasures, so too Rahya, son of Ma'az, also a native of Balkh, said, 'A Sūfī gives up all worldly pleasures. He does not desire even paradise. He desires only union with God and he cannot see any other than God'. Bayazid, another Sūfī, said, 'There is nothing apart from God. The cup, the wine and the drinker are one and the same. Sūfīsm means abjuring the world's pleasures and patiently accepting suffering'. According to Junaid of Nehawand, a Sūfī should detach himself from everything that is 'non-God'. We see in these doctrines a parallel to what Kabīr said about subduing the senses and forsaking all sense-pleasures. The Sūtīs, while being Moslems and believers of the Quran, were not so dogmatic as orthodox Moslems were. Amīr Khusrav even says:

'Though the Hindu is not faithful like me
He often believes in the same thing as I do'.[27]

And another Sūfī says:
'O you who sneer at the idolatry of the Hindu,
Learn also from him how worship is done.'[28]

As we have said, Kabīr tried to effect a synthesis between Islam and Hinduism. We find the Vaiṣṇava spirit in his verses as well as the Islamic. For example he says: 'The small thatched hut of Vaisnavaism is better better than a huge city.'[29] And again,'That lovely woman is praiseworthy who gives birth to a son who's a Vaiṣṇava, because he dwells in Rāma and so becomes fearless.... That family is good in which a devotee of Hari is born and a family which does not have such a person is as useless as an *arka* (swallowwort) or a *palasa* (*butea frondosa*) tree'.[30] For Kabīr a Vaiṣṇava chāṇḍāla (a man of the lowest caste) is to be counted as more meritorious than a brahmin, and such a one ought to be given a warm welcome and indeed considered as Gopāla himself![31] In one of his verses, after having spoken of several ways of attaining *mokṣa*, i.e., freedom from rebirth in this world, he mentions the *mulādhāra cakra* of Tantra yoga whose presiding deity is Lord Ganesha, but finally he places his trust in the *gopīs* (cowherd women) whose love for Krishna is said by the Vaiṣṇavas to be the highest from of love.[32] The *Bhāgavata Purāṇa* conceives passion as for a lover to be the highest form of devotion, 'Indeed the favour shown by the Supreme Being to the *gopīs* of Vrindāvana when in the *rāsa* sport he clasped them by the neck with his arms, was not enjoyed by Lakṣmī who is held to his heart, nor by the heavenly nymphs though blooming and odorous like the lotus, much less by other women'.[33] Thus the Vaiṣṇava faith, which is based on love for God, was predominant in Kabīr in spite of his being a strict monist.

PARTING AND MEETING

Hindi poets often express love in the form of separation and union. The difference between the poets of the *śṛṅgāra* tradition as for example Bihārī, Ghanānanda, Matirama. Senāpati and other and Kabīr, is that while they do not always speak of the pangs of separation of the soul from God and the joy of union with him—though sometimes their *nāyak* is Krishna and the *nāyikā, Rādhā, Kabīr*, even though using the same symbolism, invariably means the torment of the soul's parting with God: 'O Rāma, I who have been separated from you, ever keep looking down the pathway expecting you any moment. My heart longs to meet you and I know not a moment's rest'[34] 'I wish to burn my body, so that the smoke from it may rise heavenwards and maybe Rāma may take pity on me and cause rain to fall, so that the fire may be extinguished by it'.[35] He is even prepared to make his body a lamp and in it his heart as a wick and as the oil his own blood and light it to show the way for his Beloved Lord to come to him![36] Hari cannot by obtained by laughter and merrymaking, he says. If this were so, everyone would be able to get him. He comes only when one weeps for him.[39] This recalls Shri Ramakrishna's saying which is worth repetition 'People shed torrents of tears for their wife and children but who does so for the sake of God? If one weeps sincerely for him he will surely manifest himself'[38] The fire of separation in which the separated woman burns is often a favourite symbolism which Hindi poets use. Kabīr also speaks about this extensively: 'I am burning with the fire of separation. My agony is continual for the anguish of parting slowly consumes me as a piece of wood smouldering and giving out smoke. If I die as the wood swiftly burnt up. I will not have to suffer ceaselessly'[39] 'Parting's fire has completely consumed me. Now my mind and body is beyond the grief of separation. Only the fire which has burnt me can know of it!'[40] 'O my fellow-saints, the fire of parting in which I burn is so fiece that when I rush to the pond to extinguish its flames, the water in it too, catches fire! Say then, what should I do?'[41]

'Day and night I await your coming. O Mādhava (Krishna) I have been parted from you for long and so my mind knows no peace. Pray come to me while life yet remains, says Kabīr'.[42] And speaking of his intense longing to meet the Lord from whom he is separated Kabīr says in anguish, 'O dear friend, when will that day come awaiting the coming of which I have got this human body? When will I be able to clasp my Lord, my Lover, to my bosom?'[43]

Kabīr's descriptions of the anguish of parting are eloquent and striking, and have a Shakespearean ring in their expressiveness:

'She never told her love:
But let concealment, like a worm i' the bud,
Feed on her damask cheek : she pin'd in thought:
And with a green and yellow melancholy
She sat like patience on a monument,
Smiling at grief'.[44]

His narrations of meeting however are not so forceful. Speaking of Hari (Viṣṇu) he says: 'O friend, Hari is my Lover and without him I can't keep alive. He is my Lover and I am his beloved. He is great and I am very small. I have adorned myself to meet you. O my Lord Rāma, Why do you still not come. If I am able to meet you I will be freed from this mortal world'.[45] However, the verse reiterates the Vaiṣṇava element in Kabīr, for this is clearly borne out by his calling himself Rāma's *bahuriā* (wife). In the same way the Vaiṣṇava concept of *mādhurya* stresses the Lover-beloved or Husband-wife relationship. Kabīr says 'Wisdom dawned in my eyes and I avoided delusion and attachment, and straightaway took refuge in Rāma (Hari) my Lover. His divine grace destroyed my ignorance and evil deeds and catching hold of my hand he brought me close to himself'.[46]

THE TRANSITORINESS OF EXISTENCE

As we have said before, the Vedāntic element is quite predominant in Kabīra. The illusory nature of the world was emphasized by Śankara and his guru, Gauḍapāda. Śankara did not deny the reality of existence, but he said that it exists no longer for one who has realized *Brahman*: 'As the dream world is real as long as one is dreaming, but is proved unreal on waking, even so the world of attachment, aversion and so forth, has no longer any reality for the knower of *Brahman*. The world of appearance seems true only so long as *Brahman*, the basis of creation, is not realized...'[47] The idea is that when one realizes God, the world has no value for him. Although Kabīr did not enter into the intricacies of the world's illusoriness, and in fact accepts life as it is, he did dwell repeatedly on the ephemeral nature of existence, as many other poets and thinkers have done. Omar Khayyám says in the *Rubaiyát*:

> 'Think, in this batter'd Caravanserai
> Whose Portals are alternate Night and Day,
> How Sultan after Sultan with his Pomp
> Abode his destin'd Hour, and went his way'[48]

And Gray says:

> 'The boast of heraldry, the pomp of pow'r
> And all that beauty all that wealth e'er gave,
> Awaits alike the inevitable hour
> The paths of glory lead but to the grave'.[49]

Shakespeare often speaks of the world's ephemerality:

'we are such stuff
As dreams are made on, and our little life
Is rounded with a sleep'.[50]

Kabīr's emphasis is also on the vanity of existence. He could not have himself studied the Vedānta but must have understood its principles from the talks he had with his fellow-sadhus. In one of his verses he speaks about sleep and dreams, 'In the state of sleep the *jīva* (soul) has, as though become two, but on waking it has become one again.'[51] Evidently Kabīr's idea about the soul in dream, sleep and waking was very superficial. The state of the soul in dream has been narrated vividly by Yājñavalkya to Janaka in the *Bṛhadāraṇyaka Upaniṣad*. 'Though remaining with the sense organs, it (the soul) is yet different from them, for it is the light which lights up the mind and makes all the senses work.... It appears to think and to move about, but doesn't really, for it is only the immutable witness to thought and action. It is with the body in waking dream or deep sleep, but it also transcends these states'.[52] Kabīr's aforesaid verse depicts confusion of thought, for the soul does not split into two. It is the same through all the three states of consciousness (dream, sleep and waking) and the *turīya*, i.e., 'the fourth', or the Eternal Witness. Kabīr compares transient existence to the flower of the *palaśa* tree or that of cotton which soon withers and falls.[53] 'You have made ample provision for living' he says, 'but remember, emperor, king and beggar, all have to leave the world'.[54] 'A day will come, he warns both emperors and kings, 'when all of you will have to leave the world. Why don't you think about it'?[55] You may beat your kettledrum (drum sounded on auspicious occasions) for ten days, i.e.,. for a short while', he says, 'thereafter (when you die) you will not be able to come again to see the city and the lane which is yours.[56] And in much the same vein. 'When a man, after having sounded his drum, kettledrum, *shahanāi* and other musical instruments, i.e., after having made himself prominent; departs from the world, can anyone save him from death?[57] Mocking people who pride in their grand mansions he says 'You cast admiring glances on your huge house. Tomorrow and the day after, i.e., after the few years of your short life, you will have to face death and you will then lie under the earth and grass will grow over you'.[58] Hindu mythology records that the boy Krishna killed a huge python-shaped monster who was really a handsome and well-built lad so proud of his body that he would deride those with misshapen ones. Once a lame sage passed by and when he ridiculed him the sage cursed the handsome lad, due to which he turned into a monster. Kabīr deprecates people who have such vanity. 'Why are you so stuck on yourself?' he says. This body of yours which you prize so much is just bones encased in flesh. Those who ride swift steeds and sit under canopies, will also lie in dug up graves'.[59]

In another verse he says 'Why do you go about conceited when Death keeps hovering over your head? And you do not know even where he (Death) will overtake you, whether when you are in your home or abroad'.[60] 'The sorrow of existence is like a burning fire', he says. 'It consumes me entirely. My bones burn as faggots and my hair as dry grass, making me sad'.[61] The body is nothing but dust as the Holy Bible says: 'For dust thou art, and unto dust shalt thou return',[62] and 'Then shall the dust return to the earth as it was: and the spirit shall return unto God who gave it'.[63] In the same way Kabīr says. 'This packet (the body) encloses dust. It is a four day's wonder, (i.e., will exist only a short time), and will in the end return from the dust to dust'.[64]

A unique feature of Hindu religion is belief in rebirth, although other religions also believe that death is not the end of the soul. The world is consided by Hindus and Buddists to be a place of sorrow and death (*mṛtyaloka*) To some extent Christianity also believes that the fall of man, and the expulsion of Adam and Eve from Paradise condemned mankind to sorrow: 'And unto Adam he said.... cursed is the ground for thy sake: in sorrow shalt thou eat of it all the days of thy life: thorns also and thistles shall it bring forth to thee... in the sweat of thy face shall thou eat bread...' And to Eve the Lord said 'I will greatly multiply thy sorrow and thy conception: in sorrow thou shalt bring forth children...'[65] As we have said, the Hindus believe that human birth is obtained with great difficulty and after eighty-four lives on earth in various lower wombs. Kabīr, too, accepts this belief: 'Birth as a human being is got with difficulty' he says, 'and cannot be obtained again and again, as when a fruit falls off a branch it can't be restored to it'.[66] So what is the way out? Hindus believe that when knowledge of *Brahman* is attained there is no rebirth and the Soul becomes one with God. Kabīr, too believes that one should try to realize this state (*mokṣa*): 'As the earth the potter uses to make his pots gets beaten repeatedly to give it proper shape, so also man has to bear many tortures. if on getting human birth, he does not become aware (of the Soul) even then and misses the chance, he will have to be born again and again and suffer worldly sorrows'.[67] Thus emancipation is the goal of life and Rāma-devotion is the only way to achieve it'. But such devotion ought to be firm and whole-hearted. 'Do not take half-hearted measures to end the world's sorrows' he says. 'I have cured them by the elixir of Rāma-devotion.'[68] At the same time he throws in a word of caution. One should beware of pretenders 'who foolishly go about bragging that they are Rāma-devotees with the *tīkā* (sacerdotal) mark on their forehead, but whose minds are shallow, and who have really not an iota of devotion in them'.[69]

MUSINGS ON DEATH

If there was no death there would be no God, and religions would make no sense. Right from the beginning of human life on this earth people have tried to unravel death's mystery, but it remains elusive as ever. No one knows when or where or in what manner it will come, but inexorably right from the moment of birth one starts approaching nearer to death, and when God creates the human being, he does not give him any warranty. Kabīr says: 'Auspicious songs are sung on the birth of a child. The mother thinks "my son is growing in years." Alas, she does not know that each day his age gets less and less'.[70] Kabīr wrote about death (Yama, the god of Death or *Kāla*) in a most graphic manner. A writer says 'No other poet in India has spoken about "*kāla*", (Death) as Kabīr has done, with such tragic intensity'.[71] That is perhaps coming it strong. Death figured as Yama, its god, centuries before the birth of Christ in the *Kaṭha Upaniṣad* and the story of Naciketas going to Yama under the command of his father. It was current among the ancient Āryans, perhaps even going back to the *Ṛg Veda*. Vājaśravasa, Niciketas' father was offering old and decrepit cows to *brahmins*. This vexed the boy, who reasoned that it was wrong to gift such useless cows for form's sake. So in disgust he asked his father 'To whom will you give *me*?' When he repeated his question three times, Vājaśravasa got annoyed and said 'I give you to Death'. The boy took this to heart, and went off to Yama's abode. But Yama had left town and came back after three days, shocked to find the brahmin boy lying at his doorstep and without food and water for three days. To make amends he promised Naciketas three boons. After the boy had asked for two, he went on to the third. 'When a man dies', he said 'some say he exists and some that he doesn't. I'd like to know the truth of this'. Yama was cornered and tried to wriggle out of having to clear this matter 'Even the gods have their doubt about this' Yama said 'the question is very complex. Don't ask me, choose some other boon'. He went on to tempt the boy by offering him the choicest gifts—rare beauties, chariots, musical instruments, in brief, the moon. 'But don't ask me about death', Death's god said. Naciketas replied 'All these are most transient, O Death, they tire the senses and life is short. Man never gets satisfied with wealth. Besides, when your shade falls, i.e., when death comes, what use are these? So keep your horses, dance and song to yourself. I only wish to know about the supreme life after death. I do not wish to have any other boon'. Put in a spot, the god of Death had to tell Naciketas about afterlife, and what Yama said about the way to achieve emancipation is contained in the *Upaniṣad*. Here it is sufficient to point out that Naciketas' narration of life's transience couldn't be bettered and Kabīr's observances are not a patch on it.[72] Ovid says, 'Sooner or later to one goal we haste, (i.e., one reaches the end of his life)'.[73] A number of philosophers and poets have spoken about death and life, and it would be wearisome to quote them. This is not to belittle Kabīr's own observations, which have a rugged strength in his own characteristic power of expression. 'You say today "I will chant Hari's name tomorrow", and the next day you again say "I will chant it tomorrow". In this way time will go by and you'll never be able to chant it.'[74] 'You keep thinking thus about putting things of thinking of the morrow when you don't know what will happen the next moment! You should realize that no one can comprehend death and say when it comes, for it will pounce on you suddenly as a hawk upon a bird'.[75] If one escapes death somehow, he says so what? It'll be just as bad, for old age will bring its torments.[76] As age advances, gradually one loses the various functions of the body and finally, says Kabīr, 'O soul, soon your turn to leave will also come!'[77] 'That which grows must wither and die the bud breaks into flower and then fades, that which is built will crumble and what has been created will also know destruction'.[78] 'We human beings' he says, 'are for a short while, like a bubble blown up only to burst, or like stars which disappear when the morn comes'[79]

Musing on the uncertainty of existence, Kabīr says, 'This life is of no account. One moment it is joyful as sweet-tasting water, and the next grief-laden like water which has become brackish. They who sat the other day under auspicious canopies (pavilions rigged up for auspicious occasions), are lying now on the cremation grounds'.[80] In the *Bhagavadgītā* Krishna says, 'All creatures are unmanifest in the beginning and so too in the end. They are manifest only in the middle'.[81] In the same way Kabīr also conceives the soul, and the body it gets when it enters into a creature on earth. He says 'This pilgrim-soul has come from afar and will go again to that place from where it came. It had come temporarily to sojourn here in between its advent and departure, but Death pursues it here'.[82] Seeing that death is the inevitable concomitant of living, Kabīr turned to God as his refuge, 'For me all happiness consists in taking shelter in Rāma, for all that is other than him is just sorrow. Everyone—whether a god, a man, a demon, or a sage—is held fast in death's noose'[83] Commenting on the universality of death, he says 'I saw that those who were mourning the man's death also died, and so too those who bore the corpse on their shoulders; and those who came to offer their condolences also had to face death. Who can escape it?'[84]

Kabīr dwells chiefly on the inevitableness of death and the ephemerality of life. There is no escape from it. But he does not go beyond that, as Krishna does in the *Gītā* where the Lord says that wise men do not sorrow for those dead, for rebirth is certain for one who is dead and death is only like the discarding of old clothes and putting on new, for just as the embodied soul passes through childhood, youth and old age, so too it takes on a new body on rebirth.[85] He does speak in one of his *padas* about conquering death by the soul's merging with God but in it he speaks more about *mokṣa* (about which something will be said later) than about death. Kabīr fails to consider death and old age in their philosophical aspects as for example Browning does:

> 'Grow old along with me!
> The best is yet to be,
> The last of life for which the first was made:
> Our times are in his hands
> Who saith "A whole I planned
> Youth shows but half; trust God: see all, nor be afraid!"'[86]

Or as for example Socrates: 'Be of good hope in the face of death. Believe in this one truth for certain, that no evil can befall a good man either in life or death, and that his fate is not a matter of indifference to the gods.... And now the time has come when we must depart: I to my death, you to go on living, but which of us is going to the better fate is unknown to all except God'.[87] And in his own characteristic epigrammatic manner Epicurus says, 'Thus that which is the most awful of evils, death, is nothing to us, since when we exist there is no death, and when there is death we do not exist'

It wouldn't be fair to Kabīr, of course, to compare his thoughts about death with what the *Gītā* or philosophers like Socrates say of it, but it is desirable to strike a balance when we find critics putting his verses alongside Buddha's teachings and the Gospel of St John.

KABĪR'S CONCEPT OF MAYA

Arjuna asked Lord Krishna, 'What is it that impels a man to commit sin, as though he was forcibly driven to it, even against his will?' The Lord said 'It is desire (*kāma*), it is anger arising from passion (*rajoguṇa*). They are extremely evil and insatiable. These are the culprits'.[88] Thus there is some power over which we have no control, which holds us in its grip making us helpless to avoid doing what we very much want to . This is maya, which originally in Vedic times meant wondrous skill or mysterious willpower. Later the mystery element was given more emphasis, and it came to mean magic or illusion. This sense has stayed on and maya now means illusion or more properly, delusion. yet the element of mystery also remains, and maya is believed to be inscrutable. According to the *mayavādists* (as opposed to the followers of *śaktivāda*) it is not real for it is neither the supreme *Brahman*, nor is it altogether unreal. Therefore it is beyond one's understanding (*aniravacanīya*). The *śaktivādist*s believe it to be (*mahāmāyā)* or the divine Mother-power. According to Śankarācārya the universe is maya because it has only a phenomenal existence—*Brahman satya jagat mithyā*. According to him the object and the subject (*viṣaya and viṣayina*) are as opposed to each other as darkness and light, i.e., the 'not-I' and the 'I' are diametrically opposed, but due to false knowledge which is inborn in human beings (*naisangika*), they are paired together. Hence arises the idea of 'I' and 'mine' in them, which ceases only when this false notion (*avidyā*) is removed by the realization of *Brahman*. Maya has the power of hiding truth (*āvaraṇa*)` and of misreprenting it (*vikṣepa*) For example when one sees people all round, one's relations and friends too, dying, and still thinks 'they are dead, but I won't die'; that is maya's power of *āvaraṇa* working: and when one mistakes the body for the soul, that is caused by the truth being misreprented (*vikṣepa*).

We find in Kabīr all these elements of maya He believed that people are greatly deluded by sense-pleasures, particularly born of lust (*kāmā*) and the greed for wealth. But he did not make woman alone stand for passion as most Hindu poets and saints did. He censured lascivisousness in men too. 'The lecherous man', he says, 'wallowing in lust, forgets devotion. Living in vain he has lost the gem of Rāma-devotion. He prefers the poison (of sense-pleasures) to the nectar of devotion'.[89] Nonetheless it is for women that Kabīr reserved his most caustic invectives, calling them unwanted in the world like left-overs from a meal. Only vile men go near them, he says.[90] Women are like the pits of hell (*kabīra nārī kuṇḍa naraka kā*) or like wildcats. Very reluctantly he gave the go ahead to sex which is santified, in other words sex between wife and husband. 'Passion can unite one with Rāma' he says, 'provided one can keep it under control. When the sage Shukhdeva, himself sang about the amours of Krishna with cowherd girls, what else can Kabīr say?[91] He hastened however, to contradict this, realizing perhaps that he had overstepped the mark and his contemporary saints would never forgive the infringement of orthodoxy. So he went on to castigate sex even with one's wife, a complete crawl out of his former stand: 'If a man lies with any woman, whether his own wife or some other girl, he will go to hell. One fire is just the same as another, so do not burn your hand in either of them'.[92]

In Sāṁkha *prakṛti* (Nature) comprises the three qualities (*guṇas*)—*sattva* (purity) *rājasa* (passion or activity) and *tāmasa* (dullness). Kabīr used the Sāṁkhya symbolism in speaking of maya. 'Maya' he says 'is the huge tree yielding the three kinds of fruit (the *guṇas*). Its branches are sorrow and distress. This tree of maya is shadeless and the fruit it yields is tasteless and creates a burning sensation in the body'.[93] It is clear that Kabīr closely followed the Sāṁkhya school of Hindu philosophy despite at one stage negating the Six Systems of which Kapila's Sāṁkhya is one. This too adds to the various other contradictions in his thought. 'Maya' he says 'is the outcome of the interplay of the three *guṇas—sattva, raja* and *tamasa*— and through them of creation consisting of various creatures—those born of wombs, of eggs, heat and dampness and sprouting from the ground. Thus from the five tattvas (elements, i.e., earth, water, air, fire and ether-*chit, jala pāvaka, gagana, samīrā*) creation evolved and along with it the I-sense, arrogance vice (sin) and generosity (charity) attachment, prosperity, misfortune—all arising as bonds which held the embodied soul in captivity'.[94]

Kabīr's exhaustive treatment of the subjects he wrote about often landed him in contradictions. The main reason for this seems to be that he borrowed extensively from the various shades of thought with which Hindu philosophy is replete, but had little to offer of his own. This , however, is not strange for there is really nothing new under the sun, and all the more so in philosophies. Except for the founders of religions like Christ and Buddha, religionists keep repeating the same truths in different ways. Kabīr was against idolatry, yet he spoke of the Hindu idols, he was a monist yet we find traces of dualism in his verses, he accepted Sāṁkhya, yet did not favour the Six Systems and we find that he ridiculed the Śaktas, yet conceived maya to be the Mother of creation. The *māyāvāda* view of maya being *aniravacanīya* also found expression in his verses: 'The more you cut this maya-shaped creeper the more it spreads out' (i.e., indulging in sense-pleasures leaves one drawn to them all the more). And if you water it, it dries up, (i.e., by meditating on God one achieves detachment and has nothing to do with maya). Therefore this maya is beyond human understanding and its nature cannot be known'.[95] Maya is also like the chameleon and keeps changing: 'This maya' says Kabīr, 'is fickle and kaleidoscopic. It keeps changing each moment and ever moving as the continually blowing wind'[96] Maya causes ignorance, distress and affliction and imprisons human beings securely in its spreading tentacles. It tempts people with wealth, honour and vanity so much so that they even give their lives to achieve these things. Sometimes it assumes the form of a lovely woman and at other times as a demon. She is like a vile woman driving people to sin, and enticing them, but favouring none, much like Keats' la belle Dame sans Merci. Kabīr left no damning epithet in painting maya in the most lurid manner giving her the rap in various ways. He called her a witch (*ḍāin*) a female serpent (*sarpani*), a thief (*corati*), fiendish (*piśācinī*) a cheat (*ṭhagorī*) and so forth.[97] She has a lovely body he says, but a vicious mind. In some of his verses we find a mix-up of several concepts of Hinduism. Maya is doubtless like a poisonous snake, Kabīr says, but is also the creative power of the Lord.[98] Krishna says in the *Gītā* that he incarnates (in the human form) through his maya.[99] Kabīr also calls maya the creative power of Rāma (*līlā*, lit. 'sport').[100] He does not accept the belief that God is the material cause of the universe as the *Upaniṣads* do in some places conceiving the world issuing from him as the web from the spider's body. God is creation's immanent cause, i.e., he is present in the universe everywhere, yet not in it. As Krishna says in the *Gītā*: 'My unseen form pervades the entire universe. All beings are in me, but I am beyond them. But in truth these creatures are not contained in me. See my wondrous power (*yogam aiśvaram*) I sustain the universe yet am away from it. It is my Spirit which gives beings life'.[101] In the same way Kabīr says, '*Brahman* is one, eternal, non-Being, causeless and abode of bliss. He is qualitiless, formless and shapeless. From him is creation yet he is hid in it as though one was lost in a labyrinth'.[102]

While Kabīr conceived maya as inscrutable he was on safe ground. But when he proceeded to categorize it, he confused between maya and devotion. This was largely because of his digs and cracks concerning ritual and his eagerness to condemn all outward trappings of religious observances. He divides maya into three parts *moṭi* or gross, i.e., rituals like worship, prayer, pilgrimages, keeping long hair, wearing saffron robes and so forth; subtle or *jhīnī*, i.e., the disturbances of the mind like anger, longing, desire, greed and attachment; and the third classification, *vidyā rūpi* maya which includes both that which is manifest and that which is changeful. This has a Baudhya tinge for the Buddhists believed that everything that exists is ever changing as in a flowing river the water at any one point is not the same at any one moment, or the candle-flame though seemingly continuous keeps changing. Kabīr says 'The outward karma-shaped maya can be overcome, but not the subtle one which distracts the mind'.[103] In the *Gītā* Krishna clarified to Arjuna: '*Yagña* (carrying out of sacrifices or oblations), giving of charity and austerity are worthy of observance because they make even wise men pure'. The only condition is that these ought to be done desirelessly (*saṅga tyktvā phalāni ca*)[104] Kabīra's view was somewhat different inasmuch as he castigated all forms of external scriptural observances, and in saying *moṭi māyā saba tajai*, he obviously meant that all these *śastranakūla* karmas (observances of scriptural injunctions) are maya and should be abandoned. Where he condemned the greed for wealth and the promptings of lust, however, he is on solid ground.[105] Shri Ramakrishna also considered these—'woman' and 'gold' or as Kabīr says more appropriately *kāminī* and *kanaka*—as the main stumbling blocks in God-realization.[106] His calling down of expectation and thirst for the pleasures of the senses is also well conceived. These, he says, are very difficult to get over, even when one strives to do so life after life, for self-control is a hard row to hoe.[107] The sages, however he says, can overcome maya (for she is subservient to them, and thus reach God, but even they can do it only the hard way.[108]

Thus desire (*kāma*) and the thirst for honour and fame delude people. In addition Kabīr considered that wealth, caste clan, youth, learning and so forth also make one vain and so they become victims of maya. He likens one who prides himself on his clan or family to the bamboo tree which grows tall, but cannot have the fragrance of the short sandalwood tree, and is finally destroyed by the entire bamboo clump being burnt.[109] It's no use bragging about one's descent he says, for he who does so is surely as though hell has overtaken him. What difference does it make to him when he's dead? The only way to cross the murky sea of existence is by taking shelter in Rāma'[110] Thus according to Kabīr maya can be overcome only by placing oneself wholly at God's mercy. It is significant that despite parallel comparisons with the utterances of poets and philosophers, maya remains purely a Hindu concept. Kabīr's numerous verses on it show that he had a predilection for the Hindu religion, particularly his belief that only knowledge of *Brahman* can free one from maya's delusive power.

One of the many contradictory utterances of Kabīr, which concerns maya also, is about the means of livelihood itself being maya and thus a hindrance to realizing God. While he extolled honest labour and insisted that every person ought to work for a living, he says in one of his verses: 'O Mādhava (Krishna) maya has forced me to weave cloth, and engaging me in this occupation, has tied me to the world.... Leave this, says Kabīr to himself, and instead meditate on Rāma'.[111] 'Who will weave cloth?' he bemoans when, O maya, my mind is immersed in Rāma's love... 'I can't concentrate on my work because of it for my mind is in a whirl. It seems the warp, the woof, and the starch for thickening the threads are all revolving, making my job impossible'.[112] Again he says 'While working at the loom I wove cloth, criss-crossing warp and woof. But my heart was burning with love for Rāma. So I left the loom. Lord Rāma knows this to be true'[113] And, 'Kabīr says I have ceased weaving and, so to say, written Rāma's name all over my body, (i.e., I am lost in devotion to Rāma), which will be lost if I keep feeding thread in the shuttle and taking it this way and that'.[114] That work should be considered as maya, and thus an impediment to emancipation, is a strange and retrograde idea. For one thing work is an inevitable consequence of human existence. As Krishna says in the *Gītā*, Do your work, for to work is better than not working. Indeed without work even one's body cannot be maintained'.[115] We have already spoken about Kabīr's inistence on controlling the mind without which maya cannot be subdued, for the mind's involvement with the world is the greatest hurdle in realizing God. He often says that one should be a *jivanmṛtaka*, (i.e., 'dead to life' or 'unattached to worldliness'). The idea expressed by him is that of Christ in the Holy Bible, 'He that findeth his life shall lose it: and he that loseth his life for my sake shall find it'.[116] Kabīr says: 'He who abandons worldly pleasures and has no hope from men in the world, is looked after by Hari himself'.[117] 'I am dead to the world both in mind and body. Seeing this Hari himself comes after me saying "Kabīr, Kabīra."'[118] 'When one is dead and is carried to the cremation ground, no one bothers about him, but Hari, who cares for him as a cow would for her calf'.[119] 'If I burn my worldly house it is saved and if I protect it, it is lost! I have seen a wonder, that the man who is dead, (i.e., dead to joys and sorrows and to the enjoyment of sense-pleasures) can devour, (i.e., overcome) even death'.[120] 'The touchstone of Rāma (alone) is true, for only he can be proved genuine by it who has renounced worldly pleasures'.[121] 'The poor are humble,' says Kabīr, 'while those involved in dualities, (i.e., worldly pursuits) are vain. Rāma lives in the hearts of the poor while those of the worldly are full of poison'.[122] Kabīr's thought has parallels in both the Holy Bible the *Rāmāyaṇa* and *Śrimadbhagavadgītā*. As Kabīr says that God himself seeks out his loved devotee, so too Krishna tells Arjuna that he comes speedily (*na-cirāta*) to those who have unswerving faith in him (*mayaa āveśita-cetasām*)[123] As Kabīr commends the poor for their humility, so does the Bible: 'It is easier for a camel to go through the eye of a needle, than for a rich man to enter the kingdom of God'.[124] And, 'Blessed are the poor in spirit: for theirs is the kingdom of heaven.... Blessed are the meek: for they shall inherit the earth'.[125] Tulsīdāsa too speaks of the humble (*dīna*) people in reference to himself, 'O Rāma, I am your most humble devotee and there no one who does so much good to such persons as you. So save me from the dreadful sorrows of births and deaths in this world'.[126]

THE SAINTS AND THE UNSAINTLY

In the *Uttara-kāṇḍa* of Tulsī's *Rāmayāṇa* we come across a narration of the qualities of saints and also the nature of those who are unsaintly. The saints are compared to sandalwood and the unsaintly to the axe which cuts it.

Even while being cut, the sandalwood imparts its parfume to the axe: so also saints repay evil with good. But the axe's blade is heated red-hot in the fire to sharpen it, while sandalwood anoints the foreheads of people. Thus the unsaintly are punished for their evil while the saints are rewarded. The saints are detached from the world. They grieve at the grief of others, and rejoice to see them happy. They have conquered rage, fear and rancour and are compassionate, self-controlled, kind to the poor and needy, unaffected, calm, unostentatious disciplined, pious and free from craving. On the contrary the unsaintly persons are jealous, glad to hear someone maligned, arrogant, cunning envious of everyone, cruel, crooked and sinful. They envy all men without cause, even their well-wishers. They are all smiles, but dark inside. They are malicious, greedy, disdainful, coveting the wives and weath of other men, having attraction only for sex and food. The sorrows of others makes them elated. They have no regard for their parents and do not like the company of holy men.[127] So too Krishna describes the natures of the divine and the demoniac in the *Gītā*, on much the same lines.[128] Shakespeare speaks about saints or godly men in one of his sonnets thus:

> 'They that have power to hurt and will do none,
> That do not do the thing they most do show
> Who moving others, are themselves as stone,
> Unmoved, cold, and to temptations slow'.[129]

Kabīr follows more or less the same pattern. A section of his *Sākhīs* is about saints and their company (*Sadha kau anga*) and in another he cautions us against imposters who wander about in ochre robes and pretend to be holy men. He also speaks a great deal about Vaiṣṇavas (we have quoted from his verses about them before) for whom he had overwhelming fascination. 'The company of sadus' he says, 'is always bebeficial as when the bitter neem comes into contact with sandalwood it acquires its sweet perfume'.[130] 'Nothing is to be gained by going to places of pilgrimages', he says 'unless one seeks the company of saintss'[131]. 'Only that day is good, on which one meets a saint because if he clasps him to himself all that man's sins will go away'.[132] 'Nobody drinks the dirty water of a moat, but when that water flows into the Ganga it becomes pure and fit for drinking (even so the company of saints purifies a man)'.[133] 'O Rāma', he prays 'do not give me the company of a man who sticks to falsehood and forsakes truth, even in a dream'.[134] 'A fine white cloth always looks clean, but a black blanket is dark wherever you spread it (so is the difference between the godless and the godly)'.[135] According to popular belief Rāmānanda was Kabịr's guru, however that is in the realm of speculation. It is most likely however that whenever he had the opportunity, he took time off from his occupation as a weaver and went to meet saints, for whom he had a high regard. While he had great veneration for sages, he was also aware that many imposters went about in the garb of holy men, befooling people. So he hastened to tip the wink regarding such fourflushers. 'He whose outward appearance is like that of an ascetic but whose conduct is evil is at heart an unsaintly person'.[136] 'Do not be misled by one who's natty for he may be like the white heron, appearing to meditate, but inside evil. He will bring you misfortune and will also destroy your wisdom'.[137] He cautions men against so-called saints who speak sweet words, but who will be their doom, 'as one who shows some one the depth of a river (where it isn't deep) and then takes him on to deep waters and drowns him'.[138]

Kabīr placed greater emphasis on the advantages of the sages' company than on their qualities. His admonitions to false saints are unique and expressed in forceful language. In the age in which he lived there were many such persons who pretended to be holy but followed evil practices and who abused religious obsevances. There were the Kāpālas and the Kalāmukhas who practised a kind of degenerated Śaivism. The Kāpālas believed that one could obtain the highest bliss by concentrating his mind on the vagina, and drinking wine could confer the higest virtue and occult power. They ate all kinds of disgusting things and practised yoga only to achieve miraculous powers. They performed human sacrifices. The Kālāmukhas, who were just as bad, ate the ashes of the dead and smeared their bodies with them. They worshipped God as seated in a pot of wine or holding a club. These sects worshipped Bhairava, whose wife Caṇḍikā was shown wearing a garland of skulls. They made offerings of wine and human victims The Kāpālas and the Kālāmukhas had a large following. No wonder Kabīr cautioned devotees to shun the company of such vile people. He warned people to keep away from the Śāktas. 'The company of saints', he says, 'takes man nearer to God, but the blanket of the Śāktas is so black that no amount of washing can make it clean'.[139]

THE EMPTINESS OF RUTUAL

It is very difficult to conceive the abstract and so everything moves from it to the concrete. Love finds expression in sweet nothings, hatred in blood and tears and joy in smiles and laughter, water-vapour in clouds hail and rain and fire in ashes. Thoughts find expression in words:

'And as imagination bodies forth
The forms of things unknown, the poet's pen
Turns them to shapes, aand gives to airy nothing
A local habitation and a name'.[140]

Much the same is the case with religions. Most of them move from the abstract to the concrete. The *ṛṣīs* of the Vedas knew of no dualities. They were of course wonder-struck to see nature in its various aspects as the fire, wind, water, earth and sky and so eulogized these in their beautiful hymns, yet they believed that beyond nature was the One to which people gave different names —*ekam sad vipra bahudhā vadanti*. The *Upaniṣads* developed this concept of the One into *Brahman* (the Cosmic Absolute) of which, one could say only *na iti na iti or neti neti*, i.e., 'not this, not this—'the one which remains, while the many change and pass.' Then came the dualists (*dvaitavādists*) led by Rāmānuja and his followers, and the concept of *bhakti* (devotion) extolled in the *Bhakti-sūtras* of Nārada, giving rise to saints and devotees like Caitanya, Mīrā, the Aḷvārs, the Vaiṣṇavas and so forth. The *Bhagavadgītā* was perhaps the earliest attempt to synthesize the dual and the non-dual points of view. Krishna said: 'The devotees who meditate on me singlemindedly and with supreme faith are nearest to me. but those persons who worship the Imperishable beyond the reach of words and unmanifest. Omnipresent, Unfathomable, Immutable, Immovable and Constant, (i.e., *Brahman*) also come to me'.[141] The most controversial aspect of the *bhakti*-cult was image-worship, about which the *Vedas* and the *Upaniṣads* had maintained a discreet silence. Krishna says in the *Gītā* 'I accept whatever a man of pure heart offers me with devotion—a leaf, a flower, a fruit or water.[142] Thus worship of God in the form of idol-worship was enjoined by the *Gītā* as much as worship of the formless (*avyakta*) *Brahman*.

Religions like Christianity and Islam reacted by strongly condemning the worship of images: 'So when the sacred months have passed away, slay the idolaters wherever you find them, and take them captives and besiege them and lie in wait for them in every ambush:... The idolaters are nothing but unclean...'[143] And in the Holy Bible the Lord appeard to Moses on Mount Sinai and said: 'Thou shalt have no other gods before me. Thou shalt not make unto thee any graven image, or any likeness of any thing that is in heaven above, or that is in the earth beneath, or that is in the water under the earth: thou shalt not bow down thyself to them, nor serve them; for I the LORD thy God *am a jealous God....*'[144]

Some Hindu saints, too, fell in line with the Islamic and Christian beliefs, though without giving such a bawl out to idolators. Swami Dayananda and Kabīr were two such saints. Dayananda sought the support of the *Vedas* in his assault on image-worship, even though they just didn't say anything about it one way or the other.[145] Kabīr, with greater restraint, merely razzed the concept of image-worship, as he ridiculed all other outward show, both among Hindus and Moslems: 'Why do you climb up the minaret, O mullah', he says, 'do you think the Lord is hard of hearing. Search him in your heart to whom you call so loudly in prayer'. About idol-worship he says: 'The images are lifeless, they cannot speak, for I have called aloud to them and they are silent. The *Puraṇas* and the Quran are just words. I have seen the Truth myself by lifting the curtain of falsehood'.[146]

It is not only Hinduism which admits of rituals. According to Islam, at least in its observance, a pious Moslem is required to make a pilgrimage to Mecca once in his lifetime in any case. While there he observes three main rituals. The first, performed on arrival, is the circumambulation of the Kaabaa seven times. Then he runs seven times between two small hills across Mecca. This is to symbolically enact Hagar's frantic search for water for her son, Ishmael. The third act is going to the mount of Mercy at the plain of Aract. The pilgrims stand here before God from noon to sunset. They are forbidden to wear head-coverings, but may carry umbrellas. There are other rituals too like circumcision, the Ramadan fast, sacrifice of animals on the Bakr'Idd and so forth. The Christians go to the Grotto of Nativity and the Manger in Bethlehem Christ's birthplace. They kiss the floor, hang lamps and place small figures of Christ on a spread-out white cloth.

Thus we see that the human mind, even while desperately clinging on to the abstract, meanders into the concrete. And this is so irrespective of the creed to which a man subscribes. As Krishna says in his terse observation *avaktā hi gatir duḥkhaṁ dehavadbhir avāpyate* ('The way of the Unmanifest is fraught with sorrow for human beings').[147] Therefore the Moslem seeks salvation in Kaabaa, the Christian in Christ's Crucifixion and the Hindu in worship of images. Idolatry is merely a symbol of love. It's like keeping a photograph on the table to remind a man of his sweetheart, only in image-worship it's a stone or metal statue instead of a picture.

Kabīr was not the only person who sought to bring about a synthesis of Moslems and Hindus. Many others both dead and living, small and great have attempted it or are still doing so. There was Mahatma Gandhi. he did try a lot, but failed. 'I have no shadow of a doubt' he said 'that our hearts will meet some day. What seems impossible today for us, God will make possible tomorrow. For that day I work, live and pray'.[148] But a Moslem client and friend of his in South Africa where Gandhi practised as a lawyer left him disillusioned. When Gandhi told him 'other scriptures (the Quran and the Bible) do not move me as do the *Gītā* of Krishna and the *Rāmāyaṇa* of Tulsīdāsa', his friend, he records, 'despaired of me and had no hesitation in saying that there must be something wrong with me. His, however, is not an exceptional case because I have since met many Mussalman friends who have held the same view'.[149] Gandhi never succeeded in his endeavours and the outcome was a separate homeland for the Moslems. He also initiated the policy of their appeasement which, after Partition, has been enthusiastically pursued by scheming politicians corrupted by power. Mohammed Ali Jinnah said 'The Hindus and Moslems... belong to two different civilizations which are based mainly on conflicting ideas and conceptions. Their concepts on life and of life are quite different'. According to the Prophet every child is born in Islam, but its parents make him a non-Moslem. Islam is believed by the Holy Quran to be the chosen religion destined to triumph over all religions. According to Āyat Allāh Khomeini 'Eleven things are unclean: urine, excrement, sperm, blood, a dog, a pig, bones, a non-Moslem man or woman, wine a bear and the perspiration of a camel that eats filth (Bat Ye'or the Dhimmi, Associated University Press, 1985).[150] It is this exclusiveness and militancy of Islam that makes any compromise between it and any other religion weaving a rope of sand. Many have tried to bring Hindu and Moslem together, none has gone over the big. Among those who tried, was Kabīr, but his method was neither appeasement nor cajoling. He lambasted persons of both the faiths pointing out the absurdities of their rituals and the hypocrisy of their outward trappings. 'Hindus say Rāma to express the reality, Moslems, Khudā', he says. 'But he has really known who does not differentiate between them'.[151] 'If one abjures fanaticism', 'Kaabaa will be as Kaśī (Varanasi) and Rāma and Rahīm will be the same. Differences are resolved, as the coarse flour becoming refined and pure'. 'As for me' says Kabīr, 'I would rather eat the refined flour of non-difference than the coarse one of separation'.[152] Kabīr was against all differences, whether in social status or caste or religion. He realized the ephemerality of existence; that 'sceptre and crown' would be one with the 'scythe and spade' when death, the leveller came. 'Mighty kings have gone', he says, 'leaving behind huge palaces, tanks, and untold wealth'.[153] 'Monarchs and potentates possessing crores of horses and elephants are all miserly. Their wealth is useless'.[154] 'People are vain of their wealth and have nothing else to think about except that. They dance madly about like naked lunatics and even forget God. They don't know that nothing will go with them when they die except their souls'.[155] 'Wealth is fleeting, it ought not to create a rift between brother and brother. The rich and poor are fundamentally the same. Who knows by God's will the roles may be reversed one day and the poor man become rich, the rich man poor. Says Kabīr, only he is without wealth in whose heart Rāma is not enshrined'.[156]

Kabīr opposed all kinds of separatism and conceived the common bond which bound mankind. This is doubtless very signifant, but men seem to be intent on maintaining distinctions rather than removing them. What has emerged is a world torn with strife, splintered and divided by race, religion, wealth, caste, language and complexion; a world of violence, bloodshed and hatred with the sword out of the scabbard; a world bereft of moral values and sunk in voluptuous sense-pleasures. The saints still keep coming, but they are not like the forest-dwellers of the *Upaniṣads* who had renounced the world to seek truth. Our modern saints have oomphish girls as secretaries and wish to bring heaven on earth with houris, dance, song and wine. Kabīr was against all such jiggery-pokery. A twentieth century Bangala poet Pāgalā Kānāi wrote: 'There are two brothers both equal and of the same blood. They are born from the wombs of their mothers. One says Durga or Hari, the other Bismillah, but they drink the same water. One wears a rosary, the other is circumcised. Then why, O brothers, do you fight and ruin yourselves'.[157] Much the same was said long back by Kabīr: 'The yogīs say "Gorakh", Hindus, "Rāma" and Moslems "Khuda", but Kabīr's Lord is one'.[158] 'King or commoner all are human beings created by God. All men are brothers in whom the same blood flows. They live through the same existence, (i.e., live their allotted years of life) and have the same soul. They are born in the same way from the wombs of their mothers. They share the same creation. Then what is it that creates division between them?'[159] Saints have no answer to such a question because they see all beings with the eye of sameness. but the fanatics of religions and the politicians know why. The fanatic divides because of his instinct for self-preservation—so that he remains a cut above his brother coreligionists, while the politician's aim is to divide and rule. 'So', says Kabīr, 'when I forsook all doubts and arguments and saw the one soul in all beings and knowing this looked on all people alike, God blessed me and I was able to achieve all that was worthy of attainment'.[160] Kabīr echoes the same thought as is contained in the *Gītā*, 'The yogi whose conscience is clear and who has controlled his senses and his mind sees the same soul in all creatures that he sees in himself. Such a man is not attached to karma'.[161]

Kabīr, as we have said, was against all outward show of piety. He considered such demonstrations as mere hypocrisy. Indeed most religious conflicts are caused by such display and fanfaronade. 'What is the use of smearing one's body with ashes' he says, 'or to bathe in sacred rivers, or fasts austerities, pilgrimages, *rozā*, *namāz* going on Haj or visiting Kaabaa, ringing bells in temples or calling for prayers in mosques? Someone (the Hindu) prays with his face towards the east, another facing west (the Moslem). All this is just ritzing it and vain pretence for Rāma and Rahīm are within one's own self. The Lord dwells in everyone and Allah and Hari are my saviours—thus says Kabīr'.[162] 'The Hindu dies saying "Rāma", and the Moslem saying "Ḳhudā". Kabīr says he is really alive who is not bigoted by either of these two dharmas'.[163] 'Turmeric is yellow', says Kabīr, 'and lime white. But when they are mixed they lose their colour. Even so when persons unite themselves with Rāma, family and clan are forgotten'[164] 'One (the Hindu) burns the corpse, the other (the Moslem) buries it. These differences make me sorrowful and I keep aloof from both. Listen, O brothers, says Kabīr, neither you will remain nor I. Only that One Eternal will remain'.[165] No wonder the Hindus wished to cremate Kabīr body when he died and the Moslems to bury it! While generally Kabīr speaks of Yama, the Hindu god of death whose messengers go to bring the souls of the dead, he mentions Israel also in one of his verses. 'Of the two letters forming Rāma, (i.e., *rā* and *ma*) make *rā* your helmet and *ma* your armour, and put the gem of wisdom in your lurban. Then even if Isreal comes to take your soul, your destiny will awake, (i.e., good divine judgment will await you)'.[166]

Most of the religions are persuasive in claiming that they will benefit their followers. Even in Hinduism, which perhaps is the most catholic and accomodating of faiths, Krishna says that those persons who proclaim his message, study or follow his teachings are his loved ones and would go to auspicious spheres after their deaths.[167] In the Holy Bible the Isrealities are God's chosen people and when he appeared to Moses in the burning bush he said 'I am the God of thy father, the God of Abraham, the God of Isaac, and the God of Jacob',[168] Islam goes a little beyond persuasion, inasmuch as it not only proclaims itself to be the chosen religion, but also urges that unbelievers should be brought under its pale by active compulsion: '*Fight* those who do not believe in God nor in the latter day, nor do they prohibit what God and His Apostle have prohibited, nor follow the religion of truth, out of those who have been given the Book, until they pay the tax in acknowledgment of superiority and they are in a state of subjection'.[169] This doubtless gave great impetus to the Moslem rulers to unleash a reign of terror, for whatever their scripture might say, in actual practice the establishment of Islam became to them a sacred duty, a kind of crusade or *jihād*, and the slaying of infidels was the gateway to heaven. The hatred and cruelty this involved could not possibly be favoured by saints like Kabīr. Besides the idea of a God who was external to beings and who favoured only the 'believers' of Islam was quite different to Kabīr's Lord who resided in the souls of beings and everywhere in the world and there was nothing apart from him.[170] As cows of different colours gave the same white milk, even so there was unity in diversity. Duality ceases when the truth is known, and then all is one.[171] For the Moslems certain observances are essential, namely *namāz, rozā, haj, tauhīd* (belief in one God), *salat* (prayer) and *zakat* (giving charity to *Moslems*). Kabīr expressed himself against all such external show.[172] Thus Islam had hardly any impact on him, Nor did his attempt to bridge the chasm between Hinduism and Islam have any success. Indeed a religion which believed that one became a victor (*ghāzī*) by killing even non-combatant Hindus and thereby gained merit, perhaps even heaven, could never reconcile itself with idol-worshipping infidels. The only thing Kabīr borrowed from Islam was the abhorrence to idolatry. The Moslems were eager to bury his body when he died, but no Moslem ever bothered about him either in life or after death.

The Sūfīs, whose thinking we have narrated before, did, however, have an influence on him, particularly in their making love a bond between man and man and man and God, also their belief that the soul and God are one. Many interpretations are given of the import of the word *sūfī*. One is that they were woollen garment (*soof* - 'wool'), and another from *sūlf* 'a row', because of the belief that they would stand in the first row of men on the Day of Judgment. They believed in the Quran but gave it a new interpretation. Union with God was their creed and this was achieved by ten steps *tauba* (conversion), *majāhad* (earnest striving), *khalwa wa-'uzla* (solitariness and withdrawal), *taqwā* (the fear of God), *wara* (abstention), *zuhd* (renunciation), *samt* (silence) *khawf* (fear), *rajā* (hope) and *huzn* (repentence for for sins committed).[173] Thus the Sūfī moves from one stage to the other till finally satisfaction (*riḍā*) is achieved. Other Sūfī saints have variations of these stages. These saints did not stop at spiritual advancement. They advocated public service, removal of poverty, and so forth. Much akin to Kabīr's thought, Shaikh Nizām-ud-dīn Auliya said 'The rejection of the world does not mean that one should strip himself of his clothes or put on a loin-cloth and sit idle, instead what comes to him unasked he should accept, but not hoard it. He should not place his heart in anything. Only this is rejection of the world'.[174] The Chishti saints advised their disciple 'to take only what was absolutely necessary'.[175] Pacifism and non-violence and abstension from meat and slaughtering animals, was another Sūfī creed which recalls Kabīr's way of thinking. 'If a man places thorns in your way' said Shaikh Nizām-ud Dīn Auliya 'and you do the same, it will be thorns everywhere'.[176] Patience, endurance, elimination of anger, introspection and giving up all thoughts of revenge for any wrongdoing were qualities advocated by the Sūfīs and in all this their *think* closely resembles that of Kabīr.

The Sūfī's conceived God as omnipresent and in all creatures. Nūr Mohammed says that God is beginningless and no one is his creator. He exists in himself. None is like him and he is inseparable from the world, as the wave of the sea rises from the ocean and falls again in it. The world, says Nūr Mohammed is also of this kind. For Kabīr too, the relation between God and the world is similar. The soul is contained in God, and God in the soul.[177] But in this the influence of the non-dualist creed of Śankara is more evident than that of Sūfīsm. Where Sūfīsm and Kabīr meet is in counting love of God as the supreme goal of human existence. The soul is purified through love and is immersed in bliss.[178] It is not easy, however, to reach this state of endless bliss. One has first to purge his mind of all desires for sensual pleasures and greed for wealth.[179] As we have said, the Sūfīs, like the Vaiṣṇavas, believed in the union of the soul with God and the highest expression of this is the love of a lover for his beloved or of a husband for his wife (*mādhurya bhāva*). Kabīra has expressed this in his verses, some of which we have quoted.[180] The woman whose husband has come to the nuptial bed, (i.e., the soul which is to be united with God) can't contain her joy, and when their love is consummated she is loath to part with him. 'I will not let you go now Lover' she says, 'do with me as pleases you'.[181] Thus Kabīr uses erotic symbolism to depict his love of God. Though he may not have accepted all the principles of Sūfīsm, they had doubtless a great influence on him. But it was the Vaiṣṇavas who had the pull over the Sūfīs, and so Vaiṣṇavism was Kabīr's moving force.

Moslems, however had no link with Sūfīs, despite the fact that they too belived in the Holy Quran. They did not appreciate Sūfīsm's broadmindedness, and whether Kabīr was a Hindu or a Moslem, his closeness to the Sūfīs did not at all click with them. His idea of the Formless One to which he gave the name 'Rāma' was more akin to the *Brahman* of the Hindu *advaita* philosophy than to the Moslem view of Allah or Ḳhuda. Whether Rāmānand was his guru or not, there is a definite Vaiṣṇava trend in him.

His attempt to reconcile Islam with Hinduism failed because of the inherent militancy of Islam and their intolerance for religions other than it. The only way he could achieve such fusion was by deriding the outward show and rituals of both, but that did not bring them any closer. Hindus and Moslems remain as far apart as they ever have been. To effect a fusion between them is catching the wind in a net. As reformer Kabīr did not accomplish his objective, but it must be said to his credit that he tried with all sincerity.

THE NATURE OF KABĪR'S POETRY

Some critics of Kabīr are of the view that he was not a poet at all in the true sense of the word as his verses do not follow the traditional fashion of Hindi verse. According to Keśavadāsa there are four kinds of verse—*kauśiki, bhāratī, ārabhaṭī* and *sāttvikī*. The first is that in which merrinent. love and tenderness are belended together and in which simple and expressive words are used. The *bhāratī* verse is one in which feelings of heroism, wonder and merriment are contained, and whose meaning is delightful. The *ārabhaṭi* is the kind containing descriptions of violence, dread and loathing. There are plentiful alliterations and words having double meaning in this kind of verse. The *sāttvikī* verse is that in which wonder, heroism and calmness mingle in equal proportion and whose sense is easily understood.[182] It is true that none of these elements, except perhaps calmness, is discernable in Kabīr's verse. Nonetheless one can't confine poetry in such narrow compartments for it is a term comprising the noblest thoughts in various spheres, one of which is wisdom and philosophy. The *rītikāla* or *śṛngāra-kāla* poets of the latter medieval period of Hindi poetry (like Bīharī, Ghanānanda, Matirāma, Deva, Ṭhākur, Sanāpati and so forth) wrote mainly about love, beauty, the meeting and parting of lovers, the woman spurned, the arrogance (*māna*) of women who, because of this, cannot evoke feelings of love in their lovemaking, illicit amours and so forth. These *rītikāla* poets expressed various moods of lovers through their *nāyakas* (literally 'eminent persons') who were the lovers and the *nāyikās* the beloveds comprising women of various intensities of longing, in different situations, circumstances, beauty and form. Quite apart from the *rītikāla* poets, were the devotional poets of the mid-fifteenth century, of which Tulsi Sūr, Mīrā, Kabīr and others were exponents. These poets often used the same symbolism of love as that of *rītakāla* poetry (separation, meeting, love (*anurāga*) the pangs of longing etc.). The lover and belove were not however, a man and a woman in carnal relationship but God and the devotee or *Brahman* and *atman* (the soul) in spiritual union. Mīrā conceived Krishna, Tulsī Rāma, and Kabīr the Cosmic Absolute which he termed 'Rāma'. The poetry of these saint-poets was as inspired if not more, than that of the *rītikāla* poets. Those critics who deny that what the devotional poets wrote was poetry, are very much like the blind men and the elephant. They are only seeing one aspect of poetry and ignoring the others. The English poet Percy Bysshe Shelley says:

'Poetry is indeed something divine. It is at once the centre and the circumference of knowledge; it is that which comprehends all science, and that to which all science must be referred. It is at the same time the root and blossom of all other systems of thought ....What were virtue, love, patriotism, friendship—what were the scenery of this beautiful universe which we inhabit; what were our consolations on this side of the grave—and what were our aspirations beyond it if poetry did not ascend to bring light and fire from those eternal regions where the owl-winged faculty of calculation dare not ever soar....

'Poetry is the record of the best and happiest moments of the happiest and best minds....

'A poet, as he is the author to others of the highest wisdom, pleasure, virtue and glory, so he ought personally to be the happiest, the best, the wisest, and the most illustrious of men... the greatest poets have been men of the most spotless virtue of the most consummate prudence and if we would look into the interior of their lives, the most fortunate of men...'[183]

Kabīr was 'the author of the highest wisdom' and also 'a man of spotless virtue' and by Shelley's definition of poetry being divine, the centre of knowledge and the root and blossom of all systems of thought, his poetry was what good poetry ought to be. Poetry has a wide compass and it would be an error to restrict its scope to physical love and longing, descriptions of beauty or nature and so forth. the greatest poetry like Browning's *Abt Vogler* and *Rabbi Ben Ezra* or Wordsworth's *Ode on Intimations of Immortality* are philosophical and when Shakespeare reaches the acme of excellence he speaks of life, death and the world's ephemerality. Kabīr's observation on death that its god is powerless when the soul has merged with God (*kabīra ghara jālauṁ ūbarai, ghara vākhauṁ ghara jāi/ eka acambhā dekhiyā, maṛā kāla kūṁ khāi.*), is much like what the poet John Donne wrote:

'Death be not proud, though some have called thee
Mighty and dreadful, for thou art not so,
For, those, whom thou think'st, thou dost overthow,
Die not, poor death, nor yet canst thou kill me....
Why swell'st thou then?
One short sleep past, we wake eternally,
And death shall be no more; death, thou shalt die'.[184]

And much like Kabīr verses about his complete surrender to Rāma, Donne says:

'Both good and evil from His mouth proceeds:
Why then grieves any man for his misdeeds?
Turn we to God, by trying out our ways.
To Him in heaven, our hands with hearts upraise'.[185]

We have particularly quoted Donne because there appears to be a great deal of similarity between his poetry and that of Kabīr, in the reughness of language, the unconventional though forceful nature of their style and even in the divergence of the response they evoke in critics.

Many critics of Kabīr's verses have said that it wasn't poetry in the true sense of the word. He was a saint first and a poet afterwards. His verses lack melody and while the dharmic aspect of his verse is predominant, its poetic excellence is mediocre.[186] Others have expressed the view that Kabīr's work can't be called either poetical or literary (*sāhitya yā kāvya*).[187] It has no sustained literary merit and consists of stray *dohās* and *padas* (couplets and verses) arranged in an out of whack and a ramble-scramble manner.[188] Similarly Sir Walter Scott said about Donne's poetry that it was 'harsh and scholastic, pedantic and the unprofitable trade of combining dissimilar and repugnant ideas—barbarous, jingling, ill-regulated prose little different from the inscription on a tombstone'.[189] However Logan Pearsall Smith sums up Donne's poetry as follows: 'His harshness, his crabbed and often frigid way of writing, his forced conceits, his cynicism and sensuality, are extremely repellent to some readers; while to others his subtlety, his realism, and a certain modern and intimate quality in his poems, illuminated as they are with splendid flashes of imaginative fire, posses an extraordinary interest and fascination. There are people who hate Donne; there are others who love him, but there are very few who have read his poems and remain quite indifferent to him'.[190] Much the same can be said for Kabīr's poetry which found 'fit audience though few'. It is difficult not to appreciate his search for truth, his unswerving devotion and his rejection of all dogma, even though the way in which he expressed himself was somewhat on the free and easy.

Before we go on to give instances of Kabīr's poetical felicity, it would be appropriate to refer to the language he used in his verses. We can't of course be sure what his genuine work really was for it was his disciple, Dharmadāsa, who first wrote down the verses which he orally got from Kabīr. Some time later Kabīr's companion-sadhus added their own compositions to these, making it almost impossible to know which verses were Kabīr's and which were accretions. About the language of poetry in general Wordsworth says:

'The principal object (of his own poems) was to choose *incidents and situations from common life*, and to relate or describe them, throughout, as far as was possible in a selection of language *really used by men*, (Coleridge feels, 'really' should be substituted by 'ordinarily') and, at the same time, to throw over them a certain colouring of imagination, whereby ordinary things should be presented to the mind in an unusual aspect; and further and above all, to make these incidents and situations interesting by tracing in them, truly though not ostentatiously, the primary laws of our nature: chiefly as far as regards the manner in which we associate ideas in a state of excitement. Humble and rustic life was generally chosen... For all good poetry is the spontaneous overflow of powerful feelings....'[191].

The two points made by Wordsworth, 1.That the language of poetry should be that ordinarily used by men, and 2. The incidents and situations described by poets ought to be culled from common life, are particulary relevant in Kabīr's poetry because both of them are found in it, even though it may be doubted if by themselves they are the hallmarks. of the greatest poetry. When truth, which Keats equated with beauty, reaches its pinnacle it evades expression, vanishing like the stars in daylight; remaining what Morlowe said:

'One thought, one grace, one wonder at the least,
Which into words no virtue can digest'.[192]

Kabīr said that he never touched a pen and he composed his verses orally and they were compiled later. Still, that does no disqualify him from the aura of poetry. Milton was blind yet he wrote poetry which was sublime. Chaucer chose his own dialect in preference to Latin which was then in vogue, just as we find Kabīr rejecting Sanskrit. Shakespeare's education was haphazard and as a critic says 'he might well seem ignorant to the Masters and bachelors of Arts of the two universities'.[193] So if Kabīr was unlearned and unlettered, we can't say he could not be a poet. So indeed was the case with some other saints of his times like Ravidāsa, Pīpā and so forth. Hunt believed poetry to be 'a passion for truth, a passion for beauty, a passion for power and imaginative passion'.[194] According to him 'He who has thought, feeling, expression, imagination, action, character and continuity, all in the largest amout and highest degree, is the greatest poet'.[195] Kabīr fulfils most of these qualifications—truth, power, thought and feeling. He himself says in one of his *Padas* that he did not compose his verses for entertainment or to be set to music, he wished to speak of the knowledge of *Brahman*. He claimed that he was divinely inspired and he wrote under divine command.[196] Before we go on to illustrate the heights of Kabīr's poetry by examples of his *Padas* and *Sākhīs*, it would be well to point out that those writers who have showered encomiums on him are as mistaken as those who have refused to place him in the galaxy of Hindi poets. Speaking about the ingress of Islam, a writer says 'Had Kabīr not arrived on the scene with his reformative philosophical principles, the history of India would have taken a different turn'.[197] That is too much to say for Kabīr, even if it is conceded that he tried to bring about a rapprochement between the two faiths. Neither the poets nor the saints are born to change the history of nations. They only enrich the world's culture and spiritually show the way to truth. A French writer says, 'If not a learned poet, a *kavi* in the traditional sense, the little weaver of Benares was indeed a great poet, *one of the greatest known in India and elsewhere*'.[198] This kind of accolade is quite out of place, for though Kabīr rises to the poetic heights in snatches, his verse lacks the universality, tenderness and depth of the greatest poetry such as that of Tulsīdāsa the king of poets (*mahākavi*). Quite often his symbolism is crude as when he calls maya a prostitute (maya *besvā*), sinner (*pāpaṇī*), witch (*ḍāina*) and so forth. Human beings, he says, are the evil products of the union of the woman's ovum and the man's semen (*kabīra raj bīraj kī kalī*). The imagery may be realistic, but it is bizarre and rummy so far as poetry is concerned. Although some of the devotees of Śiva followed obnoxious practices, to call them worse than pigs was surely more the language of the drain, than good poetry—'a pig is more valuable than a Śakta, for it keeps the village clean (by eating excreta)'. He calls Hari a thug (brigand) which is irreverent and unrefined. In his eagerness to razz the ritual part of religious observances like prayer, pilgrimages, fasts, the *haj*, *namāz* and so forth. Kabīr used terms which were hardly fit for poetical expression and many of his satirical verses are crude in their phraseology. Kabīr ought to have realized that religion is not logic. For example he says about the Hindu *ekādaśī* fast, 'why does the Vaiṣṇava observe this eleventh day's fast and not the twelth'. He might have as well asked, why the Christians believe that God made creation in six days and rested on the seventh! He ridicules the *Veda* and the *gayatrī mantra* of which he must have been completely ignorant because, he had no education and as low-caste was excluded from them. In the same way he speaks disrespectfully of Moslem observances like the Ramadan fast, the visit to Mecca, the Kaabaa and so forth. To pan and scoff at what one is ignorant about is cortainly not the charactcristic of elegance. H.P. Divivedi says of Kabīr's diction that his words were 'Tender as a flower and hard as a diamond'. Perhaps they do have a rough kind of hardness, but certainly not the giitter of a diamond, and more like adamant than a polished gem. As for the tenderness, while a certain amount of it may be found in Kabīr's descriptions of meeting, parting and ecstatic union, they take on a philosophical hue depicting the merging of the soul with God, its quest for *mokṣa* and its agony when it is not able to reach the divine. The beauty of nature and its changing moods seldom seems to figure in his verse, which is surprising, for as a weaver he would have been village-based and must have observed the glory of sunset and sunrise, the loveliness of fields green and yellow and the charm of the full moon and the canopy of stars. A saint-poet like Mīrā sang both of God and nature with infinitely greater tenderness than Kabīr. As we have said in the preface, the reason for this could be that while for Mīrā, Krishna was someone on whom she could shower her love and adoration and even conceive his image as being alive, and for Tulsī, Rāma was the Lord incarnate, Kabīr's Rāma, like Allah, was formless shapeless and never conceived materially, and like *Brahman*, a negation of everything that one might say of him. When Krishna says in the *Gītā* that to worship the Unmanifest is fraught with sorrow—*avaktā hi gati duḥkam*— one can imagine how difficult it would be to make it the subject of poetry, of which the main elements are love, beauty and tenderness of feeling. So Kabīr had to adopt a language that could describe the indescribable, and poetry was a poor medium for such expression. Kabīr himself realized the difficulty of worshipping the Unmanifest, as Krishna pointed out in the *Gītā*. 'The path to Rāma's house is long and rugged and he lives very much afar. To reach him is tough going, so O sages, how can one reach that hard to come by Lord?'[198] 'I find it very difficult to think of the Lord's name, (i.e., meditate on him).[199] It is like an acrobat balancing himself on the sharp blade of a javelin from which if, not being able to stay, he falls, there is no other place for him'.[200] It is true that even Homer nods, and a poet of the stature of Wordsworth could at times sink to bathos and write:

> 'I've measured it from side to side:
> 'Tis three feet long and two feet wide'![201]

But with Kabīr this kind of thing happens too often to be ignored. We have given some examples and may add another verse in which he says 'hearing Death thunder even Brahmā's throne starts shaking'![202] In one of his *Padas* he says: 'Why do you go about flaunting yourself? Why do you forget that for ten months you were lying as an embryo in your mother's womb? If you were burnt you would become ashes and if you were kept (buried) you would be full of maggots. Your body is like water in a jar of half-baked earth, what's so great about it? You have done as the bee which gathers honey, (i.e., you have accumulated wealth, which, when you die people will say "take it, take it!" (i.e., it will be of no use to you). After your death they will say "why keep this corpse any longer?" And, seeing your mourning wife, some comrades of yours may go with your dead body to the cremation ground, but your soul will go alone by itself. Then too you don't remember Rāma! Why do you cast yourself into a dark pit. Says Kabīr, you have tied yourself to the world as a parrot sitting on a branch'.[203] The wisdom of what Kabīr puts across in the verse can't be denied, but it sounds more like a preacher's sermon than the flight of imagination that constitutes great poetry. And that is the characteristic pattern on which his verse is formed. He mostly either harangues or sermonizes. In the aforesaid verse Kabīr says, *maraghaṭ ghāṭ khaiṁca karirākhe* ('they will *pull* the corpse and put it on the pyre'). The word *khaiṁca* is very harsh for no one would exert such force on a dead body of one who was loved by the mourners. The ten month's lying in the mother's womb is also queer and out of place. Saying that the aggrieved relations take the corpse only when they see the widow's (sorrow) is also odd, for they would have to take it anyway. The simile of being tied to the world as a parrot sitting on the branch of a tree, too, is not very appropriate, for obviously the bird perches for a short while only . Kabīr was at his best in his verses on separation and union in which he used the example of the lover and the beloved in the Vaiṣṇava style. He closely resembles Mīrā in these verses though they do not have the poignancy and wistfulness of her thought or the fluidity of her language. An *abhisārikā nāyikā* is a girl who dresses in blue and accompanied by her companion, goes to meet her lover at midnight. Kabīr uses the example of the *abhisārikā* to denote the union of the soul with God and brings out the difficulties in achieving it by a comparison which, though adequate, is not very refined. The *abhisārikā* is a *krishnābhisārikā*, i.e., one who goes to the tryst on a dark night (as distinguished from the *śuklābhisarikā* who goes on a moonlit night. Adopting the conventional figuration of the *rītikāla* poets,he says: 'The girl, filled with longing to meet her lover, was going to the rendezvous when suddenly clouds gathered and it started raining. It became pitch dark and the girl and her companion lost the way. The girl covered her head with a blanket (the mention of a blanket is queer and spoils the picture) to shield herself from the rain, but it became heavy as the rain soaked it and the frail girl could not bear its weight. All these impediments prevented her from uniting herself with her lover'.[204] In a similar vein Kabīr conceives the union of the soul with God in the Vaiṣṇava *mādhurya* manner drawing on the analogy of the love of a wife for her husband or lover: 'Come to my house, lover, my body aches for your embrace. Everyone says I am yours but I have my doubts about it for what kind of love can you have for me unless you share my bed? Anger and sleep have fled and I go about restless in my house, tormented like a woman deprived of her lover, or like one thirsty having no water to drink. Is there anyone so kind as to convey my longing to Lord Hari? I can't live on any longer, says Kabīr without meeting (having *darshan* of) him'.[205] Likewise using the same symbolism he says 'O eternal Lord, protector of saints, when will you come to me? I weep for you and am hungry for your sight. I stand with my eyes glued to the pathway, expecting you each moment. Ever since you left my heart longs for you and ever dwells at your feet. I feel restless without you, writhing as a fish without water. Daylong I have no desire for food and I spend restless nights, waking. My house gives me no comfort without you here. I have to lie alone in bed tossing about for, Lover, you are not there to share it. I am your slave, you are my husband-lover. Lord, be gracious to me and come. If you do not come I can't live on. Kabīr your devotee says "Separation from you torments me greatly. Come soon now, Lord, and fulfil my longin" '.[206] 'In the rainy season', Kabīr says, 'the heron (*kraumca* bird) sheds so many tears on being separated from its mate, that they fill all the ponds! When this is the agony experienced by it, one can imagine the state of the soul which is separated from God for many lifctimcs" '.[207] And giving the example of the male and female ruddy goose (*cakavā and cakavī*)—another favourite symbolism used by Hindi poets, Kabīr says, 'The *cakavā and cakavī* are separated from one another in the night, and they come together again in the morning. But the *jīva* (the embodied soul) remains parted from God night and day'.[208] In the distant past communication was not so developed as now. There were few good roads and mostly dirt-tracks and pathways So when a man went away for some work it was not possible to know of his welfare—there weren't any phones or postal services. The only way was to inquire about it from someone who had gone to that place and had returned. So women whose husbands were abroad would eagerly question any traveller coming back, about him. Giving this analogy Kabīr says, 'As the separated woman stands on the pathway expectantly awaiting someone who might come and give her news about her husband's welfare, even so the soul is eager to meet some saint who can tell it how to reach God'.[209] But there is none who can give her such news. She waits in vain and the dark comes clouding her eyes. She calls out to him till her tongue is sore. Even so, says Kabīr, there is none to guide the seeker to God. The search for him is long and torturous and it is a wait that lengthens till one despairs of finding him.[210] The eyes keep raining tears continually like water being drained from a well by the *rahaṭ* and she keeps calling out for God like the cuckoo saying "pī, pī", yet he does not come. Even so the soul keeps vainly calling to God'.[211]

In portraying the quest of the soul for realizing God, Kabīr has used the comparison of a woman immolating herself on the funeral pyre of her dead husband. For example, he says 'As the woman whose husband is dead sits on his funeral pyre and says "beloved, now all are forgotten and there are only you and me", so the embodied soul is one with God'.[212] She lies on the pyre as the soul surrenders itself completely to God.[213] In this way she makes the supreme offering to her departed husband. The soul unites with the divine in like manner and there remains no distinction between the two.[214] Incidentally, this verse (containing the idea of oneness depicts Sūfī infuence. The comparison of the soul's union with God in this manner is not at all a happy one, for it conjures images of this ludicrous and repulsive custom which has been the bane of Hinduism. Women were aften forced to burn themselves on their dead husband's pyre and on one occasion the emperor, Akbar, when informed of a *satī* about to be burnt, rode a long distance on horseback to save the poor woman. Even if there was no compulsion, the social opprobrium cast on a widow was such that death were better than such living. So Kabīr's choice of the metaphor even if appropriate, hardly deserves any appreciation. The other comparison used by him is more appropriate, namely that of a war, for as Whitman says:

> 'Know'st thou not there is but one theme for ever-enduring bards?
> And that is the theme of War, the fortune of battles,
> The making of perfect soldiers'.[215]

This war is not fought on the battlefied but in the mind of the seeker of God, and the foes which are combated are desire, anger, greed for weath, malice, enmity and so forth. But it is not by relinquishment of the world and escapism that the challenge is met.[216] The field of battle is the world itself and one has to squarely face the five adversaries—craving and passion, rage, arrogance, greed and ignorance. Thus one gets rid of duality.[217] 'This war', says Kabir 'is fought by the Soul-shaped warrior riding the horse of love, wielding the sword of wisdom. Thus ready for battle, the warrior wages war and beheads the birth-and-death shaped foe'.[218] This thought is very much similar to that of the *Gītā* in which Krishna exhorts Arjuna: 'Therefore, O Arjuna, take hold of the sword of wisdom and slay with it that doubt which has arisen from ignorance and resort to yoga'.[219] 'The true warrior never leaves this struggle and fights on to the last even though he may be hacked to pieces'.[220] The real devotee, says Kabīr surrenders himself fully to God. God himself aids such a person and comes to him.[221] The figurative language of Kabīr is doubtless expressive, but he overelaborates the comparisons, and this tendency is noticeable almost all through his verse. It may be all right to do so in scriptures such as in the *Upaniṣads* because there the idea is to effectively indoctrinate, but in poetry such overdoing does not lend it grace.

Then there are the verses in which Kabīr adopts the conventional symbolism of wine, so extensively used by poets like Omar Khayyam and in modern times Bacchan (in his *Madhushālā*). Kabīr says 'The love for God is like life-giving nectar, but it is not easy to drink it for he who gives it demands the sacrifice of life itself'.[222] 'The intoxication of wine lasts only a while but that of love for God is everlasting and after drinking it one is not even aware of his existence'.[223] This nectar of Rāma (*rāma-rasa*) is far superior to the wine of worldliness—*rāma rasa pīyā re tātem̐ bisari gae rasa aura*. On drunking it one becomes filled with consciousness of the divine and the three worlds are revealed to him.[224]

Kabīr's verses do not have the consistency of poets like Bihārī, each couplet of whose *Satasaī* is concentrated with meaning so much so that they have been likened to the sharp points of barbs (*nāvaka ke tīra, dekhan mem̐ chote lagaim̐ ghau karaim̐ gambhīra*), or rise to Tulsī's or Mīrā's poetic height. Kabīr's darts are sharp only when he is attacking religious rituals or outward show But condemnation is the domain of the preacher, not of the poet. And even where the poet castigates he takes away the hurt by his wit. But not so Kabīr. His barbs are not tipped with wit's healing balm. Nonetheless Kabīr's verses often have depth of thought. 'The divine is not attained by laughing' he says. 'Those who reach him have to shed tears. If Hari was got by merrymaking there would be none deprived of him'.[225]

In the same strain he says, 'If one could attain Hari (God) by laughter and merrymaking who would undergo agony like the blade of a knife being sharpened on the hone? Only he can reach God who has forsaken passion, rage and craving'.[226] 'The arrows of Rāma's love' says Kabīr, 'are sharp and piercing. Who can relate the pain of him whom they strike? I have searched for the wound they cause all over my mind and body so that I may put healing balm on them, but all in vain. All comely girls have loveliness, but who knows which one is the Lover's beloved? On whose brow is that auspicious sign which marks out that girl to be the chosen one?'[227] And in another verse Kabīr eloquently expresses his yearning for God. 'My hopes have been belied. Who is there who can absolve one of the consequences of my karma, except him? The pond is full of water yet how can that water quench the thirst of the *cātaka* bird? She remains filled with gloom. Likewise the burden of my karmas is heavy and I remain ever athirst (for Hari) yet I have no news of him. He gives his favour to whom he wills and draws that person to him. Only his presence can banish sorrow In shallow water the fish finds no peace, even so O Krishna, without you Kabīr's agitation cannot end'.[228]

As a metaphysical poet Kabīr is outstanding, but when we view poetry in its common parlance, we can only consider him mediocre. His comparisons are not very apt, as when he speaks of fish in shallow water, having insufficient to drink—*udara na bharaī nīra,* or the blade's agony when sharpened on a hone, or the lake beginning to catch fire when the separated woman burning with the fire of separation approaches it! *(birah jalaī maiṁ jalau jalati jalahari jāuṁ/moṁ dekhā jalahari jalai, santauṁ kahāṁ bujhāuṁ).* Kabīr desires God's vision during one's lifetime, not at the moment of death as Krishna says in the *Gītā.*[229] The comparisons in his verse to express this however are often facile as for example he says if the iron should turn into stone and thus lose its elemental character, what use will the *pārasa* be?(which turns iron into gold according to legendary belief). So too, what will be the use if one finds God after he dies?[230] Sometimes his metaphors are mixed and lack clarity. For example he says, 'Existence is such a vast uncrossable ocean that one can't get across it except by means of the boat of Rāma's love. but this boat is also the serpent-shaped worldly enjoyments which if indulged in, will destroy the seeker of God'.[231] Here combining the two metaphors of the serpent and the boat seems rather odd. Although Kabīr draws his metaphors from common life, they do not have aptness and grace, and his diction is laboured and harsh.

As we have pointed out Kabīr's verses are primarily philosophical and didactic. They lack two essential elements of poetry, namely love (as separate from the mystical union of God and the soul) and nature. He would not have shared Bihārī's view that those who dive deep into the ocean of music and song and the rapture of levemaking are not drowned; those are drowned who keep away for these.[232] Kabīr remains far from the melody of music and the rapture of physical lovemaking. Nor does his poetry have the requirements enumerated by Ghanānanda, 'A peerless lover knowing the elegance of poetry... who is ever drenched in love's essence... who can master language, yet is not a stickler for convention. The person who is a great lover and speaks a language suffused with love hearing which acute desire awakens in men's minds. Those who do not know such love are for ever bewildered'.[233] Though Kabīr, too sings of meeting and parting, as we have said it is not that of lovers but the pangs of the soul's longing for God and the desire to achieve union with him. He never speaks of love in its ordinary connotation. Nor do we find in Kabīr's poetry the usual elements of beauty and descriptions of nature. Shorn of these his poetry doesn't have class. We may take for example Wordsworth's lines in which he conceives nature to be almost on a par with the divine:

> 'Wisdom and Spirit of the universe,
> Thou Soul, that art the Eternity of thought,....
> A motion and a spirit that impels
> All thinking things, all objects of all thought,
> And rolls through all things'.

This is practically deifying nature, mich like the primordial nature (*prakṛti*) of the Sāṁkhya. We find very vivid and stirring descriptions of nature even in poets like Mīrā who are otherwise purely devotional, for example: 'Toads and peacocks are drunk with glee, the cuckoo and the *papīhā* (the pied-crested cuckoo) sing in a sweet voice. The rumbling clouds gather and pour down on the parched earth. The lightning streaks as though shamelessly making love to the clouds. The bare earth adorns herself and puts on a new dress as though to meet Indra (heavens king)'[234] Or taking another example 'Black clouds, yellow clouds are massed together.... all in a moment they pour continually till it's water all over. The thirsty earth drinks the rain and dricd plants revive and are again green'.[235] The omission of nature either in its personified aspect as in Wordsworth, or its ordinary descriptive vein as in poets like Mīrā,

Kalidāsa and others, does not give his poetry wings to fly. Although he reaches the pinnacle at times, generally he is on flat ground. Besides, in considering the nature of his poetry we have to take into account that notwithstanding scholarly attempts to compile Kabīr's verses in anthologies, it can't be said with any amount of certainty which are his and which were added on by enthusiastic disciples of his or others who liked to put his stamp on their compositions. Kabīr himself confessed in a verse of his that he never held a pen and his utterances are 'by word of mouth'. Indeed his verses show such great variation that it is impossible to conceive they are of just one person. However, seeing what we have—the *Bījak*, the *Sākhīs*, the *Padas* and the *Ramaiṇīs*—one can conclude that as embodying his philosophy and devotion, he was certainly among the great poets, but in expression and poetic art he could be called just middling. Some critics have showered encomiums on him. For example Dr Ramakumara Verma says, 'He (Kabīr) fails to express his ideas because their charm is so great. These thoughts can't be expressed in ordinary words. The intensity of his think is so powerful that ordinary words can't bear its weight'.[236] Dvivedi goes one better calling Kabīr the 'dictator of language' (*vāṇī ke* dictator) and makes the highfalutin comment that 'language seems to become helpless before Kabīr (*bhāṣā kucha kabīra ke samane lācāra-sī nazarāti hai*)'.[237] This is sheer spread-eaglism. Language is never a slave and no one can ride roughshod over it, least of all a poet like Kabīr, for words are like tools which if used skillfully will do the task and if not, will hurt the hands which work them. It's like paint, which if spilled on the canvas will only blotch it up, but if dabbed by expert hands will produce a masterpiece. It is the same with the sculptor working on stone, the musician with notes and tunes, and so too with a writer and poet with words. There is usage of course and new words keep creeping into lexicons in their exotic forms; yet it is language which remains the master and those who do not pay it proper homage would be writing only words, words, words. Nor is language ever unable to bear the weight of ideas, however great they might be. In fact ideas by themselves are like birds with clipped wings, and as the bard says, unless turned into shape, they are 'airy nothings'. So it's the other way about and words aren't helpless before the poet (Kabīr is no exception), it is the poets who are helpless without words. While not deprecating Kabīr's poetry in any manner, it may be made clear that such paeans about it are quite out of place.

KABĪR'S LANGUAGE

The kind of language Kabīr used in his verse is as problematic as everything else about him. Various classifications have been made. One view is that it was *khaṙī-bolī,* i.e., Hindi in which some Sanskrit words have been adapted, or Urdu derived from Arabic and Persian words. Others believe it to be *Bhojpurī* (the language of Bhojpur) and yet others take it to be Rājasthānī (the language spoken in Rājasthān). Other views are that is a kind of Brajbhāṣa (Braj country dialect). P. Chaturvedi feels it is the dialect used by yogis and siddhas and R.C. Shukla and other scholars, that it would be most appropriate to call it the jargon of sadhus. Yet other views are that it is a kind of mixed dialect *(bemela khichaṙī—khichaṙī* being a kind of dish comprising rice and pules). Some writers (for example Charlotte Vaudeville) think it is Avadhi or Pūrabī, the language spoken in the Moslem kingdom of Jaunpur. Other versions are 'Hindui' which seems a concocted term implying 'the language of the bazaar' which appears meaningless for it's anybody's guess which bazaar and where. Other competitors for the Kabīrean language are Punjabi, Gujarati, Bundeli (the dialect of Bundelkhand) and the spoken dialect of folksong and ballads. Of these it appears that the term *kichaṙī* (potpourri) would be the most appropriate, for Kabīr's language seems to defy classification, which some critics have praised as being its admirable quality when really it is a kind of blemish. As for Kabīr himself, if we take it from the horse's mouth, discarding speculations and fanciful interpretations of 'eastern', it seems clear he considered that his verse was in Pūrabī: 'My language is of the east and can be understood by one familiar with that tongue'.[238] Scholars differ in interpreting this couplet. According to Charlotte Vaudeville 'Yet the meaning of the above-quoted *dohā,* (i.e., the one in question) which both Grierson and Ahmad Shah have taken literally is far from obvious. A literal interpretation appears hardly plausible: the idea that no one (in the west?) understands eastern Hindi is a rather flat statement'.[239] Vaudeville goes on to quote P. Chaturvedi's argument that *pūraba disā* 'the eastern region' symbolizes the ultimate spiritual stage which is the aim of the yogis, and therefore takes Kabīr's language to be 'a cryptic language understandable only to the yogis and *siddhas* who are the dwellers of that mysterious country' Charlotte supports Chaturvedi's view on the basis of a mention in the *Bījak* of a verse which says *puraba disā haṁsa gati hoī,* "The eastern reagion is the resort of the *haṁsa*".[240] The word *gati* means 'motion' or 'movement', hence all this means is that the movement of the *haṁsa* is eastward. A *haṁsa* or *haṅsa* means either 'the swan' or 'the sun.'[241] The verse of the *Bījak* could mean either the swan flies from the east, westwards, as swans do near about sunset, or that the sun's movement is from the east to the west (its rising and setting). Mystery could be attributed to the fabulous *rājahaṅsa* who is believed to dwell in Mansarovar lake and feed only on pearls. But that has nothing to do with Kabīr or his verse. Equally unlikely is the view of Dr Chaturvedi, for Kabịr wrote for the common man of the world and his 'east' has nothing to do with any spiritual state such as yogis aimed at. It would therefore be most rational to take *pūraba* in its most obvious sense. Besides dialects of the west and east of India have distinct characteristies. For example the Jats of the west stress the 'ṭ' (in *roṭi,* 'bread') as 'ṭṭ' so that *roṭī,* 'bread', is pronounced as *roṭṭī.* The westerner speaks of an old-fashioned person as *taparghasa* which no easterner can understand. And the dialect of Benares has *ailī gailī* for 'coming' and 'going', which no westerner would be able to decipher, while the Benarasi dish of *phunnī-dānā* (gram, sliced onion and parched rice') wouldn't make sense to him.

It seems Kabīr made use of several languages and dialects of northern India, or maybe it would be nearer the truth to say that the various compositions which pass off as his, were couched in various tongues. This being so we might call it a mixed language with *pūrabī* predominating, but with a large number of Punjabi, Bhojpuri, Rajasthāni, Braj, Sanskritized Hindi (despite his deprecation of Sanskrit), and Urdu words thrown in. It must also be observed that though his verse has some Arabic and Persian words too like in the ones quoted by Dr Tiwari, namely *garīb, majlīs, sekh, khelakhāsī, khilkhanā, ādāma, nazir, rahimānā* (Arabic words) and *gudarāve, salara, paigambara, diwānā, bhisti, bajgāri, panāh, najiki* and so forth (Persian words), this is the exception rather than the rule.[242] Irrespective of the controversy about Kabīr being a Moslem or a Hindu, his verse is influenced more by Hindi and Sanskrit than by Urdu, Arabic or Persian. He never studied Hindi systematically, nor deliberately introduced embellishment (*alankāra*) in his verse, yet we do find word and meaning combining to produce at times exalted poetry. Quite often he gives an unusual twist to words making them sound exotic, as for example *sabada* for *śabda*, *agani* for *agni*, *hari ki bahuriā*, *pīra* for *pīra*, *bātī*, *kūṁ*, *dinana* and so forth. He often uses *ba* for *va* and *ṇa* for *na*. Though he did not deliberately introduce such variations, they give his verses a harshness which could be avoided, and also make the text difficult of interpretation. Besides, many words he uses are archaic. What Longfellow said would aptly apply to Kabīr, '(He) spoke full well in language quaint and olden'.[243] Kabīr's poetry also lacks variety, and his comparisons (which form the greater part of the figures of speech he uses), are often obscure. They are at times so abstruse that they hang heavy on the reader's mind. For example expressing the various stages of life from youth to old age he says:

raini gaī mata dina bhī jāi
bhaṁvara uṙe baga baiṭhe āi

(The night has gone, the day will also go: the bumblebees have flown and the heron has alighted') Here 'night' stands for 'youth', 'day' for middle age and the bumblebees (which are black) giving place to the heron signify black hair turned white. The verse is quoted by critics to illustrate the felicity of Kabīrs comparisons, but it shows more the complexity, for the metaphors are far-fetched. So too is the case with another verse (in the *Sākhī*) depicting the extinction of life when the soul departs—'The breath stops and the embers are extinguished. The anvil is quiet when the blacksmith departs'.[244] In these verses Kabīr vies with Keśavadāsa in being terse and abstruse beyond comparison—*kaṭhina kāvya ke preta* ('the spirit of difficult verse'), but the comparison of the *jīva* to the blacksmith is bizarre and lacks refinement.

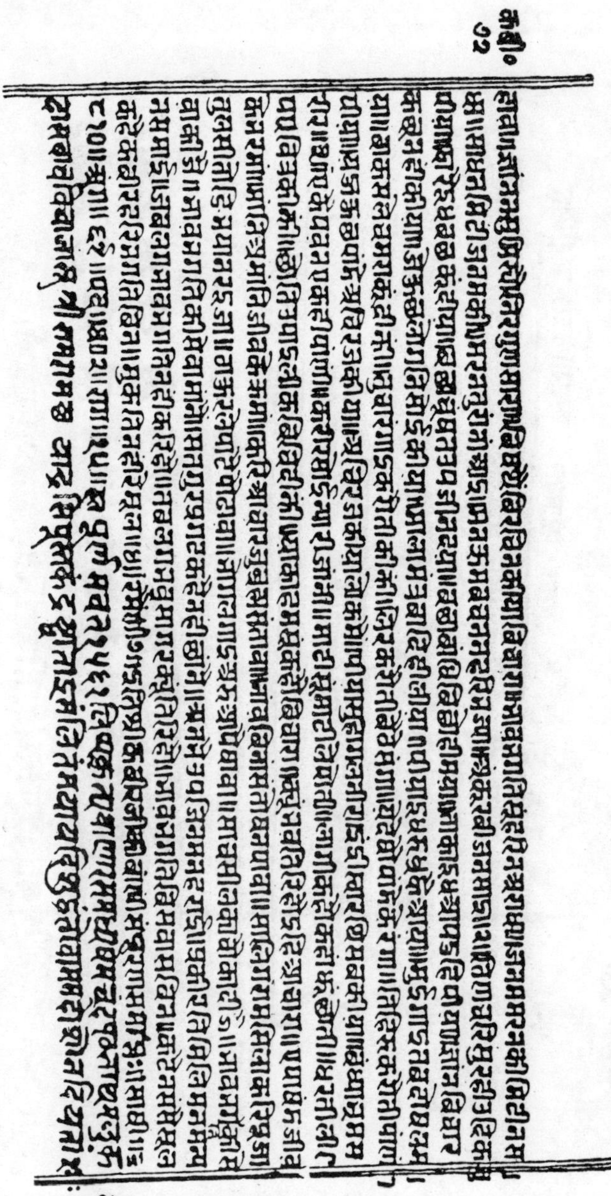

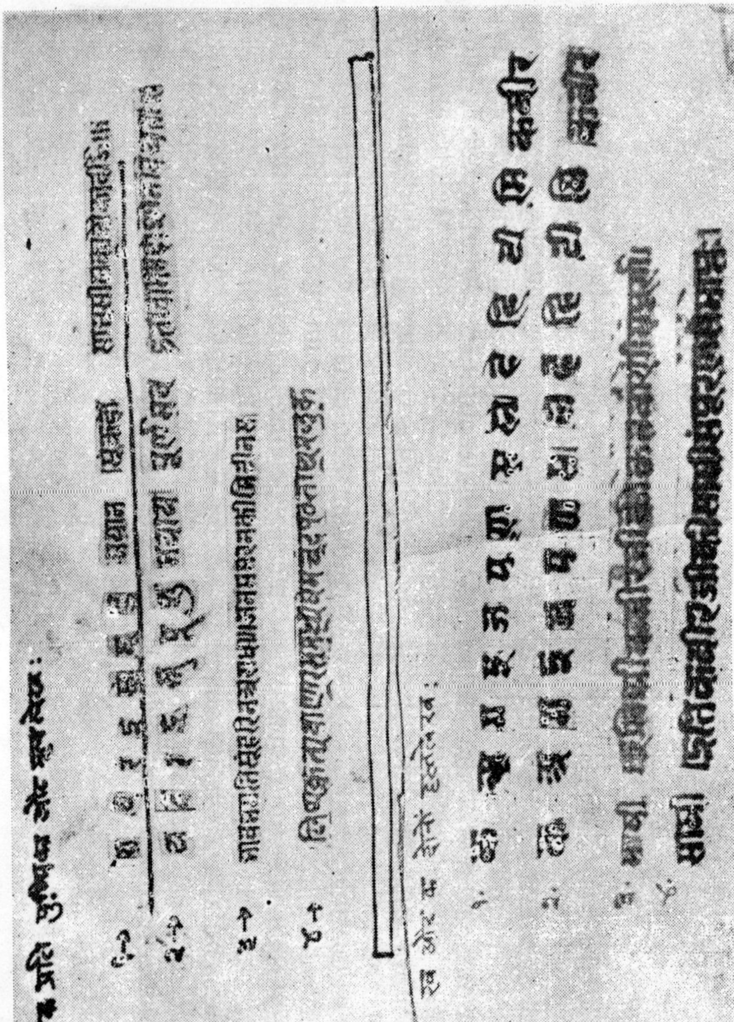

SOURCES

Dr. Parasanatha Tiwari has, after a great deal of research, enumerated eleven sources from which Kabīr's verses can be gleaned:[245]

1. Dādū-*panthi* (followers of Dādū).
2. *Niranjani.*
3. Contained in the *Guru Grantha Sahib.*
4. From the *Śabdāvalī* of Kabīr-panth.
5. The *Bījak* of Kabīr.
6. The *Śabdāvalī* of the Belvedere Press, Prayaga.
7. The Collection of Kabīr's *Sākhīs.*
8. The *Sākhīs* of Belvedere Press, Prayaga.
9. The *Sākhī* of *Sīyābagh.*
10. The *Sarbangī.*
11. The *Guṇaganjanāmā.*

However, there have been many anthologies of Kabīr with various classifications. For example Dr Mataprasada Gupta classifies the *Sākhīs* themselves into 59 sections according to their topics like *sumiraṇa, viraha, maya, kāmīṁ nara, jīvata mṛtaka* and so forth, the *Padas* under sixteen *rāgas*, the *Ramaimṇīs* with six sub-divisions.

Ramakumara Verma has given a detailed analyis of the various sources from which Kabīr's poems have been complited. His views are as follows.[246] The Bclvedere Press edition is based on the compilations made by various saints and mahatmas, but no handwritten manuscript which could have authority is mentioned in this anthology. The *Bījak* of Kabiracaura Benares doubtless mentions ancient documents as its basis but they relate primarily only to the ones found there. Yugalananda (Kabīr-panthi's Kabīr's *Sākhī*), has drawn from several sources which he considers to be authentic, particularly a manuscript of the library of Bakshi Gopalalala ex-minister of Śivahar principality which is said to date back to *samvat* 1600, (i.e., A.D.1543). But then he claims that his *Sākhī* includes all the relevant ones of the poet, and does not explain why the other *Sākhīs* which do not figure in his collection and yet are acknowledged genuinely to be Kabīr's, are not in it. The *Sākhī* of Sīyābagh, Baroda, is an orderly edition with a detailed introduction and index but the basis on which they have been compiled is nowhere mentioned and so the compilation can't be taken to be authorative. The *Bījak* of Sadhu Pūrandāsa (A.D.1837) is renowned, but when it was first published in Lucknow in Gangaprasada Verma's press it was found to have many errors which were pointed out by scholars. Ramakumara Verma mentions another handwritten manuscript of the *Bījak* of Burhanpur which he obtained from Sadhu Kashidasa, but this gives neither the year in which it was written, nor the source. However, he remarks it is doubtless an old manuscript.

Kabīr Granthāvalī of the Nāgarī Pracāriṇī Sabhā had two handwritten editions (A.D.1504 and A.D.1824). The manuscript was edited by Dr Shyāmasundaradāsa, but it contains very few of Kabīr's verses and does not appear to be authentic for, apart from other reasons, the concluding words of the chapters have been written in a script different from that of the rest of the text.

It seems that most of the handwritten manuscripts can't actually be ascribed to Kabīr for as he himself admitted he was not only unlettered but seems to have disdained bookish knowledge too.[247] He says in one of his verses that he had no systematic education, and in fact in his occupation as a weaver and that too of the lower caste (they were excluded from scriptural study), he hardly had any need for book knowledge.[248] That is the difficulty with his verses. They were obviously conveyed orally to some sages in whose company he moved And it must be borne in mind that such transmission by word of mouth was not like that of the *Vedas* or the *Upanisads* which were chanted time and again by devout disciples who memorized them, so that they were transmitted from generation to generation exactly as they were. But the same can't be said for Kabīr. Who knows how many of the verses which have been so laboriously compiled, commented on and extolled by learned scholars and on which researches have assiduously been made; are actually Kabīr's own and how many accreditions or inaccurate versions of his recitations? The inconsistency of language and imagery, too, makes this all the more likely for in places the verses show a felicity of expression while on the other hand some are harsh and tuneless to the ear. For example, repeating a few lines of a poem of his we have already quoted, we can discern in them the smoothness of poets like Mīrā:

> *maiṁ to tumhārī dāsī hoṁ sajanā, tuma hamare bharatāra*
> ***dīna dayāla dayā kari āvau, samaratha sirajanahāra***
> *kaiṁ hama prāna tajata haiṁ pyāre kai apanī kari lehu*
> *dāsa kabīra biraha ati bārḍyau abatau darasana dehu*

This is surely poetry beyond compare, particularly the second line is superb in imagery expression and embellishment (*alankara*). But let us see another verse of his:

> *kabīra keso kahi kūkiye, na soī asāra*
> *rāti divasa kai kūkaraiṁ, kabahūṁ lagai pukāra.*[249]

Despite the alliteration (ka) and that too of a harsh sound, there is no tenderness or felicity of expression here. The word *asāra* meaning 'continually' is neither approriate nor has ease of expression. The second line does not adequately explain the sense, so much so that in his version Dr Gupta was constrained to add '*mat*' after '*kūkanaiṁ*'.[250] Or, taking another verse which depicts the Islamic influence on him, which too we have quoted before in another context, in which he exhorts the *jīva* to wake up, as thieves abound. 'Keep watch' he says, 'making *ra* of the word *rāma* your turban, *ma* your armour and keeping the gem of Rāma (devotion) in your turban. Than even if Israel sends someone to take your soul. Hari will protect you. Kabīr says, one should always be awake, whether he is a householder or a hermit'.

> *jāgi re jīva jāgi re/corana kau ḍara bahuta kahata haiṁ, uṭhi uṭhi paharai lāgi re*
> *rarā kari ṭopa mamāṁ kari bakhtara, jñāna ratana kari pāga re*
> *jaisai jau ajrāila mārai, mastakiāvai bhāga re*
> *jaisī jagaṇī je ko jāgani ta hari dei suhāga re*
> *kahai kabīra jāgyā hi cahiye, kyā griha kyā bairāga re.*

In the lines both the idea and expression are of a low order. The expression, 'there is said to be a great fear of thieves', is peculiar and so too the juxtaposition of Israel and Rāma. The aforesaid verses have been quoted not to deprecate Kabīr in any way, but just to bring out the inconsistencies. It can be seen that the possibility of different hands writing them and of different minds conceiving them is very strong indeed.

An investigation made by the Nāgarī Pracariṇi Sabhā revealed that there are 85 handwritten manuscripts existing between the years 1901 and 1922, but except one they do not give the year in which they were written. According to Ramakumara Verma eight such manuscripts also exist in the library of the Jodhpur *rājya*, which too are of doubtful authencity.

As regards the Kabīrpanthi manuscripts these also appear to be mythical and more the flights of imagination of the sadhus of this school than compilations of Kabīr's verses. One of them for example, depicts Kabīr conversing with Chitragupta and Gorakhnāth! Another is even more fanciful and conceives him to be an avatar in the Kali-age! The *Bhaktamāla* which dates to 1585, has a verse on Kabīr (which we have reproduced at the beginning of this introduction and so is not being repeated.). It is evident, therefore, that Kabīr's time was before 1585. Another stanza of it makes it obvious that the poet was a disciple of Rāmānanda. The point is being emphasized because some commentators, chiefly those abroad have not accepted the discipleship of Kabīr to this saint, dismissing it as a 'Hindu tradition'.[251] Many other saints who were contemporaries of Kabīr have also been mentioned in it. The *chāppya* (stanza) is as follows:

śrī rāmānanda raghunātha jyoṁ dutiya setu jagatarana kiyo
anantānanda kabīra sukhā surasurā padyavati narahari
pipā bhāvānanda raidasa dhanā sena surasara kī tharahari
aura śiṣya praśiṣya eka teṁ eka ujāgara
viśva mangala ādhāra sarvānanda daśadhā ke āgara
bahuta kāla bapu dhāri kai, pranata janana kau pāra diyau
śrī rāmānanda raghunātha jyoṁ dutiya setu jagatarana kiyo.

Kabīr's name finds place in the *Ain-i-Akbarī* 'He was a Mohammedan for his catholicity of doctrine and illumination of his mind, and when he died, the brahmins wished to burn his body and the Mohammedans to bury it'. And 'Some say that at Rattanpur (Subah of Oudh) is the tomb of Kabīr the asserter of the unity of God, the portals of the spiritual discernment were partly opened to him and he discarded the effete doctrine of his own time. Numerous verses in the Hindi language are still extant of him containing important theological truths'. Ignoring the cant about cathocity being a Mohammedan attribute, we may take this as confirming that Kabīr's advent was before 1598 the date of the *Ain-i-Akbari*. The sage Tukārāma (b.1598) also mentions Kabīr, though strangely enough emphasizing the low caste of other saints he spoke of (he himself was of a low caste too): *'Gorā, raidāsa camāra, Kabīra musalmān, senā nāī, kanhopātrā veśyā... cokhāmelā achūta, janābaī kumārī apanī bhakti ke kāraṇa īśvara meṁ līna ho gaye haiṁ* ('Gorā the potter, Raidāsa the *camāra* a low caste, Senā the barber, Kanhopātrā the prostitute, Cokhāmelā the untouchable and Kumari Janabāī have, because of their devotion to God, been merged with god').

Kabīr is also mentioned in Anantadāsa's *Kabīr Sahib kī Paracaī*. Anantadāsa's tract has two, parts, the first about Pīpā and Raidāsa and the other about Kabīr. The first portion (which does not mention Kabīr) was written in 1600. It stands to reason, therefore, that the one concerning Kabīr was also written at the same time. However, Ramakumara Verma claims to have obtained some handwritten manuscript of the same name dated 1785 which gives the information that Kabīr was a weaver living in Kāśī (Varanasi), his guru was Rāmānanda, the rajah of Baghel, Vīrasingh Deva was his contemporary. Sikandar Shah visited Kāśī and he behaved cruelly toward Kabīr and the saint-poet lived up to the age of 120 years. Even if we do not treat this manuscript as authentic, as is indeed admitted by Verma himself-*yah vāṇī hajara nau ke guṭakā kā bhāga hai* 'It's part of Vāṇī Hajāra Nau'), it does give vital information about Kabīr.[252]

The Guru Granth Sahib, the Sikh scripture, was compiled by the fifth guru, namely Guru Arjuna Singh. In some of its verses we find mention of Kabīr as for example one of Nānaka—*nāma chībā kabīra julāhā pūre gurute gati pāhi* (Kabīr the weaver, achieved liberation by the blessings of a guru preceding him'). The pointer by the expression *pūre* guru may be to Rāmānanda, though some, like Dr Mohan Singh, interpret it as 'becoming merged in *Brahman*'.

We have already mentioned Nābhādāsa's commentary on the *Bhaktamāla*. This is of assistance firstly in definitely fixing Kabīr's time for it was written in A.D.1585 and the poet must have lived before this date. Secondly, it proves that he was living in the age of Sikandar Shah (1489-1517) of the Lodi dynasty, and the Sultan, not favouring the poet's liberal views, inflicted many cruelties on him. Orthodox Islam could neither reconcile itself with the Vaiṣṇava tendencies of the Sūfīs, nor tolerate their esoteric liberalism. Sikandar Lodi, who was a zealous Moslem, was as much a bigot as other Sultans and the historian tells us:

'He (the Sultan) utterly destroyed diverse places of worship of the infidels and left not a vestige remaining of them. He entirely ruined the shrines of Mathura, the mine of heathenism and turned their Hindu places of worship into caravan serais and colleges. Their stone images were given to the butchers to serve them as meat-weights, and all the Hindus of Mathura were strictly prohibited from shaving their heads and beards and performing their ablutions'.

We will have to say more about Sikandar's treatment of his Hindu subjects when we go on to narrate about Kabīr's times But it would be relevant here to mention that he strongly disapproved even liberal Moslems. A writer records, the Sultan stopped the annual procession of Sālār Mas 'ūd Ghāzi's lance, the visits to tombs of saints by Moslem women and the carrying of *tāzias* during Moharrum. His intolerance was thus not confined to Hindus but also extended to broadminded Moslems.[253] A brahmin named Laudhaṇ of village Kaner was killed because 'he thought that Islam was true, as was his own religion'![254] This being the thinking of Sikandar Lodi, the account of the tortures inflicted by him on Kabīr is very plausible, as conveyed by Nābhādāsa's commentary in the *Bhaktamāla*[255] Nabhādasa's commentary further testifies that Kabīr was a weaver, but at sometime left the profession in order to devote himself to Rāma-devotion, that by God's grace he was endowed with miraculous powers and the Sultan and his begam were amazed by seeing a demonstration of them; that he was Rāmānanda's disciple; and he lay down on a bed of flowers and was merged with God, at Maghara. Nabhādāsa's commentary, however, does not give any information about the poet's birth, family and other such matters.

We have mentioned Anantadāsa's *Kabīr Sahib ki Paracai*. This also confirms many of the facts about the poet, namely :

1. Kabīr was a weaver, and lived in Kāshī.
2. He was Ramananda's disciple.
3. Sikandar Lodhi visited Kāshī and imposed many tortures on Kabīr.
4. Kabīr was a contemporary of Rajah Virasingha of Baghela who became the saint's disciple.[256]

We have mentioned the literary compositions of Kabīrpanthīs which mention some traditional and often incredible beliefs about Kabīr, as indeed are apt to become current about many Indian saints and mystics. The work known as *Anurāga Sāgara* for example has it that Kabīr was a baby found by a weaver, Nīrū and his wife Nīmā. The baby was found abandoned near a tank, believed to be the Lahartāla (*tāla* -'lake') lake of Kāśhī.[257] Another such Kabīrpanthi work is *Kabīr Caritarabodha* which, even though it can't claim absolute trustworthiness, is yet noteworthy, for it gives information about the probable date of birth of Kabīr, which in one of its verses, is said to be the *samvat* year 1455, i.e., A.D.1398.[258] These works are, however, so greatly exaggerated that they degenerate into honeyfogle adulation. One of the verses of *Bhavatarana* of the saint Dharmadāsa, for instance conceives Kabīr to be an avatar of the Kali-age, which is pure nonsense and incredibly freakish.[259]

TRADITIONAL BELIEFS ABOUT KABĪR

Tradition has a very prominent place in the lives of Indian saints and all kinds of beliefs which are fantastic are not only current but are eagerly swallowed hook, line and sinker by critics and those writing about them. The following exist about Kabīr:

1. It is said he was the son of a brahmin widow who once went with her father to seek the blessings of the sage Rāmānanda. The sage blessed her by saying *putravati bhava*, (i.e., 'may you be the mother of a son'). The sage was obviously unaware of the fact that she was a widow. The words of the saint had to be proved true and so she gave birth to Kabīr in Kāshī where she lived. The *Bhaktamālā Ramarasikāvalī* of Maharaj Ragurāja Singh gives a slightly different version. According to this the woman lived in Rāmānanda's hermitage, engaging herself in the sage's service. One day when the sage was lost in meditation he had 'divine' communion with the widow resulting in Kabīr's birth. Yet another version has it that she was gathering flowers in the hermitage's bower when Rāmānanda chanced to come that way. Seeing him there, she hid the flowers making a bundle of them in her sari, and told the sage that her belly was distended because she was pregnant. 'Be it so' said the sage and as his words could not be falsified, she really became pregnant and gave birth to Kabīr.

   As the brahmin woman was a widow she feared public opprobrium, and abandoned the baby near a tank, from where a weaver and his wife, finding him lying there, adopted him. The baby grew up to be known as Kabīr, the weaver.

2. Another traditional belief is that Swami Aṣṭānanda went one day towards the Lahara lake and saw something gleaming brightly on the waters. He hurried to Rāmānanda and told him of this strange phenomenon. The sage said that it was really a baby, and because he had so spoken, his words came out true and the baby was Kabīr. Rāmānanda declared that the child would be greatly honoured and spend his life in serving the people. According to the Ahmad Shah, the man who 'saw the light' was really Kabīr's father, and it wasn't any light, but his own baby child who had been abandoned by the widow woman, whom, because of fear of public consure, he wasn't willing to acknowledge as his wife. It is said that when Kabīr died he was again mingled with this mysterious light.

Such accounts, forming part of mere traditional belief, lack authenticity, and are all in the mind. Two other beliets that popularly exist are about Kabīr's obtaining the *dīkshā* (initiation) from Rāmānanda and the other about his death. According to the first, Kabīr was eager to be initiated into discipleship by Rāmānanda, but feared he may not be able to get it as he was of a low caste. So once when the sage was going to have his early morning bath in the Ganga river, Kabīr lay on one of the steps leading to the river-bank. Since it was yet dark, the sage did not see him and stumbled againt him, exclaiming 'Rāma! Rāma!' Kabīr took that to be the initiation *mantra*. However this account is most unlikely, and being what he was, Kabīr would never resort to such a stratagem. The other belief is that when he died, the Hindus wanted to burn his dead body and the Moslems to bury it. But when they reached the spot, all they found was a heap of flowers! This fanciful story is still less likely and deserves summary dismissal. Kabīr was obviously as alike in birth and death as any other man.[260] We go on to narrate the poet's life and times.

LIFE

'Who ever took Rāma's name in our family? Ever since the rosary began to be counted here (by Kabīr), we have known no happiness. What a wonder, this accursed lad has left off interest in weaving (which is his livelihood)'...[261]

Kabīr's mother cursing Kabīr

BIRTHPLACE

As in the case of other Indian saints and sages, Kabīr's life is shrouded in mystery. We have little to go by apart from stray utterances about him and even the little he said about himself has been twisted by critics to conform to their own views. For example he referred to Magahar several times as the place of his early life and said that later he went to Kāshī (Varanasi) 'First I had a vision of God in Magahar and then I went to live in Kāshī'. Yet some critics believe Benares to be his place of birth, for at one place he said 'As is Magahar, so is Kāshī. They are the same to me'. The fact of his spending his early years in Magahar cannot of course be taken to mean that it was the place of his birth. Nonetheless it would be a strong indication of it. The different places suggested are:

1. Magahar, a village near Benaras rather poor, backward and wretched.
2. Village Belaharā in the district of Azamgarh, an Eastern district in the province now known as Uttar Pradesh.
3. Benares town by the Ganga river (now Varanasi).
4. Kuraha village in the province known as Takka.
5. Lahartāla which is in Benares about two miles from Kabīr Caurā.
6. Mithila.
7. Chandavār, in the district of Ballia (again an eastern district of Uttar Pradesh).

Various writers have drawn on their own sources to support their views. Barthawal is for Magahar because mainly weavers lived there. But then weavers aren't confined to that place alone, they are spread all over northern India. Kabīrpanthīs, relying on legend believe the poet was born in Lahartāla. Subhadra Jha relying on a line of the *Bījak* is for Mithila. Dr. Ramajilal 'Sahayak' believes Kabīr's birthplace was decidedly Benares, basing his conclusion partly on legend and partly on isolated lines from various compilations attributing them to be Kabīr's. Dr Mataprasada Gupta thinks it can't be Benares, for Kabīr calls his birthplace *kuraha*, (i.e., *kulakṣya or kudeśa*—'an evil country') and he could never have used this term for Benares which is considered to be a holy city.[262] Dr. P.N. Tiwari suggests Chandavār on the basis of some obscure Kabīrpanthī works. Dr Parasanath Chaturvedi believes all the different versions are mere claptrap, a view shared by others too, like Gupta, who concludes that nothing definite can be said, (Dr Jayadeva Singh and Dr Vasudeva Singh). Considering all factors, Magahar seems most likely.

DATE OF BIRTH

Equal uncertainty prevails about Kabīr's date of birth. The verse regarding this, which has already been quoted (*caudaha sau pacapana sāla gage* etc.), would point to the year *samvat* 1455, i.e., A.D.1398 This has been accepted by some writers (as for example Ramajilal 'Sahayak' who gives Rāmānanda the dates A.D. 1328 to A.D. 1448). That would mean the sage lived 120 years. This might not sound so incredible as seems to western writers for the longevity of ancient Indians has been commented on by Ktesias: 'The age to which they live is 120,130 and 150 years, though the very old live to 200'.[263] Since we find mention in Kabīr's verses about Rāmānanda, it would be rational to conclude that they were contemporaries. Nonetheless Kabīr's date of birth as A.D.1398 presents difficulties inasmuch as Sikandar Shah reigned from 1448 to 1517. That he visited Benares is historically confirmed. According to John Briggs the Shah's army crossed the Ganga river in the Moslem year Hijri 900, i.e., 1494 in order to fight with Hussain Shah Sharki and the two armies faced each other about 27 miles off Benaras. In his commentary on the *Bhaktamāla*, Priyadāsa also mentions about the ill-treatment of Kabīr by Sikandar Lodi, and in confirmation of the many ways in which the king tried to get rid of the poet it is mentioned in these verses that elephants were brought out so that they would trample on Kabīr and he was bound in chains and cast into the Ganga river, but was miraculously saved.[264]

Thus it is clear beyond doubt that Sikandar Lodi visited Benares and perpetrated many tortures on Kabīr. Writers who dismiss this as moonshine are mistaken. The Sikhs believed that Kabīr had met Nanak also. Hence the dates for the poet (Kabīr) given by Farquhar and confirmed by Keay, namely A.D.1440 to 1470 seem to be most reasonable. This would also account for Kabīr's meeting with Nanak (b.1469). That way Kabīr would be forty-eight years old when Sikandar Lodi ascended the thone and the fact of the Sultan's oppression would be borne out. As for those learned scholars who dismiss the whole controversy by saying that historical evidence is lacking, it may be said that the scope of history in too limited to incorporate minor details. Besides, we have to reconstruct the facts about the lives of saints, who were singularly reticent about such things in the best possible manner, as a man in a dark room has to make his way by the dim light available to him. So it would be most rational to accept the dates for Kabīr suggested by Keay and Farquhar, namely b.1440 and d.1518.

FAMILY AND NAME

Fanciful stories are related by some critics about the 'previous lives' of Kabīr. It is said that in these he was born a brahmin.[265] Due to some sinful acts he had to take birth as a weaver in a low caste. As we have related, according to legend the poet was the illegitimate child of a brahmin widow, who abandoned him, and he was adopted by Nīmā and Nīrū who found him, and these two became his foster-parents. 'Sahayak' has also put forward an existing belief according to which Kabīr's father was a Korī weaver and his mother a Moslem. However, there does not appear to be any foundation for such beliefs, and the truth most probably is that the poet was born in a Moslem family and was a Moslem. Ravidāsa, also of a low caste says 'In Kabīr's family the festivals of Idd and Bakr'idd were observed and cows were sacrificed. Shaiks and Pirs were honoured. By his good deeds Kabīr achieved merit in such a family'.[266] Ravidāsa, himself a butcher, ought to have known. As we have said. Kabīr's mother was annoyed by her son's vagaries, observing that the name of Rāma was never taken in her family. All this conclusively shows that Kabīr was born in a Moslem family and his parents, too, were Moslems, their profession being weaving. Having said this, it cannot be denied that the influence of Hinduism, and particularly of the Vaiṣṇavas among them, was ponounced, and even though the poet was a Moslem living in a Moslem family his thought, ideas and language were more akin to Hinduism than to Islam.

There is no controversy about Kabīr's name. The word *kabīra* means 'eminent' or 'great' in Arabic, and it is said that on his birth when the *qāzī* opened his book to seek a name for the child, the first word which came up was Kabīra and so he was given the name Kabīr. There are some minor variations of it, namely Kabīrā, Kabbīr, Kabīra, Dāsakabīra, Kabīradāsa and Kabīrū, but these are mainly to be in consonance with the metre or rhyme of his verses. Sometime he is also called Kavīr.

EARLY YEARS

We do not know much about his early days. He was described by Garībadāsa as a handsome child having a lovely golden complexion and fair.[267] There was nothing to show that he would turn out to be a saint and a poet of distinction; no sign of any precocity or genius. The boy Kabīr spent his time with his playmates, the children of his neighbours, as he later recollected rather sadly—*bārah barasa bālapana khoyo* ('I let twelve years of my childhood pass by uselessly'). But what more could be possible for a poor child belonging to a family so low in status? There were quarrels too with his playmates and apparently Kabīr was an aggressive lad for there were complaints of his having thrashed his chums.[268] His parents would beg their forgiveness for their son's behaviour.[269] He was their only child and naturally all the company he got was from the children of his neighbourhood. Right from childhood Kabīr was a lover of all living creatures and the animalist that he later became, found expression. Even though belonging to a Moslem household, he abhorred the killing of animals. He said about this later that those who consume meat and liquor can never achieve emancipation. They go to hell.[270] Even as a child he was so repulsed by meat that when guests were invited and meat dishes served, he wouldn't enter the house. When asked by his mother why he kept away, he would reply that he did not like to be present where meat was being eaten![271] It is said that his parents were so affected by his stern resolution that they never again ate meat in his presence. Ahiṁsā (non-violence) and abstaining from slaying animals is foreign to Moslems and this trait of the child shows his bent towards the Hindu culture for ever after the Mīmāmsic-ridden Vedic period, sacrifice has been unknown to Hindu India, except in rare cases where the custom lingers (as at Vindhyacala).

According to the Islamic custom every Moslem boy has to be circumcised. But to Kabīr the rite was repulsive and he refused to be circumcised presaging his opposition to all convention, which was to become his nature.[272] He was one of those rare persons for whom commonsense and and logic overrode blind superstition and he had the courage to defy orthodoxy. If circumcision was that vital, he reasoned, why weren't women also circumcised? Besides, if for Moslems it was essential, God himself would have caused them to be born thus. The reasoning was, of course, specious, but he must have been a child when the rite was to be performed and firstly it was remarkable that at that age he could think so clearly and secondly that he could have the strong will to oppose such a custom, which was as essential for Moslems as *mundan* for Hindus.

HOUSEHOLDER AND SAINT

It seems the turn towards devotion (*bhakti*) came early in Kabīr's life, much to the chagrin of his Moslem mother to whom his 'Rāma' was meaningless and sages lousy people good for nothing. Of this call of the Divine Kabīr wrote 'My mind was no longer in weaving, I was engrossed in Hari (God)'.[273] When his mother found herself powerless to divert his mind to his occupation, which was indeed necessary to support his family, she could do nothing but sit and weep.[274] Kabīr has been praised for this, but it is doubtful if such praise was deserved. For a man who prided himself in carrying out his duties, it was criminal neglect to ignore the wants of his family. He may be eulogized as a perfected saint, but hardly earns any credit for being a dutiful father. He spoke of his own grief at being pulled up for his *bhakti* and association with his fellow-sages.[275] But he never appeared to have any remorse for the neglect of his family,particularly his marital relationship with his wife Loi, who even though said to lack beauty, was after all his wife. It was natural for her to feel neglected and she complained to him about it.[276] Although there is no mention of the other wife, Dhaniā, who was also known as Ramjaniā (he married two, the Molsems being allowed four), she too must have suffered because of his cold indifference. It could be that he was not so inattentive to her, for unlike Loī, she was very lovely, of a higher family and, according to some writers, possibly a prostitute in her early years, and so the more sexually inviting of the two. There is nothing to show that Kabīr was any less sexy than other men. It is doubtful if saints can be exonerated from the duty they owe to their wives and families. Even Lord Buddha tricked his wife, leaving her and their son asleep, and sneaking away quietly in the night. From one point of veiw saintliness is no passport to such deceit or indifference. particulary towards those who are so intimately connected and have such complete trust in the deceiver. Swami Rama Tirtha was once admonished by his devotee, Puran Singh, when he hesitated to meet his wife and son who had come a long way to see him. So too Ramana Maharshi who refused to give any answer to his mother, Alagammal, had to be ticked off by his own devotee, Pachaiyappa Pillai. 'Your mother is weeping and praying, why don't you at least give her an answer?[277] So one can't absolve Kabīr of his neglect. His son and daughter, he had two children, (though some writers like Dr Jayadeva Singh mention two sons and two daughters), often went without food because he would give it away to the saints who stayed at his house. They had to be content with fried gram.[278]

It is generally believed that Kabīr's guru was Rāmānanda, even though there is no positive evidence for it. Nonetheless there are many indirect references to his being Rāmānanda's disciple. The *Bhaktamāla* of Nābhādāsa and Priyadāsa's commentary on it both are of this view. Others mentioning this fact are *Anatadāsa*[279] and the *Kabīrpanthī* sources.[280] In the *Dabistān-i-Majahib* of Mohsina Fani we find the following observation: 'It is said that when Kabīr was set on the path ot the non-dual, he went (for instruction) to many learned and virtuous Moslems and Hindus, but he could not find anyone worthy enough. Then someone told him to seek the blessing of Rāmn̄anda, the aged bṛahmin and renowned sage'.[281] Many critics, among them Dr Ramakumāra Verma, Dr Hazariprasada Dvivedi, Dr Shyamasundaradasa and Dr Barthawal, are also of the same view. Thus there is quite a great deal of secondary evidence to point to Rāmānanda being Kabīr's guru.[282]

The other claimant to being Kabīr's preceptor is Sheikh Takī. There were two Sūfī saints of this name, one of the Chisti branch, the other of the Suharwardis. One of them lived in Karā Mānikpur and the other in Jhūsī. The former has been suggested as Kabīr's guru, but it seems it was the other way about and it was Kabīr who instructed Takī, as one of the poet's verses shows.[283] Besides, it was Takī who was instrumental in getting Kabīr tortured by Sikandar Lodi and was disappointed when these attempts failed.[284] When Sikandar Lodi got the poet bound in chains and cast in the Ganga river, the current broke the chains and Kabīr was found sitting on a deeskin and meditating by the river-bank. Thus by no stretch of the imagination can Takī be deemed to be Kabīr's guru. There is a reference in one of the poet's verses to some *pītambara pīra* ('a saint dressed in a yellow silk robe') living on the bank of the Gomti river who, he says is his guru. But he does not say where.[285] However this may be an allusion to Rāmānanda, particularly because of the mention of the ochre robe.

It has been said that Kabīr was a great traveller and visited many far-off places.[286] It is said there is a samādhi in Jagannatha Puri, so this pīra was the poet's disciple.[287] But there is no evidence of the existence of Kabīr's grave there despite the claims of Moslem divines. In one of Kabīr's *Sākhīs* there is also a vague mention of the poet having been to Mecca, the holiest place for Moslems to be visited at least once in a lifetime by the devout.[288] But it seems that the verse only shows Kabīr's devotion to that sacred spot. Even seeing off a Hājī on his *haj* is considered by Moslems to confer merit. So maybe the verse conveys that alone. Kabịr was against all outward show—fasts austerities, sacerdotal marks and empty display of religious zeal. Speaking of Mecca he said 'The Hindus died paying homage to spirits and the Moslems on their way to Mecca', and 'Mecca lies in the mind'.[289] How could such a person go to Mecca? Kabīr does not appear to have been at all affected by wanderlust. His occupation and family life never permitted him the luxury of outings, nor could he have money to spare for them. Whenever he could, he chose to befriend the holy men who thronged Benares and it's a safe bet he found many who were not so holy, only pretenders.

EDUCATION

Kabīr himself admitted that he had no truck with pen, ink or paper, and described the 'greatness of the four ages' verbally. He appeared to have a contempt for learning, terming Sanskrit as 'the water of a well', i.e., stagnant. While one can admire his frankness in admitting his own shortcoming, decrying learning is not a commendable quality. It is true that *bhakti* (devotion) has nothing to do with learning. Once Chaitanya was going somewhere, when he noticed a man sitting by the roadside with a book. He would open it, glance at a particular page and be filled with ecstasy, and then close it again. Amazed, Chaitanya desired to see the book and was astonished to find it completely blank, except for one page on which was written the word 'Rāma'. On questioning him, the man said 'what use for me will this book be if "Rāma" is not in it, and if "Rāma" is there of what significance is all else written in it'. So too Kabīr says, 'All who read books, died without being learned, but he has real wisdom who has been able to decipher even one syllable of love'. For him love was something spontaneous, got by complete self-surrender and single-minded devotion. It demanded the sacrifice of all else. It was not something 'which could be grown in an arbour or be bought from the bazaar'.[290] Having spoken about the insufficiency of learning, it would have suited the humility of a sage like him not to have extolled his own. But we regretfully notice the streak of vanity still persisting when he goes on to say about his own *Sākhīs* that they are 'the eyes of wisdom' and without them 'there is no end to strife in the world',[291] and that the words which issue from his lips are as endless as the leaves of a big tree or the grains of sand on the Ganga-bank![292] Surely this is self-praise and what a contrast it is to the utterance of that *mahākav*i ('king of poets') Tulsīdāsa—*kabita bibeka eka nahiṁ moreṁ/satya kahuṁ likhi kagada koreṁ.* ('My poetry does not have even an iota of poetic knowledge, i.e., excellence. I swear it hasn't').[293] Nonetheless we find such a mine of wisdom and felicity of expression in Kabīr that it has elicited the admiration of lovers ot poetry and produced a mass of critical literature on the utterances of an illiterate weaver. There are a few conclusions that can be reached as possible solutions of this riddle. One view expressed is that since he was Rāmānanda's disciple, the grace of the *sadguru* (guru) gave rein to his poetic genius even though he was uneducated. 'I held the dice of love' he says, 'making my body the dice-board. My guru told me what move I should make and I played the game as he instructed me to'.[294] And again 'I learnt mind-control from my guru and through yoga and meditation perfected myself'.[295] It was through the wisdom imparted to him by his guru that he achieved success, which was possible only by the guru's grace.[296] There is surely a great deal of truth in these observations, for all wisdom (as indeed all else) comes from God—*tvameva vidyā*. As Tulsī also says in the *Mānasa*, 'Even the meritorious poetry of a good poet does not get splendour without Rāma's name, as a moonfaced beauty even though having all adornments, cannot look lovely without putting on a dress. And as against that even the most faulty verse having no good qualities, but which sings the praises of Rāma, is prized by wise men and recited and heard with reverence, for saints savour such poetry as bumblebees suck nectar from flowers'.[297] Nevertheless, in Kabīr's case one has to keep in mind the fact that all his poetry was communicated by him to others by word of mouth and how much of it was distorted, how much composed by others and passed off as his, and how much of it genuinely his own, could be anybody's guess. With this reservation we must remain content with what has been handed down to us and that which has been laboriously sifted from the spurious by learned scholars and researchers of Kabīr. What is material is the quality of great utterances, not the person or persons whose work they are. A pearl is prized for its iridescent gleam even though it is made by a lowly oyster to ease the irritation caused to it by a grain of sand, and gems repose under the earth we tread on. So Kabīr's lack of education has nothing to do with the greatness of the *Sākhīs*, the *Ramainīs* and the *Padas* of the *Bījak*. There are disputes about the authorship of many ancient books of philosophy, religion and literature, but no one can, because of that, question their greatness. So too with Kabīr.

Though content with the barest minimum to eke out a livelihood, one can't live on *bhakti* (devotion) alone, as the *Gītā* says: *śarīrayātrā pi ca te na prasidhyed akarmaṇaḥ* ('you cannot even exist if you do not work').[298] Therefore Kabīr said in one of his verses 'One can't devote himself to God on an empty stomach. O God, if you do not give me food take away my rosary'.[299] He didn't ask for much, though. Just 'two seers of flour, a quarter seer ghee and salt and half a seer of pulse' This, he said, would be enough for two meals a day. For his simple living he desired just a pillow to place beneath his head, a cotton-filled sheet and a blanket. 'With these I am content', he said, 'I have not borrowed or taken anything from anyone. Having got these articles I will find peace in the name of Hari'.[300] He seems to have got what he wanted, but not all the time. And it is curious that he didn't include his family in his prayers, as indeed he ought to have done, particularly as they were sharers in his poverty. Quite often his generosity to others snatched the food from their mouths. After weaving, he had to take the finished product, the coarse cloth to sell and from the money he got he purchased the necessities of living. One day he took a large piece of cloth (*thāna*) to the bazaar. On the way he met a holy man who begged alms, and Kabīr gave him the whole *thāna*. But thinking of the hungry mouths at home who were expecting him to sell the cloth and bring back money to feed them, his heart was sorrowful and tears came to him eyes. Anantadāsa's *Paracai* gives the account:

> *dinhīṁ turata bāra nahiṁ lāī, taba kabīra mandira nahimāī.*
> *dyausa tini ke mānasa bhūṣe, bāke rovai bahuta bidūṣe.*

He was ever engaged in serving the sick and the needy, and once when a man came with a highly infectious disease he nursed him without hesitation despite the fact that he too caught the infection and fell ill. But no harm came to him and he was well again. Hadn't the Lord promised in the *Gītā—na hi kalyanakṛtkśrid durgatim tāta gacchati* ('One who engages himself in doing good to other, O friend (Arjuna) can never come to grief')?[301] Kabīr believed in helping his friends and neighbours in every way for if one does not extend such help it is a great shortcoming: *pārosī se rusaṇāṁ tila tila sukha kī hāni*. As we have said before, he believed in the unity of mankind. Though he was a Moslem, he had no differences with Hindus and in fact his nature was more akin to the Hindu psyche than to the Moslem. He didn't believe in caste distinctions either, and we, who are prone to be divided into narrow compartments of religion and caste, can take a lesson from his view of the oneness of humanity.[302]

JOURNEY'S END.

As in the case of Kabīr's date of birth, there is also considerable difference of opinion in reckoning the date of his death. According to Dr Ramajilal 'Sahayak' the poet lived to an age of 120 years (from 1398 to 1518). This, according to him, is supported by a verse of the poet which speaks of his old age in which he says his limbs have begun to tremble, his voice falter and watery eyes have started impeding vision.[303] Four verses have been quoted by Dr Ramajilal which refer to his death.[304] Thus the dates are *samvat* 1505 or 1515 or 1569, i.e., A.D. 1448, 1518 or 1512. It is said that 1518 is acceptable. But the writer has taken the poet's date of birth as A.D. 1398 (*samvat* 1455) on the basis of the lines about his old age This would be 120 years and in consonance with the description of his limbs shaking and so forth. However this does not appear to be reason enough for the deduction because it is obvious that with the kind of living which was Kabīr's—he often went hungry and with his family worries, the condition he describes could also be much earlier than the assumed age of 120. We have agreed with the dates suggested by Keay and Farquhar as A.D. 1440 to 1518 which would mean a life-span of 78 years and the stings of old age could very well have set in them. Thus we would accept the date of Kabīr's death as A.D. 1518 as we have discussed before when speaking of his date of birth.

As regards the place of the poet's death, the most likely place is Magahar. The *Kabīr Paracai* of Anantadāsa points to this.[305] Kabīr's own verse on this subject, too, confirms this view.[306] However a little controversy exists regarding the exact location of this place. Some critics are of the view that it was in Basti, an eastern district of Uttar Pradesh because a *samādhi* (tomb) of the poet exists there, but as Dr 'Sahayak' rightly points out, the '*Ain-i-Akbarī* has it that there is a *samādhi* of the poet in Ratanpur and Puri; so how can he have died at three different places? However, it can't be said that Kabīr deliberately chose Magahar as the place to die, simply to disprove the stigmā attached to the place for the popular belief was that one who died in Magahar became a donkey in his next life![307] It could hardly be possible that one would deliberately go all the way to a certain place to die, merely to expose the absurdity of a notion. Besides, no one chooses the place of his death. Some of the Moghul monarchs chose from before the place of their mausoleums, but they did not necessarily die there. The place of death as too its manner, is predestined and beyond human control. Kabīr did not subscribe to the belief that dying in Benares conferred *mokṣa*. He obtained emancipation only who was close to God.[308] Priyadāsa mentions a place across the Ganga river adjacent to Benares, which went by the name of Maggar (another way of writing Magahar). It appears this place is in Ramanagara which is in Benares but across the Ganga river, where now the ex-rajah of Benares lives. This place is about six miles from the main city and so beyond the *pancakośi*, the five mile radius surrounding a holy city. It is believed that he who dies within this area attains emancipation. But, of course, as Kabīr said, this is pure superstition and arrant nonsense. What matters is the individual's love for God.

According to a tradition Kabīr went round this place to have *darśana* (pay obeisance) of the many temples there. He went to the room of a saint and lay down pulling a coverlet over himself and thus his soul became one with God:

apanaiṁ paracaiṁ lāgī tārī, āpana paiṁ āpa samānā.
kahai kabīra jūṁ āpa vicārai, miṭi gayā ānā jānā.

THE CONTROVERSY ABOUT DISPOSAL OF KABĪR'S MORTAL REMAINS

Tradition and blind belief is so strong in India that very few saints are granted the favour of a natural death. In the case of one like Swami Ramakrishna the truth that he died of cancer of the throat could not be hid because there were observant biographers to watch and record each stage of his life and in Mahendranath, the elusive 'M' he had found his Boswell. But others are believed to fly to heaven or merge in some idol—all except a rightfully earned peaceful death in bed. Enthusiastic biographers seem to forget that even Lord Krishna's end came when he lay down in a forest and caused a hunter's arrow to pierce through his heel, thus bleeding to death and Christ died on the Cross to uphold that truth which had left Pilate puzzled.

So for Kabīr we are asked to believe that his dead body miraculously turned into flowers, for which the Hindus and Moslems made a dash, and finally compromised by each taking away half of them, the Moslems burying them and erecting a grave and the Hindus doing the cremation rite (probably by ceremonially casting them in the Ganga river).[309] All baloney. After a six mile hike old man Kabīr (seventy-eight) must have been pegged out and perhaps thought he'd have a rest at the dwelling of some fellow-saint. Maybe he got a heart attack and took the last count there. The claritication given by Dr Ramjilal 'Sahayak' about the flowers seems to be logical, for among Hindus 'flower' (*phūla*) also signifies the ashes left after the corpse is burnt, and these are taken away by the mourners to be immersed in a sacred river, most often the Ganga on which the bank of which Benares is situated. That of course does not explain the Moslems, making a bid for the flowers, but it is very doubtful if they showed any particular interest in one who said about the *azān* 'O Mulla, why do you climb the minaret? Do you think the Lord is hard of hearing?' and The *Purāṇas* and the Quran are mere words'.[310] And worse still, 'Give up the Book and worship Rāmā'.[311] So we may assume that after Kabīr's death his body was cremated according to Hindu rites and his ashes immersed in the Ganga at Benares, where he spent the most part of his life in devotion to the Cosmic Absolute (his Rāma). Whether he got the *mukti* (*mokṣa* or emancipation) that he desired and so often spoke of, will be known only to God. But if purity of thought and good deeds are of any importance in this world of birth and death. (*mṛtyuloka*) we can be sure he did—*parhita basa jinha ke mana māhiṁ, tinakahuṁ jaga duralabha kachu nāhiṁ*. 'For one whose mind is always engaged in the good of others, nothing in the world is difficult to get'.[312]

THE TIMES OF KABIR

They collect armies and surround forts and create much suffering and destruction. The Sultans wreck many such forts, but for them this is just sport and game.[313]

KABĪR

POLITICAL

About this time there arose in my heart the desire to lead an expedition against the infidels, and to become a *ghazi*; for it had reached my ears that the slayer of infidels is a *ghāzī* and if he is slain he becomes a martyr.

Tīmūr-I-lang, 1398

We have explained the divergence between Islam and other religions, chiefly Hinduism. Moslems believe that Islam is so superior to all other religions that it ought to be accepted by all human beings. A contemporary writer on the Islamic law of war and peace says 'The question has been raised as to whether it is not inconsistent with Islam's objective, seeking ultimate supremacy of the true religion, to accept payment in money (*jizyah*) for persistence in unbelief. Sarkhasī held that the object is nor pecuniary consideration, but the invitation (given to) unbelievers (those who aren't Moslems) to live among Moslems. By being allowed to live among the Moslems the *dhimmis* (non-Moslems paying the *jizyah* poll-tax) **will be attracted by the beauties of the Moslem faith**, and they may willingly accept it'.[314] And in case the infidels (*kaffirs*) did not accept Islam voluntarily a crusade (called *jihād*) was to be fought with them and they were to be eliminated as unfit to live on the earth—*jihād* by the sword (*jihād bi's-sayf*). This was what Francis Bacon condemned: 'But we may not take up the third sword, which is Mahomet's Sword, or like unto it; that is to propagate religion by sanguinary persecutions, to force consciences;...[315] Describing his attack on the fort of Hanumangam Tīmūr wrote in his *Memoirs* 'the heads of ten thousand infidels were cut off. **The sword of Islam was washed in the blood of the infidels'**. Thereafter Tīmūr turned his attention to the city of Sarsuti *because 'the people of the place were strangers to the religion of Islam'*.[316] In his sack of Delhi, Tīmūr got all the Hindus killed while sparing the Moslems: 'Next day I gave orders that the Musalmān prisoners should be separated and saved, but that the infidels should all be despatched to hell with the **proselytizing sword**. I also ordered that the houses of the *sayyids, shaikhs* and learned Musalmān prisoners should be separated but that all the other houses should be plundered and the fort destroyed. It was done as I directed and a great booty was obtained'.[317] There were 100,000 Hindu prisoners in Tīmūr's camp. Regarding them the *amīrs* said 'on the great day of battle (for the capture of Delhi) these 100,000 prisoners could not be left with the baggage and *it would be entirely opposed to the rules of war to set these idolaters and* ***foes of Islam*** *at liberty*'.[318] So Tīmūr got all those innocent and helpless prisoner slain, in a bloodbath unparalled in the history of the world. In his *Memoirs* Tīmūr wrote, 'Maulana Nāsir-ud-dīn' Umar, a counsellor and a man of learning who, in all his life had never killed a sparrow, now, in execution of my order, slew with his own sword, fifteen idolater Hindus who were his captives'.[319] Thus Islamization by the sword persisted throughout the rule of the Moslems in India, exposing the weakness of a religion which, failing to convince, had to be imposed by brutal force. In fact Islam dangled before its adherents the tempting bait of heaven, as Tīmūr said: 'My principal object in coming to Hindustan had been to accomplish two things. The first was to wage war with the infidels and to acquire some claim to reward in the life to come. The other was to give a chance to the army of Islam to gain something by plundering the wealth and valuables of the infidels; *plunder in war is as lawful as their mother's milk to the Musalmāns*'.[320]

We have mentioned Tīmūr's invasion which took place at the end of the fourteenth century (A.D. 1398) as, though we have accepted Kabīr's dates from 1440 to 1518, according to a good few critics he lived earlier (A.D.1398 according to Dr Ramajilal 'Sahayak'). By the beginning of the fifteenth century the Tughluq dynasty had ended and that of the Sayyids and the Lodis begun with the installation of Khizr Khan as emperor(1414). He was followed by Mubarak Shah (22 May 1421) and his successors, Sultan Mohammed Shah and 'Ala-ud-din, and on 19 April 1453 Bahlul, the first of the Lodis asanded the throne. He was a tolerant ruler, a happy exception to bigotry, who respected religions other than Islam too.[321] But this was not so with his successor, Sikandar Lodi, whose name was Nizam Khan and who was ironically the son of a Hindu goldsmith's daughter, thereby evoking Powell-Price's comment 'It seems as if these Muslim sons of Hindu mothers always had to satisfy the father in them by the denial of their mother's faith'![322] We have already related Sultan Sikandar Shah Lodi's ill-trreatment of Kabīr. The account occurs in various verses of the saint-poet.[323] This fits in with Sikandar Lodi's character which had a strong streak of bigotry in it. We have mentioned about this previously but it is worth repetition. 'Abdulla has this soapy observation about the end of his honeyfogling panegyric on the Sultan's reign. 'It was a wonderful age! The Musalmāns were dominant, the **Hindus depressed**'.[324] When a Moslem divine dissuaded the Sultan from raiding the Hindu tanks at Thāneswar and slaying all the bathers, it made Sikandar hot under the collar, and he burst out 'You side with the infidels! I will first put an end to you and then massacre the infidels at Kurkhet'.[325] Elliot and Dowson record 'He was so zealous a Musalmān that he utterly destroyed diverse places of worship of the infidels and left not a vestige remaining of them. He entirely ruined the shrines of Mathura, the mine of heathenism, and turned their Hindu places of worship into caravanserais and colleges. Their stone images were given to the butchers to serve them as meat-weights, and all the Hindus in Mathura were strictly prohibited from shaving their heads and beards and performing their ablutions'.[326] The Sultan was of course only following his own scripture, the Holy Quran which has the following injunction for Moslems: 'So when the sacred months have passed away, slay the idolaters wherever you find them, and take them captive and besiege them and lie in wait for them in every ambush; but if they repent and keep up prayer and pay the poor-rate leave their way free to them, for God is Forgiving, Merciful'.[327] And in another part of the Holy Quran we find the following observation 'that (Islam) is the right religion, but most people do not know it'.[328] The significance of this is that Islam is the natural religion of human beings, but the poor ignatzs who happen to be non-Moslems do not realize this and so the 'Forgiving Merciful God' commands the Moslems to slay these bullet-heads unless they turn to Islam. So when Laudhan, a brahmin of Kaner village, expressed the view that '*Islam was true, as was his own religion*' Sikandar Lodi got the man who dared equate his religion with Islam, immediately beheaded. It is strange that though Kabīr mentioned the Sultan's ill-treatment toward himself, he says not a word about these acts of persecution perpetrated by Sikandar on Hindus. Maybe busy as he was in his occupation, he could not know about them.

The Moslem officials of those times were rude and unsympathetic, though we can't say that through the long centuries we have even after freedom, improved much upon them. Taking for instance, justice. Cases in twentieth century India even at the fag end of it in which we are today living, drag on for generations without a decision. Sultan Sikandar Lodi, the ruler in Kabīr's times ensured speedy justice for his subjects often personally intervening to prevent delays. On one occasion he came to know that a dispute had lasted two *months*. He asked the judge 'What has happened to you that you cannot settle this affair?' He ordered that no one would leave the court till the matter was decided.[329] But of course this was a personal trait, not necessarily emulated by the Sultan's officers. Another aspect which prevailed in the age of Kabīr when the

Sultanate was in power, was the inequality of society, and this has lasted throughout Indian history, and is again as true today as it was in the 14-15th century:

'Weavers, naked themselves, toiled to clothe others. Peasants, themselves hungry, toiled to feed the town and cities. India, taken as a unit, parted with useful commodities in exchange for gold and silver, or in other words, gave bread for stones. Men and women, living from season to season on the verge of hunger, could be contented so long as the supply of food held out; when it failed, as it so often did, their hope of salvation was the slave trader and the alternatives were cannibalism, suicide, or starvation. The only way to escape from this system lay through an increase in production, coupled with a rising standard of living, but this road was barred effectively by the administrative methods in vogue, which penalized production and regarded every indication of increased consumption as a signal for fresh extortation'.[330] In the reign of 'Ala-ud-din (A.D.1445) the condition of Hindu society was abjectly miserable: 'The Hindu chiefs and headmen were so much impoverished that no gold and silver was to be found in in their houses; they (the Hindus) could not afford to procure horses or weapons and their wives had to serve for wages in the houses of the Moslems'.[331]

We find little of this mentioned in Kabīr's verse, except, of course, Sikandar's attempts to kill him and in which he pictures himself as a hero who, by his miraclous powers thwarted them. But of the misery of the Hindus, he has nothing to say. And as for the Sultan's causing Hindu idols to be used as meat-weights, perhaps he did not think much of it as he was a hater of images himself.

SOCIAL

The social fabric was being torn apart and people had become immoral as Kabīr observed:

para nārī rātā phire, corī biḍhatā khāhiṁ
divasa cāri sarasā rahaiṁ, anti samūla jāhiṁ.

Thus prostitutes wandered about the streets at night seeking clients, and thieves roamed nightlong. People were characterless and indulged in all kinds of vices. They were covetous of the wealth of others, full of greed and avarice and engaged in apple-polishing:

> *kali ka svamī lobhiyā, manasā dharī badhāi*
> *rāja duvārām youm phirai, jyūm harihāī gāi.*

Many evils existed from before in Hindu society such as caste, child-marriage, looking down on widows and cruelty to them, lack of education, superstition, magic witchcraft, spells, incantations and so forth. Palmists and astrologers who had no knowledge in these sciences went about fooling and defrauding gullible poeple. The caste-divide was so great that Hindus of the higher castes would not let even the shadow of an untouchable touch them! Sudras were segegated and got a rough deal. So important were caste distinctions for Hindus that in the allusion of Kabīr by the saint Tukarāma, which we have already quoted before, the caste of each savant had been specified—*Gorā* ***kumhāra,*** *Ravidāsa* ***camāra,*** *Kabīr* ***Musalmān,*** *Sena* ***nāī,*** *Kanopatra* ***vaiśyā,*** *Cokhā Melā* ***achūta,*** *Jānābāī kumari apanī bhakti ke karaṇa īśvara mem līna ho gaye.* Human sacrifice, wine, lasciviousness and degraded practices indulged in by men who pretended holiness, were rampant. These hypoorites would put on yellow robes, take a rosary, wear sacerdotal marks and a *tilak* on their foreheads and go about all day hoodwinking gullible people and extracting money from them, and in the night they would disport in the arms of their mistresses and become soused with liquor. Kabīr stormed against these dissemblers in strong terms, castigating Hindus who worshipped evil spirits the Nāthpanthis with shaven heads and wearing big wooden earrings and calling the Śāktas who had sex with women, drank and carried out abominable practices under the guise of Tantra, worse than pigs.

The Moslems added to the ills of Hindu society by forcing Hindu girls to marry Moslem boys, and very often royal princesses of Hindu kingdoms were carried off by victorious Moslem kings as prizes for their harems. That was the reason for the mass immolations (*jauhars*) of Hindu queens and women of the royal household, such as the one which occurred at Chitor when Padminī and the other queens numbering several thousands burnt themselves after 'Alā-ud-dīn's sack of Mewar.

The Moslem conquest had a great impact on Hindu society. The view that many low caste Hindus embraced Islam willingly because of their ill-treatment by those of the upper caste, is quite mistaken.[332] The fact is that the condition imposed by Moslems 'Islam or the sword' was very terrifying , and many, irrespective of caste, could not face death. It was only later that, finding it impossible to extermunate Hinduism this way, the device of charging *jizyah* advocated by the Holy Quran was enforced. A historian of note says 'as the rigours of the caste system weighed heavily upon the lower classes among the Hindus, they would naturally be attracted by the position of absolute religious and social equality which Islam offered to every Hindu, irrespective of class or creed, who embraced the new faith'.[333] As we have said it wasn't exactly that. Qanungoship for becoming a Moslem, chiefs of ruling families adopting Islam retaining their position, civil disabilities being imposed on Hindus, exemption from slavery; were some of the temptations offered for conversion, and even then if Hindus resisted the faith of 'the believers', as Mahamūd's secretary Al-' Utbi frankly recorded, 'Islam or death was the alternative that Mahmūd placed before the people'.[334] The other influences of Moslem rule were the introduction of purdah (the veil) and the intensification of slavery. Slavery was in vogue among Hindus from long before and slaves find mention in the *Smritīs* in which four kinds of slaves are enumerated—those born in the household, purchased, acquired, or inherited. A slave could get back his freedom by winning his master's favour. If the master had sex with a woman slave and she had a child by him, both the child and the woman were freed from slavery. With the Moslem rulers a difference cropped up inasmuch as after every victory Hindu girls were carried off as slaves, and they made no distinction between a common girl and one of a high family, for them all of them were infidels. Even princesses were carried off to swell Moslem harems Mohammed bin Tughluq sent to the Chinese emperor 'one hundred men as slaves and one hundred slave songstresses dancers from among the indian infidels'. As regards purdah, so far Hindu women veiled themselves only at home when before the elders of the family. But when the Moslems came they adopted purdah in society too, partly in imitation of the ruling class and partly to protect themselves. But the Hindu women of the lower class still went unveiled. The Moslem custom was based on the Holy Quran: 'Say to the believing women that they cast down their looks and guard their private parts... and let them wear their head-coverings over their bosom'.[335] Thus Moslem women had to follow the injunction of the Holy Quran and the Moslem rulers ensured their strict compliance. Poet Akbar comments on some women he saw who were not veiled, 'Seeing some women yesterday going without their veils, I was rooted to the ground with shame. On asking them where their veils had gone, the women said "They have dropped upon the minds of men"!'[336] God's curse on Adam seems to have been forgotten, but that on Eve still lingers on. Whatever the race and civilization, women have always received a rough deal—raped, exploited, portrayed in salacious poses and various stages of undress to sell all kinds of commodities from mosquito-repellants to perfumes. So was the case with Hindu and Moslem women, who had to dance to please potentates, be forced into sex with lust-hungry victorious soldiers and lascivious monarchs and their hencemen, sold in slave-markets, compelled to become concubines, cowives and share between them one and the same husband.

Hindu society was in a bad way. People mistrusted one another, as Kabīr noticed,[337] Selfishness, mine and thine and vanity swayed people.[338] Sensual pleasures overrode spirituality and was the bane of society.[339] All this was keenly observed and effectively recorded by Kabīr in his verses. As we have noted before, there was great divergence between the rich and the poor, the aristocracy, and common people of which Kabīr was one too, for he always had to live hand-to-mouth.[340] He realized the disregard and contempt which the rich showed to the poor.[341] The Sultans taxed their subjects and bled them white, but almost nothing went to their welfare or development, instead they squandered it on their own sensual pleasures. As Amir Khusrav wrote, 'Each pearl in the crowns of rulers has been made possible by the blood and sweat of the peasants whose money earned by their hard labour pays for the pleasures of royalty'.[342]

RELIGIOUS

'One person chants the Veda, another wanders about as a hermit. One adopts the yogic postures, another sits naked and practises austerities. One pretends to be charitable and gives alms, another thinks consuming liquor leads to God. One finds his fulfilment in *tantra* and *mantra*, another in the control of breath. One has faith in pilgrimages, another kindles incense and his body whitens with its smoke. Says Kabīr all this is useless. *Mokṣa* is only got by chanting the name of Rāma'.[343]

No wonder Kabīr was amazed. There were numberless creeds all claiming superiority and Benares being the nerve-centre of religion, it was full of men who engaged in all kinds of practices. We have already quoted the relevant verse about this: *rojā karaiṁ namāj gujāraiṁ kyā haj kābai jāyeṁ* etc., so it is not being repeated here. The Baudhya faith had made some ingress and *Tantra* and *Mantra* yoga, the worship of spirits, trees and so forth; in brief polytheism in all its aspects. Some of the rites observed were most repelling and religion was made an excuse for lasciviousness and sensual enjoyment. Some Tāntric practices, although well-meaning and having a spiritual aim, were nevertheless open to abuse, and many unscruplous votaries took what was meant to be symbolic, in the literal sense, making love to young girls (*kumārīs*), eating meat and fish and drinking liquor, all the time beguiling people that they were only following religious rites. But Kabīr refused to be taken for a ride and condemned such corrupt practices.[344] Thus Kabīr's times were years of religious degeration, and this impelled him to condemn and criticize this aspect of false pretence and hypocricy. And such criticism often puts on the garb of satire. His verses are replete with sardonic comments on these.

It is surprising that despite being unlettered and consequently having no acquaintance with Sanskrit, Kabīr should yet refer so frequently in his poetry, to Upaniṣadic terms like, *mokṣa*, *sṛṣṭi*, maya, *ātmā* and *paramātmā*. Where could he get them from? According to critics the tradition of the Vedānta, which took its rise from the *Upaniṣads*, is the gift of the old teachers and sages of Hinduism,[345] or as Dr. Pītambar Dutt Barthwāl says 'the spiritual current that always ran through Hindu spiritual life'.[346] But how did this gift come Kabīr's way?

One of the the sources through which the poet came to know of the Vedānta was his saint-companions, many of whom must have been familiar with Sanskrit, the script of the *Gītā*, *Upaniṣds* and the *Brahma-sūtras*. Another factor was the Vaiṣṇava influence. After the death of Rāmānuja there was a sectarian split in the Vaiṣṇava school and by the end of the fourteenth century two groups were formed—the Vaḍakalais and the Tenkalais. For Rāmānuja the *Gītā Vedas, Upaniṣads* and Vedānta in Sankrit were worthy of the same reverence as the Tamil *Prabandhas*. But after him, while Vaḍakalais continued the Sanskrit tradition, the Tenkalais didn't. Other fundamental differences arose between them which were primarily as follows:

1. The Vaḍakalais gave importance to self-effort. It is only when this fails, that one should resort to self-surrender. The Tenkalais, on the other hand, believed that God's love was spontaneous and no self-effort was needed.
2. The Vaḍakalais believed in karma and its consequence, the Tenkalais in God's grace. According to them such grace could forgive all sins.
3. The former believed Lakṣmi to be indistinguishable from the Lord, while the Tenkalais believed she was only a mediator.
4. The Vadakalia believed that only brahmins and the upper castes could study the holy scriptures. The Tenkalais were more liberal and admitted the Sudras

and other low caste Hindus also.

Thus even while both schools believed in the Vaiṣṇava *dharma*, the Tenkalais abjured Sanskrit and gave *bhāṣa* (the local dialects) more promirence. Kabīr's poetry should be interpreted in this light. He gave expression to his thoughts in the language spoken in the countryside, the language of the common people as Wordsworth wanted poetic expression to be, but being at heart a Vaiṣṇava, and consorting with sadhus of the Vaḍakalais tradition for whom Sanskrit was still of prime importance, he spoke about Vedānta too in unmistakable terms. He rebelled against outward observances because primarily he believed that salvation could only be got by looking inwards and funding peace within oneself. God did not dwell in temple or mosque but in the souls of beings, and when he was within oneself what was the use of going about searching for him all over the place?

būṁda samānī samunda maiṁ,
so kati herī jāi
samanda samanā būṁda maiṁ,
so kata heryā jāi

ātama maiṁ paramātama darasai
paramātamā maim jhāim
jhāiṁ maiṁ parachāim darasai
lakhai kabīra sāiṁ

KABĪR'S PERSONALITY AND ACHIEVEMENT

He who abandons prayer, knowledge and hope, craves not for honour nor minds dishonour, he for whom gold and iron is the same; is the loved one of God.[347]

KABĪR

Despite the fact that a whole lot of literature has developed round Kabīr, almost everything about him is shrouded in darkness—his dates, place of birth and religion, death, parentage, and even his works and language. One signiticant outcome is that we are kept guessing how much of what has come down to us under his name is really his own. There have verious collections, to recensions and anthologies and researches to separate the grain from the chaff, yet nothing can be said with any degree of finality. However it is certain that he was a weaver, miserably poor living a hand-to-mouth existence and a family man, spent most of his time in Benares, and had no systematic education and was unlettered. With these handicaps, it was certainly marvellous that he composed so many verses in various metres observing the convention of rhyme and some of them tops in spiritual wisdom. According to one of his biographers he had a charming personality, fair with a golden complexion, a shapely nose, rosy heels and tall, about six and a half feet high (*tīna hāth eka aradhāī*-'three hands and a half').[348]

We have already detailed the main sources of Kabīr's works and of his biographical references. As regards the principal anthologies, these are mainly as follows:

1. The *Bījak*- This is the Eastern recension of the *Vāṇīs* of the poet. It contains a fair number of corrupt verses relating to the cosmogony and concepts of Kabīrpanthīs. One edition of the *Bījak* is that of Udayashankara Shastri.Another is the Barabanki edition with a Hindi paraphrase made later by Sadhu Abhilashadasa. The satirical and paradoxical verses (*ulṭabāmsī*) are of particular interest. The *Bījak* vorses were translated by Reverend Prem Chand (1890) and Ahmed Shah (1917), though not very successfully.
2. The *Kabīr Granthāvalī* of Dr Shyamasundara Dāsa (Nāgarī Pracariṇī Sahhā 1930) based on the handwritten manuscripts of A.D. 1504 and 1824, the latter being perhaps written by some follower of Dādū.
3. The *Kabīr Granthāvalī* of Dr Pārasanatha Tiwārī (1961. Hindi Parishad Prayaga Visvavidyalaya). This was brought out in two parts, the first consisting of 200 *Padas*, 20 *Ramainīs* and 744 *Sākhīs* and the second with *Padas* under 16 heads and *Sākhīs* under 34 heads. Apparently in deference to his guru, Dr Tiwari included the verses he himself considered

genuine in the first part with critical appraisal classifying the various variants in the text, and lumped together the other verses occurring in the version of Dr S.S. Dāsa which he didn't credit as genuine, in the second part. There have been other *granthāvalīs* too as that of Pushpalal Singh (Delhi 1965), L.B. Ananta (Delhi 1969) and Dr Mata Prasad Gupta (Allahabad 1985).

Basically, the different divisions of Kabīr's verses are as follows:

1. *Ramainīs*- This expression conveys three different senses (a) that through which the souls of the world experience bliss, (b) that which brings beings in tune with the essential element of the universe and (c) a particular stanza of verse in each line of which there are sixteen feet. The *Ramainīs* speak principally about the embodied souls (*jīva*) the universe and creation. In the *Ramainīs* the *caupāī* and the *dohā* (couplet) form of verse finds place. Before Kabīr, Mohammed Daud wrote in this form and later Tulsīsdāsa used it in the *Mānasa* and so too some Sūfī poets.
2. *Sākhīs*- The word comes from the Sanskrit *sākṣī* meaning 'eye-witness', i.e., something which one sees and experiences himself. Thus the *Sākhịs* of Kabīr express his own experience.

The word '*sabad*' has been used by Kabīr in two senses, firstly for the elements of the universe (*paramatatva*) and secondly for '*pada*'. This does not, however exhaust the forms of verse used by him. He has also used the *kaharā, basanta, beli, boirhulī, cācari, hiṁḍolā, cauṁtīsī, vipramatīsī* and so forth. However, it will ever remain doubtful how many of all these verses attributed to Kabīr could be his or the accretions of enthusiastic Kabīrpanthīs.

For Kabīr 'love' and '*bhakti*' were identical terms. Besides as Krishna said in the *Gītā*, love and wisdom were not opposed but complementary. Krishna says at one place that no one is so beloved of him as the man of wisdom, and nothing purifies a man so much as that — *na hi jñānena sadrśam pavitramiha vidyate* (4.38), Kabīr finds the letter of love from his beloved in the lane of wisdom, and in it there is the message of fathomless love.[349] The beloved devotee's eyes become weary watching for the lover's arrival. The tongue is sore calling out again and again for him. She puts all her love for him as though oil in the earthen lamp and making a wick from her lovelorn heart sets the lamp alight to enable her lover to find his way to her. Thus uphill is the meeting of the soul with God and it can be obtained the hard way only.[350]

God cannot dwell in a dirty place, so before one can aspire for his grace, his heart must be pure. Untruth, theft, greed for wealth immorality, wickedness and cruelty, violence, lust, passion, jealousy, hate, hypocrisy, honeyfogling, showing off, display and all such vices and evils should be shunned for they are spurred on by maya, which makes people slaves to 'gold' and 'woman' *kanaka, kāminī,* (i.e., money and passion). Kabīr likens them to fire covered with cotton, so that it ever keeps smouldering.[351] The *Rāmacaritamānasa* also says that to obtain God's love one must first clean his heart and mind by getting rid all evils like sense-pleasures attachment ignorance and so forth, and it is such yogis who are really awake and not sleeping the sleep of worldliness:

> *ehi jaga jāmini jāgahiṁ jogī paramārthī prapanca viyogī*
> *janiya tabahiṁ jīva jaga jāgā jaba saba viṣaya vilāsa virāgā.*
> *hoi bibeka moha bhrama bhāgā taba raghunātha carana anurāgā.*[352]

The mind indeed is a hindrance to reaching *prema-bhakti* (love and devotion). As Arjuna told the Lord frankly in the *Gītā,* the mind is obstinate and stubborn and as difficult to control as the wind:

> *Cancalaṁ hi manaḥ kṛṣṇa*
> *pramāthi balavad dṛḍham*
> *tasyā 'haṁ nigrahaṁ manye*
> *vāyor iva suduṣkaram*

To which the Lord answered, yes, so it was. But it could be brought under control by sustained practice and non-attachment (*abhyāsena ca vairāgyeṇa*).[353] So too Kabīr says that apart from forsaking vices like passion, rage and so forth, control of the mind is essential, and to illustrate the difficulty of subduing it, while Arjuna gave the example of the wind, he likens it to the monkey which jumps about from branch to branch, but the tamer (*bander kā nautch wallah*) tames it and makes it dance according to his (the tamer's) will.[354] To obtain real *prema-bhakti* (love of God and devotion to him) one has to know his own Self. This is not so easy as it seems. it was only after the Lord gave the entire message of the *Gītā* to Arjuna that the Pāṇḍava warrior could know himself—*naṣṭa mohaḥ smrti-labdhā sthitha-asmi* (18.73); as Shakespeare also says 'this above all to thine own self be true'. To achieve devotion to God one has to indentify himself with all the world's creatures and to see the same soul in all. He has to leave all thoughts of 'mine' and 'yours'. Then only can he experience the bliss of God's love.[355] Love demands the greatest sacrifice, even of one's life. We have already quoted Kabīr on this and it is repeated here:

rāma rasāina prema rasa, pīvata adhika rasāla
kabīra pīvaṇa dulamba hai, māṁgai sīsa kapāla.[356]

Thus one who has true love for God, has already surrendered his life for him. He no longer fears death.[357] So too the bard conceives love admitting no compromise:

'Love is not love
Which alters when it alteration finds,
Or bends with the remover to remove:
Oh, no! it is an ever-fixed mark
That looks on tempests and is never shaken;
It is the star to every wandering bark
Whose worth's unknown, although his height be tak-
en....
Love alters not with his brief hours and weeks,
But bears it out even to the edge of doom.

If this be error, and upon me prov'd
I never writ, nor no man ever lov'd'.[358]

Satisfied with the little life gave him, Kabīr realized both the value of money as also its limitation. He knew that while money could buy comfort, it could not buy happiness. While it was necessary for existence, no one not even the richest of persons could carry it with him, when the soul departed—*hansa gayā kachu saṅga na jāī*. He did not believe in distinctions of any kind, rich and poor or high and low, nor in caste animosities or religious distinctions. He was against all outward show and rites, for unless the mind and heart were pure such things like fasts, pilgrimages, temples, mosques religious fairs, *haj* etc., could not uplift men. If the heart is full of guile what is the use of speaking words of wisdom? What is the use of going on pilgrimages and bathing in waters deemed sacred if there is evil in the mind? Purify your heart and then only by God's grace you can get across this worldly sea of sorrows.[359]

Although a Moslem, Kabīr's thinking had more of the Vaiṣṇava and Sūfī element than the Islamic tradition. He couldn't have any acquaintance with the Holy Quran, and even if he had he couldn't possibly agree with many of its tenets. His concept of God was that of an impersonal entity, *Brahman* or Allah. Nonetheless his trend of thought was devotional and he often speaks of the Lord as Hari or Krishna. Thus in practice both monism and dualism were acceptable to him, though he emphasized monism more. He did much to reform both the Hindus (as Dayananda tried to do) and the Moslems. But religions and religious beliefs are very tenacious and to negate them is like gathering grapes from thorns.

Kabīr lived a simple life and believed in honest labour. he neither cursed his lot nor envied others more fortunate:

mīṭha khaṇa madhukarī, bhāṁti bhāṁti kā nāja
dāvā kisa hī kā nahiṁ, bina bilāiti rāja

Yet he believed that God would always assist him in supplying his needs. A saint never accumulates money, he said. He only retains what he requires for his livelihood for he has full faith that God will help him in fulfilling his needs.[360] Sometimes God did assist him, sometimes he didn't; but Kabīr never complained.

His verses cover a wide canvas and deal with many aspects of life, mostly however spiritual. They vary greatly in felicity of expression, raising the suspicion that many could be spurious. His satires are biting but lack wit. Though they have caught the admiration of western critics, they are the least commendable of his verses. He is at his best in singing of love and devotion, the illusion of maya and the greatness of God:

āpā para sami cīnhiye, dīsai saraba samāna
ihiṁ pada narahari bheṭiye, tū chāṁṛi kapaṭa abhimāna

INTRODUCTION

NOTES

1. This aspect of Kabīr will be dealt with in greater detail while commenting on his language.
2. For example:
   a. *tū bāmhana maiṁ kāsī kā julāhā*
   b. *hari ke nāū bina kina gati pāī, Kahai julāhā kabīrā*
   c. *ati julāhā mati kā dhīra, sahajī guṇa ramai kabīra*
   d. *mere rāma kī abhai pada nagrī, kahai kabīra julāhā*
3. *a. hari ke nāu abhai padadātā, kahai kabīrā kori*
   b. kahahiṁ karam so jorī, sūta-kasūta binai bhala korī
4. Quoted in Charlotte Voudeville. *A Weaver named Kabir*. Oxford University Press, 1993, p., 114 (Only the jist of the verse quoted is reproduced)
5. Thomas Browne. *Hydriotaphia or Urn-Buriall* 1658.
6. It is believed by Hindus that the soul has to go through 84 lakh births in different wombs, before taking birth as a human being.
7. The illusions are to Krishna of the Yadava race, born in Mathura, but taken to Gokula to escape from the tyrant Kaṅsa who had put Krishna's mother Devakī and father Vasudeva in prison. At Gokula he was brought up by Nanda a cowherd and Yasodā his (Nanda's) wife.
   Goverdhana was a mountain in Vrindavana which Karishna persuaded the cowherd men and women to worship. This annoyed Indra, who sent a deluge to drown them, but Krishna held up the mountain on his little finger for seven days, thus saving them and humbling Indra (heavern's king).
   The seven seas are mentioned in the *Purāṇas*
8. Quoted in Dr Mata Prasad Gupta. *Kabīr Granthāvalī* Allahabad; Sahitya Bhavan Pvt Ltd.,1985, p. 36.
9. John Donne. *Holy Snnets*. XIV.
10. *Bṛhadāraṇyaka Upaniṣad 4:3*
11. *bahuta dinan thaiṁ maiṁ prītam pāye*
    bhāga baṛe ghari baiṭheṁ āye
    mangalacāra maṁhi mana rākhauṁ
    rāma rasāina rasanā cakhūṁ
    mandira māhi bhayā ujiyārā
    le sūtī apanaṁ piva piyārā
    maiṁ ra nirāsī jē nidhi pāī

hamahiṁ kahā yahu tumahi baṟāī
kahai kabīra maiṁ kachū na kīnhāṁ
sakhī suhāga rāma mohi dīnhāṁ

12. *Suni sakhī supanaiṁ kī gati aisī, hari āye hama pāsa*
sovat hī ja jagāiyā, jāgat bhae udāsa
calu sakhī bilambha na kījiye, jab laga sāsa sarīra
*mili rahiye jaganatha sūṁ, yūṁ kahai dāsa kabīra**

* (Dr M. Gupta (*Kabīr Granthavalī*) however interprets *bhae udāsa* as '*he*, i.e., the Lord was disappointed'. But how can God be so! Therefore the sense has been taken to be 'I was disappointed').

13. The Holy Bible. *St John*. 1.1-5.
14. *avadhū jogī jiga thaiṁ nayārā*
mudrā nirati surati kari sīṁgī, nāda na sanḍhai dhārā
basai gagana meṁ dunīm na dekhai, cetani caukī baiṭhā
caṟhi akāsa āsana nahiṁ chāṁṟai, pīvai mahārasa mīṭhā
paragaṭa kanṭhā mahai jogī, dila meṁ darapan jovai
sahastra ikīsa chaḥ sai dhāgā, nihacala nākai pīvai
brahma agina meṁ kāyā jārai, trikuṭī sangam jāgai
kahai kabīra soi jogeśvara, sahaj sunani lyau lāge
15. *Kaṭha Upaniṣad* 3.14 *kṣurasya dhārā niśitā duranyayā durgam pathastat*
16. *sahaja sahaja saba koi kahai, sahaja na cīnhai koi*
jnha sahajaiṁ viṣayā tajī, sahaja kahījai soi
sahaja sahaja saba koi kahai, sahaja na cīnhai koi
pāṁcū rākhai parasatī, sahaja kahịjai soi
sahajaiṁ sahajaiṁ saba gaye, suta vita kāmaṇi kāma
ekameka hvai mili rahā, dāsa kabīrā rāma
sahaja sahaja saba koi kahai, sahaja na cīnhai koi
jinha sahajaiṁ hari jo milaiṁ, sahaja kahījai soi
17. *tāraṇa tiraṇa tiraṇa tūṁ tāraṇa aura na dūjā jānuṁ*
kahai kabīra saranāṁī āyauṁ, āna deva nahīṁ mānuṁ
18. *rāma rasāina prema rasa, pīvata adhika rasāla*
kabīra pīvaṇa duralabha hai, māṁgai sīsa kalāla
kabīra bhāṭhī kalāl kī, bahutaka baiṭhe āi
sira sauṁpai soī pīvai, nahīṁ tau piyā na jāi
19. *kabīra yaju ghara prem kā, khālāṁ kā ghara nāhiṁ*
sīsa utārai hāthi kari, so paise ghara māhīṁ
20. *St Mark. viii.36*
21. *kabīra satī bicārī sat kiyā, kāṭhauṁ seja bichāi*
le sūti pīva āpanāṁ, cahuṁ disi agni lagāi
22. *Gītā* 2.60
yatato hyapi kaunteya puruṣasya vipaśritaḥ
indriyaṇi paramāthīni haranti prasabham manaḥ

23. *kabīra maraum̐ mana kūm̐, ṭūka ṭūka hvai jāi*
viṣa kī kyārī boi kari, luṇata kahā pachitāi
24. *kabīra mṛtaka kūm̐ dhījaum̐ nahim̐ merā mana bīhai*
bājai bāba bikāra kī, bhī mūvā jīvai
kabīra kāṭi manchalī, chī kai dharī cahoṛi
koi eka aṣira mani basyā, daha maim̐ paṛī bahoṛi
(The sense *daha* is not very clear. May be he means that even when cut up the fish's fish-like smell remains).
25. Śankarācārya. *Vivekachuḍāmaṇī*, 300.
26. *Bhagavadgītā* 6. 34-35.
27. Quoted in K.A. Nizami. *Some Aspects of Religion and Politics in India in the Thirteenth Century*. Asia, 1961, p, 263.
28. ibid.
29. *baisnaum̐ kī chaparī bhalī, nām̐ khakhat kā baṛa gāum̐*
30. *kabīra dhani te sundarī, jini jāyā vaisnaum̐*
pūta rāma sumari nirabhai huvā, saba jaga gayā aūta
kabīra kula tau so bhalā, jihim̐ kula upajai dāsa
jihim̐ kula dāsa na upajai, so kula 'āka palāsa'
31. *kabīra sākhit bām̐haṇa mati milai, baisuṇau milai candāla*
ank māla de bhem̐ṭiye, jānū mile gopāla
32. *mūla bandha ika pāvā tahām̐ sidha gaṇesvara rāvā*
tisa mūlahi mūla malam̐ūngā tau maim̐ bahurina bhaujali ām̐ūm̐gā
kabīrā tāliba torā tahām̐ gopi harī gura morā
tahām̐ heta hari cita lāgūm̐gā tau maim̐ bahurina bhaujali ām̐ūm̐gā
33. *Bhāgavata* X. 47.54.
34. *kabīra bahuta dinana ki jovatī, bāta tumhārī rāma*
jīva tarasai tuma milan ko, mani nāhīm̐ bisrāma
35. *kabīra yajhu tana jālaum̐ bhasi karaum̐, dhum̐ra jāi saraggnī*
mati vai rāma dayā karai, barasa bujhavai aggni
36. *kabīra isa tana kā dīvā karaum̐, bātī melahūm̐ jīva*
lohī sīcaum̐ tela jyūm̐, kaba mukh dekhaum̐ pīva
37. *kabīra hasi hasi kanta na pāie jini pāyā jini roi*
je hāsaim̐ hī hari milai to nahim̐ duhaganim̐ koi
38. Shri Ramakrishna Paramahaṁsa to Vivekananda (Naren). (We have referred to this in the Preface also).
39. *kabīra haum̐ birahakī lakaṛī, samajhi samajhi dhūm̐ dhāum̐*
chūṭi paṛaum̐ yā biraha taim̐, je sārī hī jala jāum̐
40. *kabīra tana mana yūm̐ jalyā, biraha agani saum̐ lāgi*
mṛtaka pīra na jāṇaī jāṇaigī vaha āgi
41. *kabīra biraha jalāī maim̐ jalau, jalatī, jala hari jāum̐*
mo dekham̐ jalahara jalai, santaum̐ kahām̐ bujhāum̐
42. *ho bala yām̐, kaba dekhom̐gī tohi*
ahinisa ātura darasana kārani, aisī vyāpai mohi
bahuta dinana kaim̐ bichure mādhau, mana nahīm̐ bām̐dhai dhīra
deha chatām̐ tumha milahu kṛpā kari, ārativanta kabīra

43. *vai dina kaba āvaiṁge māi*
jā kārani hama deha dharī hai, milibo angi lagāi
44. Shakespeare. *Twelth Night*. ii.iv
45. *hari merā pīva māī, hari merā pīva*
hari bina rahi na sakai merā jīva
hari merā pīva maiṁ hari kī bahuriā, rāma baṙe maiṁ chuṭaka lahuriyā
kiyā syaṁgāra milan ke tāiṁ kāhe na milau rājā rāma gusāṁī
aba kī bera milan ko pāūṁ kahai kabīra bhau jali nahīṁ āṁūṁ
46. *merī aṁkhiyāṁ jāna sujāna bhaīṁ*
devara bharam sasura saṅg taji kari, hari pīva tahāṁ gaī
balapanaiṁ ke ke krama hamāre, kāṭe āṁni daī
bāṁha pakari kari kripā kīnhiṁ, āpa samīpa laī
(Note— *devara* (brother-in-law) signifies attachment to the world while *sasura* (father-in-law) signifies detachment).
47. Śankarācārya. *Ātmabodha* 6-7
48. *Omar Khayyám*. Trans., Edward Fitzgerald. 20.
49. Thomas Gray. *Ellegy Written in a Country Churchyard*.
50. Shakespeare. *The Tempest* 4.1.
51. *kabīra supinaiṁ raiṇa kai, pārasa jīya maiṁ cheka*
je soūṁ tau doi jaṇāṁ, je jāgūṁ tau eka
52. *Bṛhadāraṇyaka Upaniṣad* 4.3
53. *Sākhī cittavaṇī*, verses 8 and 13.
54. *kabīra thoṙa jīvaṇā, maṁḍa bahuta manḍāṇa*
sabahiṁ ūbhā melhi gayā, rāva ranka sulitāna
55. *kabīra eka dina aisā hoigā, saba thaiṁ paṙai bichoha*
rājā rāṇa chatrapati, sāvadhāna kina hoi
56. *kabīra naubati āpaṇīṁ, dina dasa lehu bajāi*
e pura pataṇa e galī, ba huri na dekhai ai
57. *kabīra ḍhola damāṁmā daudabaḍī sahanāī saṅgi bheri*
ausari calyā bajāi kari, hai koi rākhe pheri
58. *kabīra kahā garabiyau, ūṁce deki avāsa*
kālihi parayuṁ bhuiṁ leṭaṇā, ūpar jāmai ghāsa
59. *kabīra kahā garabiyau cāma paleṭe haḍa*
haiṁbara ūpara chatra siri, te bhī debā khaḍa
60. *kabīra kahā garabiyau, kāla gaheṁ kara kesa*
nāṁ janṁṇau kahaṁ mārasī, kai ghara kai paradesa
61. *hāṙa jalai jyūṁ lakaṙī, kesa jalai jyuṁ ghāsa*
saba tana jalatā dekhi kari, bhayā kabīra udāsa
62. *Genesis* 3.19.
63. *Ecclesiastes* xii. i.
64. *kabīra dhūli sakelikari, puṙī jaa baṁdhi eha*
divasa cāri kā pekhaṇā, anti kheha kī kheha
65. *Genesis*. 3.17-19 and 16.

66. *kabīra manişā janam dulambh, deha na bārambāra*
taravara thaiṁ phala jhaṙi paḍyā, bahuri na lāgai ḍāra
67. *kabīra māṭī malaṇi kumhāra kī, ghaṇī sahai siri lāta*
ihi ausari cetyā nahīṁ, cūkā aba kī ghāta
68. *kācī kārī jini karai, dina dina badhai biyādhi*
rāma kabīrai ruch bhaī, yāhī oṣadi sādhi
69. *kabīra isa sansāra meṁ, ghaṇai maniṣa matihīṇa*
rāma nāma jāṇai nahīṁ, āue ṭāpa dīṇa
70. *eka suānu kai ghari gāvaṇa*
jananī jānata baṙā hotu hai
itanāku na jāni ji dina dina avadha ghaṭatu hai
71. Charlotte Vaudeville. *A Weaver Named KabIr*. New Delhi: Oxford University Press, 1993, p.106.
72. Naciketas on life and death: *śravobhavā martyasya yadanta kaitat sarvendriyāṇā jarayanti tajaḥ /api sarvam jīvitamalpameva tavaiva cāhāstava nṛtyagīte(26)*
na vittena tarpaṇīyo manuṣyo lapsyāmahe vittamadrākṣma cettvā gīviṣmo yāvadīśiṣyasi tavam varastu me varaṇīyaḥ sa eva(27)
ajīryatāmamṛtānāmupetya jīryan martyaḥ kadaḥ sthaḥ prajānan/abhidhyāyan varṇaratipramodā-natidīrghe jīvite ko rameta(28)
73. Serius ant citius sedem properamus ad unam (*Metamorphoses*, x, 33)
74. *kabīra āja kahai hari kalihi bhajauṁgā, kālihi kahai phira kālihi āja hī kālihi karantiyā ausara jāsī cāli*
75. *kabīra pala kī sudhi nahīṁ, karai kālha kā sāja*
kāla acyantā jhaṙapasī, jyūṁ titara kauṁ bāja
76. *kabīra maiṁ akel ae doi jaṇa, chetī nāṁhīṁ kāi*
je jama āgaiṁ ūbarauṁ, to jurā pahūṁtī āi
77. *kabīra bārī bārī apaṇīṁ, cale piāre myanta*
terī bārī re jiyā, neṙī āvai nayanta
78. *kabīra jo ūgyā so āṁthavai, phūlyā so kumilāi*
jo ciṇiyā so ḍhahi paṙai, jo āyā so jāi
79. *kabīra pāṁnī kera budabudā, isī hamārī jāti*
eka dina chipi jāṁhiṁge, tāre jyuṁ parabhāti
80. *kabīra yahu jaga kucha nahīṁ, ṣina ṣārā ṣina mīṭha*
kalihi ju baiṭhā māḍiyāṁ, āja masāṁṇāṁ dīṭha
81. *Gītā*, Chapter 2, verse (śloka) 28.
avyaktādīni bhūtāni vyakta-madhyāni bhārata/avyakta-nidhanāny eva tatra kā paridevanā
82. *kabīra yahu jiva āyā dūra thaiṁ, ajauṁ bhī jāsī dūri*
bica kai bāsai rāmi rahyā, kāla rahyā sara pūri
83. *kabīra saba sukha rāma haiṁ, aura dukhāṁ kī rāsi*
sura nara muniyara asura saba, paṙe kāla kī pāsi

84. *kabīra rovaṇahāre bhī bhūye calāṁvanahāra*
hā hā karate te bhūye, kāsini karauṁ pukāra
85. *Gītā*. Chapter 2, verses 11,13 and 22.
86. Robert Browning. *Robbi Ben Ezra*.
87. Socrates trans, Kathleen Freeman. Fighting Words, Beacon Press, 1952.
88. *kāma eṣa krodha eṣa*
rajoguṇa-samudbhavaḥ
mahāśano mahāpāpmā
viddy enamiha vairiṇam
Bhagavadgītā. Chapter 3 vv., 36-37
(Only v., 37 Quoted in Sanskrit text)
89. *kabīra bhagati bigārī kāmiyāṁ, indrī kerai svādi*
hīrā khoyā kīha thaiṁ janama gaṁvāyā bādi
kabīra kāmīṁ amīṁ na bhāvaī, viṣa ī kauṁ lai sodhi...
90. *kabīra jorū juṭhaṇi jagata kī bhale bure ka bīca*
uttima te alage rahaiṁ, nikaṭi rahaiṁ te nīca
91. *kāma milāvai rāma kūṁ je koi gāṇai rāṣi*
kabīra bicārā kyā karai, jo sukhadeva bolai sāṣi
92. *kabīra nāri paraī āpaṇīṁ, bhugatya narakahi jāi*
āgi āgi saba eka hai, tāmaiṁ hāth na bāhi
93. *kabīra māyā taravara tribidha kā, sākhā dukha santāpa*
sītalatā supinaiṁ nahiṁ, phala phīkā tani tāpa
94. *sat raja tama thaiṁ kīhīṁ, cāra khāni vistāra upayā*
pancha tata le kīnha bardhāa, pāpa puṁi māna abhimāna
ahankara kīnheṁ māyā mohū, sampati bipati dīnhīṁ saba kāhū
95. *jo kāṭoṁ to ḍahaḍahī, sīchauṁ tau kumhalāya*
isa guṇavantī bela kā kucha guṇa kahā na jāya
96. *kabīra māyā ḍolani pavana bahai hivadhāra*
jina biloyā tina paiyā avana bilovanahāra
97. *kabīra māyā pāpaṇī, lālai lāyā loga*
pūrī kinahūṁ ana bhogai, inkā ihai bijoga
98. *sarapanī te ūpari nahī balīyā*
jini brahmā bisuna mahadeo chaliā
māru māru sripanī niramala jali paiṭhī
jini tribhavaṇu ḍasīale gura prasāda ḍīṭhī
('No one is mightier than the serpent-shaped maya which has deluded even the gods, Brahmā, Viṣṇu and Śiva. This serpent-like maya has entered the soul. Kill it, kill it! By the grace of the guru I have seen that maya which has bitten even the gods'.)
99. *saṁbhavāmy ātma-māyayā Gītā 4.6.*
100. *tū māyā raghunātha kī, khelana calī aheṟe*

101. *Bhagavadgītā* chap. 9 vv. 4-5
mayā tatam idaṁ sarvaṁ
jagad avyakta mūrtinā
matsthāni sarva-bhūtānī
na cā ham teṣv avasthitaḥ
na ca matsthāni bhutānī
paśya me yogam aiśvaram
bhūtabḥm na ca bhutastho
mamā 'tmā bhūtabhāvanaḥ

102. *tetau ādi nināra niranjana, ādi anādi na īmnā*
kahana sunana kauṁ kīnha jaga, āpai āpa bhulāṁnā

103. *moṭī māyā saba tajai, jhīnī tajī na jāye*
pīra paigambara auliā, jhīnī sabani ko khāya

104. *Bhavadgītā*. chap. 18, vv. 5-6.

105. *raja bīraja kī kālī, tāpari sājyā rūpa*
rāma nāma bina buṙihaiṁ, kanaka kāṁminī kūpa

106. *eka kanaka aru kāmanī jaga meṁ doi phandā*
inapai jo na bandhāvaī, tākā maiṁ bandā

107. *māyā muī na mana muvā, mari mari gayā sarīra*
āsā triṣṇā nāṁ muī, yauṁ kahi gayā kabīra

108. *māyā dāsī santa kī, ūṁ bhī deha asīsa*
bilasī aru lataum chaṙī, sumira sumīra jagadīsa

109. *kabīra ūṁcā kula kai kāranaiṁ, bansa badhyā adhikāra*
candana bāsa bhedai nahīṁ jālyā saba parivāra

110. *kabīra jagat ahamdam raciyā, jhuṭe kula kī lāja*
tana binasaiṁ kula binasihai, gahau na rāma jihāja

111. *mādhau cale bun āna 'māhā jaga jītauṁ jāi julahā....*
chaṙi pasārau rāma kahi baure, kahai kabīra samajhāī

112. *ko bīnai prema lāgau rī māī ko bīnai*
rāma rasāiṇa māte, rī māī ko bīnai
karagaha baiṭhi kabīrā nācai, cūhā kaṭyā
tānāṁ rī māī, ko bīnai

113. *tānāṁ tani kari, bānāṁ buni karī*
chāki parī mohi vyāṁnā
kahai kabīra maiṁ buni siranāṁ
jānata hai bhagavānāṁ ho rāma

114. *tananāṁ bunanāṁ tajyā kabīra,*
rāma nāma likha liyā sarīra
jaba laga bharauṁ nalī ka beha,
taba laga tūṭe rāma saneha

115. *Śrimadbhagavadgītā*. chap. 3, v.8.
niyataṁ kuru karma tvam
karma jyāya hy akarmaṇaḥ
śarīrayatrā 'pi ca te
na prosidhed akarmaṇaḥ

116. *St Mathew.* X.39.
117. *kabīra jīvata mṛtaka hvai rahe, tajai jagat kī āsa*
taba hari sevā āpaṇa karai, mati dukha pavai dāsa
118. *kabīra mana mṛtaka bhayā durabala bhayā sarīra*
tava pāchai lāgai hari phirai kahata kabīra kabīra
119. *kabīra mari maṙahaṭi rahyā, taba koī na bujhai sāra*
hari ādari āgaiṁ liyā, jyūṁ gaū back kī lāra
120. *kabīra ghara jālauṁ ghara ūbarai, ghara rakhauṁ ghara jāi*
eka acambhā dekhiyā, maṙā kāla kūṁ khāyi
121. *kabīra kharī kasauṭīrāma kī, khoṭā ṭikai na koi*
rāma kasauṭī so ṭikai, jo 'jīvat-mṛtaka' hoi
122. *kabīra dīna garībī dina kauṁ, dūndara kau abhimāni*
dūndara dila viṣa sūṁ bharī, dīna garībī rāma
123. *Gītā.* chapter 12, v.7
124. *St Mathew.* xix.24
125. ibid. v.3 Sermon on the Mount.
126. *Rāmacaritamānasa.* Uttara-kāṇḍa, 130 (K)
mo sama dīna na dīna hita tumha samāna raghubīra
asa bicāri raghubansa mani harahu biṣama bhava bhīra
127. *Uttara-kāṇḍa* 36:3 to 41. Gītā Press ec.
128. *Śrimadbhagavadgītā.* Chapter 16.
129. William Shakespeare Sonnet.
130. *kabīra sangati sādha kī, kade na triphala hoi*
candana hosī bāvanā, nīṁba na kahasī koi
131. *kabīra mathurā jāvai dvarikā, bhāvai jau jaganātha*
sadha sangati hari bhagati bina, kachū na āvai hātha
132. *kabīra soī dina blalā, jo dina santa milāṁhi*
ank bhare bhari bheṁṭiye, pāpa sarīrauṁ jāhiṁ
133. *kabīra khāī koṭa kī, pāṁṇī pivai na koi*
jāi milai jaba ganga maiṁ, taba saba gangodika hoi
134. *kabīra jāni būjhi sācahi tajaiṁ, kareṁ jhūṭa sūṁ neha*
tākī sangati rāma jī, supinaiṁ hīṁ jini deha
135. *kabīra bhagati hajārī kapaṙa, tāmaiṁ mala na samāi*
sākhita kālī kāṁmlī, bhāve tahāṁ bichāi
136. *kabīra bheṣa atīta kā, karatūti karai aparādha*
bāhari dīsai sādha gati, māhaiṁ maha asādha
137. *kabīra ujjala dekhi na dhījiye, bāga jyūṁ maṁḍai dhyāna*
dhorai baiṭhi capeṭasī, yūṁ le buṙai jñāna
138. *kabīra jetā mīṭhā bolaṇā, tetā sādha na jāṇi*
pahlī thāha dikhāi kari, ūṁḍai desī āṇi
139. The verses on *Śāktas* find place in the Gurū Grantha Sahib.
140. William Shakespeare. *A Midsummer Night's* Dream. Act 5, scene 1.

141. *ye tv akṣaram anirdeśyam avyaktaṁ paryupāsate*
sarvatragam acintyaṁ ca kūṭastham acalaṁ dhruvam
Gītā. Chap. 12, v.3.

142. *patraṁ puṣpaṁ phalaṁ toyaṁ yo me bhaktyā prayacchati*
tadahaṁ bhaktyupahritamaśnāmi prayatātmanaḥ
Gītā. Chap.9, v.26.

143. *The Holy Quran*. Chap. 9.5 and 27 The Immunity. Trans. Muhammad Ali. Lahore: Ahmadiyya Anjuman-I-Ishaat-I-Islam, 1928. p., 191 and 194.

144. *Exodus*. At Mount Sinai. 20. 4-5. (italics author's).

145. See *Swami Dayananda* by Prem Lata. New Delhi: Ess Ess Publication for a detailed analysis.

146. Poems of Kabīr.

147. *Bhagavadgītā* 12.5.

148. Mahatma Gandhi. *To the Hindus and Muslims*. Gandhi Series. vol.,III. Karachi: Anand T. Hingorani, 1942, p.,387.

149. id. pp., 192-93.

150. These accounts are from Harsh Narain. *Jizyah and the Spread of Islam*. New Delhi: Voice of India, 1990.

151. *Hindū bhūye rāma kahi, musalamāna khudāi*
kahai kabīra so jīvatā, dui maiṁ kade na jāi

152. *kābā phira kāsī bhayā, rāmahi bhayā rahīma*
moṭa cūna maidā bhayā, baiṭhi kabīrā jīma

153. *maiṙī mahal bābaṙī chājā, chāṁṙi gaye saba bhūpati rājā*

154. *koṭī dhaj sāha hastibandh rājā, kripana kau dhana kaunaim kaja*

155. *dhana kai garaba rāma nahīṁ jāṁga hvai janma pai gudarāṁnāṁ*
kahu kabira cetahu re bhāi, hansa gayā kachu saṅgi na jāī

156. *nirdhana saradhana donoṁ bhāī*
prabhu kī kalā na meṭī jāī
kahi kabīra niradhana hai soī
jāke hiradai rāma na hoī

157. *sakaleri eka rakta eka ghare āśraye*
eka māyera dudha khaiye eka dariyāye yāye....
pāni khete yaye eka dariyāye
mālā paite eka jana ghare, keha bā sunnata kore
tabe bhāi-bhāite mārā kare
yācchisa kena saba gollāya
Pāgalā Kānāi : *Hindu-Muslim*

158. *jogī gorakha gorakha karai, Hindū rāma nāma uccarai*
musalamāna kā eka khudāī, kabīra ka svāmī rahyā samai

159. *ūṁ kāra ādi hai mūlā, rājā parajā ekahi sūlā*
hama tumha māṁhai ekai lohū, ekai prāna jīvan hai mohū
eka hī jananīṁ janyāṁ sansarā, kauna gyāṁna thaiṁ bhaye ninārā

160. *sarvabhūta ekai kari janyā, cūke vāda vivādā*
kahi kabīra maiṁ pūrā pāyā, bhaye rāma parasādā
161. *yogayukto viśudhātmā vijitatmā jitendriyaḥ*
sarva bhūtā tmabhūtātmā kurvannapi na lipyate
Gītā. Chap. 5, śloka 7.
162. *kyā le māṭī bhuī sūṁ mārai, kyā cala deha nhāvai*
jora karai masakīna satāvai, guna hiṁ rahai chipāye
kyā tū jū japa manjana kīyeṁ, kyā masīti sira nāṁye
rojā karai nimāja gujarai, kyā haj kābai jāye
brahmaṇa gyarasi karai caubīsoṁ, kāyī mahram jāna
gyārah māsa jude kyūṁ kīye, ekahi mahiṁ samāna
jau ra khudāi masīti basat hai, aura mulika kisa kerā
tīrath mūrati rāma nivāsā, duhu maiṁ kinahuṁ na herā
purab disā harī kā bāsā, pacchima allah mukamoṁ
dil hī khoji dilai ḍila bhītari, ihāṁ rāma rahimanā
jetī aurati maradāṁ kahiye, saba meṁ rūpa tumhārā
kabīra pangurā allah rāma kā, hari gura pīra hamārā
163. *kabīra hindū mūye rāma kahi, musalamāna khudāi*
kahai kabīra so jīvata, duha maiṁ kade na jāi
164. *kabīra haradī pīyarī, cūnā ujala bhāi*
rāma sanehī yūṁ mile, dunyūṁ barana samāi
165. *ye le jāre vai le gāṛi, ini dukhi ini doū ghar chāṛe*
kahata kabīra sunahu re loī, hama tumha binasi rahaigā soī
166. *rarā kari ṭopa mamāṁ kari bakhtara, gyāna ratan kari pāga re*
jaise jau ajarāil mārai, mastaki āvai bhāga re
167. *Śrimadbhagavadgītā*. 18. 68-71.
168. *Exodus*. 3.6.
169. The Holy Quran. The Immunity. Islam shall triumph. chapter 9: 29. Trans, Muhammad Ali. Lahore: Ahmadiyya Anjuman-I-Ishaat-I-Islam, 1928.
170. *khālika khalaka khalaka maiṁ khālika, saba ghaṭa rahyau samāī*
eka rāma dekhya sabahin meṁ
171. *tāraṇa tiraṇa jabai laga kahiye, jaba laga tat na jānā*
eka rāma dekhyā sabahina maiṁ, kahai kabīra mana mānā
172. *rojā karaiṁ nibāj gujāraiṁ, kalamaiṁ bhisat na hoī*
sattira kabe ika dila bhītara, je kari janaiṁ koī
173. *The Risāla of al-Qushayrī* (This is the classic description of Sūfism).
174. *Fawā' id-ul-Fuad*, p.,9.
175. id. p.,130.
176. id. pp.,86-87.
177. *sirjanahāra eka hai, kāhū na soī*
āpa na kāhū soṁ janā, vaha samana nahiṁ koī
saba vahi bhītara vaha saba ṁahiṁ, sabai āpu dūsara kou nāhīṁ

dūsara jagata nāma jina pāvā, jaise lahariudadhi kahāvā
jñāna naina jo dekhai koī, bāridha binā āni nahīṁ hoī

178. *kabīra prema kā hama para barasā āi*
antara bhogī atmā harī bhaī banarāi

179. *kabīra nija ghara prema kā, māraga agama agādha*
sīsa utāri paga taji dharai, taba nikaṭi prema kā svāda

180. *dulahina gavahu mangalacāra, hama ghari ȳe ho rājā rāma bharatāra*

181. *aba tohi jāna na daihūṁ ranka piāre,*
jyūṁ bhāvai tyūṁ hohi hamāre

182. The *Rasikpriyā* of Keshavadasa.

183. P.B. Shelley. *A Defence of Poetry.*

184. John Donne. *Divine Poems.* X.

185. id. chap. III. L, 38-41.

186. Ramakumar Verma. *Sant Kabīr.* Allahabad: Sahitya Bhavan, 1947, pp., 1-2. (Trans. author's).

187. Dr Jayadeva Singh. *Kabīr Vāṇī Piyūsa.* Varansasi: Vishvavidalaya Prakashan, 1976, p.,58. op. cit. (Trans. author's).

188. id *Hindi Sāhitya kā Itihāsa.* (Trans. author's).

189. *Poetry and Prose of John Donne.* ed., A. Desmond Hawkins. London: Thomas Nelson & Sons, 1938 Introduction.

190. Logan Pearsall Smith. In the above quoted anthology of Donne's poems (on jacket).

191. William Wordsworth. *Poetry and Poetic Diction* (amendment of the word 'real' in Coleridge. *Wordsworth's Theory of Diction).* Italics mine.

192. Cristopher Marlowe. *Conquests of Tamburlaine.*

193. *A History of English Literature* E. Legouis and Louis Cazamian London: J.M. Dent, 1930, p., 427.

194. James Henry Leigh Hunt. *An Answer to the Question What is Poetry?*

195. id.

196. *kabīra cālā jaī thā, āge milā khudāi*
mīrā mujhasauṁ yauṁ kahā, kina phuramaī gāi

197. *yadi kabīra apne darśanik sidhānta aur sahajdharma kī saral sādhanā padyati lekara na āye hote to bhārata kā itihāsa kucha aura hī hotā*—Dr. Ramajilal 'Sahayak' and Dr Dindayal Gupta. *kabīra-daraśana* Hindi Vibhag Lucknow Visvavidyalaya. p.,411. (Trans. author's).

198. Charlotte Vaudevile. *A Weaver Named Kabir* New Delhi: Oxford University Press. 1993, p.,130. (Italics author's).

199. *kabīra lāṁbā māraga dūri ghara, bikaṭ pantha yahu māra*
kahau santauṁ kyūṁ pāiye duralabha hari dīdāra

200. *kabīra kaṭhināī kharī, sumiratāṁ hari nāma*
sūlī ūpar naṭ vidyā, giraum ta nāhīṁ ṭhāma

201. William Wordsworth. *The Thorn*. Coleridge: Wordsworth's Theory of Diction.

202. *brahmā kā āsana khisyā, sunata kāla kī gāja*

203. *phirata kat phūlyau, phūlau, phūlyau*
jab dasa māsa uragha mukhi hotau, so dina kahe bhūlau
jau jarai tau hoī bhasama tana, rahata kṛma hvai jāī
kācai kumbhi udika bhari rākhyau, tinakī kauna baṛāī
jyūṁ māṣī madhu saṁci kari, jori jori dhana kīnauṁ
mūyaiṁ pācheṁ lehu lahu kari, preta rahana kyūṁ dīnauṁ
jyūṁ ghara nārī saṅga dekhi kari, taba laga saṅga suhelau
maraghaṭ ghāṭ khaiṁca kari rakhe, vaha dekhau hansa akelau
rāma na ramahu madana kahā bhūle, parata aṁdheraiṁ kūvā
kahai kabīra soī āpa baṁdhāyau, jyūṁ nalanī kā sūvā

204. *unai badariyā sañjhā, aguā bhūle banakhaṇḍa manjhā*
piyā anete dhani anate rahaī, caupari kamari māthe gahaī
phulavā bhāra na lai sakai, kahai sakhina so roya
jyauṁ-jyauṁ bhījai kāmarī, tyauṁ-tyauṁ bhārī hoya

205. *bālam āu hamare geha re*
tumha bina dukhiā deha re
saba koi kahai tumhārī nārī, mokau yaha andeha re
ekameka hvai seja na sovai, taba laga kaisā neha re
anna na khāvai nīṁd ṅa āvai griha bana dhara na dhīra re
jyauṁ kāmī kau kāminī pyārī, jyauṁ pyāse kau nīra re
hai koi aisa para-upagarī, hari soṁ kahai sunāī re
aba tau behāla kabīra bhae hai, binu dekhe jiu jāī re

206. *avināsī dulahā kaba milihauṁ, sama santana ke pratipāla*
jala upajī jala hī sauṁ nehā, raṭata piyāsa piyāsa
maiṁ birihani ṭhāṛhi maga joūṁ, rāma tumhari āsa
chaṁḍyau geha neha lagi tumase, bhaī caran lau līna
talābeli hota ghaṭa bhītara, jaise jala binu mīna
divasa na bhūkha rain nahiṁ nidrā, ghara aṁgana na suhāi
sejariyā bairini bhai maukauṁ, jagata raini bihāi
maiṁ to tumhārī dāsī hau sajanā, tuma hamare bharatāra
dīna dayala dayā kari āvau, samaratha sirajanahāra
kai hama prana tajata haiṁ pyāre, kai apanī kari lehu
dāsa kabīra biraha ati baṛhyau, aba to darasana dehu

207. *ambara kunjāṁ kurariliyaṁ, garaji bhare sabatāla*
jina te govinda bīchuṭe, tinakauṁ kauna havāla
Hindi poets have very often illustrated the agony of separation by giving the example of the *kroṁca* bird. (also called *kunjā* or *kurarī*). Speaking of Sītā's separation from Rāmā, Tulsī says, *vilapat ata kurarī kī nāī*— Her agony is like that of the *kurarī* bird'.

208. *cakaī bichurī raini kau, āī milī parabhāti*
je jan bichuṭai rāmasauṁ, te dina mile na rāti

209. *birahini ūbhī pantha siri, panthī būjhai dhāī*
eka sabada kahi pīva kā, kabara milaumge āī

In the *Gītā* Krishṇa tells Arjuna to sit at the feet of saints and respectfully question them about *Brahman tradvidhi praṇipātena paripraśnena sevayā, upadehṣyanti te jñāninastattva darśinaḥ*
Bhagavadgītā 4:34

210. *aṁkhiyana to jhāṁī parī pantha nihāri nihāri*
jibhyā meṁ chālā parā, rāma pukāri pukāri

211. *nainā nījhadāiā, rataṭa phayai nisa dhāma*
papīhā jyauṁ piu piu karai, kabare milahuge rāma

(A *rahaṭa* is a device for drawing water from a well. It consists of small buckets tied on to a belt which keeps revolving. As each bucket goes down below the water level it fills up and when coming up empties the water into an open iron pipe for irrigating the fields.

212. *satī pukāre sali caṙhī, sunu re mīta maṁsāna*
loga baṭāū cali gaye, hama tuma rahe nidāṁna

213. *satī bicārī sat kiyā, kāṭhau seja bichāi*
le sūtī piu āpanāṁ cahuṁ disi agini lagāi

214. *satī jarana kauṁ nīkasī, cita dhari eka amekha*
tana mana sauṁpā pīva kau, antara rahī na rekha

215. Walt Whitman, *Leaves of Grass.*

216. *kone parā na chūṭhai, sunu re jīva abūjha*
kabīra mari maidāna meṁ, kari indrina soṁ jūjha

217. *kabīra soī sūrivāṁ, mana soṁ māṁḍeṁ jūjha*
panca piyāde pāri kai, dūri karai saba dūja

218. *kabīra ghoṙa prema kā, cetana caṙhi asavara*
jñāna khaḍaga gahi kāla sira, bhalī macāī māra

219. *tasmād ajñāna-saṁbhūtam*
hṛtsthaṁ jñāsinā 'tmanaḥ
chittvainaṁ saṁśayaṁ yogam
ātiṣṭho 'ttiṣṭha bhārata

220. *surā tabahī paraṣie, laṙeṁ dhanī kai heta*
purajā purajā hoi pare, taū na chaṁṙai kheta

221. *surai sīra utāriyā, chāṁṙī tana kī āsa*
āge taiṁ hari mulakiyā, āvata dekhā dāsa

222. *rāma rasāina prema rasa, pīvata adhika rasāla*
kabīra pīvana duralabh hai, māṁge sīsa kapāla

223. *harirasa piyā jānie, je kabahuṁ na jāi khumāra*
maiṁmatā ghūmata phirai, nāhīṁ tana kī sāra

224. *avaḍhū merā mana mativārā*
unamani caṙhā magana rasa pīvai, tribhuvana bhayā ujiyārā
225. *kabīra hasi hasi kanta na pāie, jini pāyā jini roi*
je hāṁsai hī hari milaiṁ, tau nahīṁ duhagani koi
226. *kabīra hasī khelauṁ hari milaiṁ, kauṇa sahai khara sāṁṙa*
kāma krodha trisnāṁ tajai, tāhi milai bhagavāna
227. *rāma bāna aniyāle tīra, jāhi lāge so Jānai pīra*
tana mana khojūṁ cota na pāūṁ, auṣadi mūrī kahāṁ ghasi lāūṁ
ekahi rūpa dīseṁ saba nārī, nā jānūṁ ko pīyahi piyārī
kahai kabīra jā masitaka bhāga, nā jānūṁ kāhū dei suhāga
228. *āsa nahīṁ pūriyāre, rāma bina ko krama kātaṇahāra*
jala sara jala parpūratā, cātiga citahaṁ udāsa
merī viṣama krama gati hvai parī, tāthaim piyāsa piyāsa
siddha milai sudhi nā milai, milai milāvai soi
sūra sidha jaba bheṭiye, taba dukha na vyāpai koi
bochaiṁ jali jaise machikā, udara na bharaī nīra
tyūṁ tumha karani kesabā, jana tālābelī kabīra
(The *cātak* drinks only the first raindrops which are rare in winter in India. So it remains thirsty despite the pond being full of water).
229. *anantakale ca mameva smaranmuktvā kalevaram*
yaḥ prayāti sa nadbhāavam yāti nāstyatra sanśayaḥ
Gītā, chap, 8,v. 5
230. *muvāṁ pīchaiṁ jini milai, kahai kabīrā rāma*
pāthara ghāṭā loha saba, pārasa kaune kāma
231. *bherā pāyā sarapà kā, bhausāgara ke māhiṁ*
je charāuṁ ḍūbihauṁ, gahauṁ ḍasihai bāhiṁ
232. *taṅtrināda kabitta rasa, sarasa rāga ratiraṅga*
anabūṙe būṙe, tire je būṙe saba aṅga
233. 1. *nehīmahā... sundaritāhi ke bheda kauṁ jānai*
cha ke ranga maiṁ bhijyau hiyo, bichuraiṁ,
milaiṁ prītama sānti na mānai
bhaṣā-prabīna, suchanda sadā rahai...
2. *prema sadā ūṁco lahai su kahai ihi bhaṁī kī bāta chakī*
suni kai saba ke mana lālac daure, pai baure lakhaiṁ saba buddhi chakī
jaga kī kabitāi dhokheṁ rahai hyā ṁprabinana kī mati jāti jakī
samujhai kabīta ghanānanda kī hiya-āṁkhina neha kī pīra takī
234. *dādur mora papīha bolai*
koyala madhura sāja
umamgyau indra cahuṁ disi barasai
dāmaṇi chorī lāja
dharatī rūpa nava nava dhariya
indra milana kai kaja

235. *kalī-pīli ghaṭā uṁmarī, barasyo eka gharī*
jita jauṁ tita pāṇī pāṇī, huī bhumi harī

236. Dr J. Singh and Dr V. Singh. *Kabīr Vāṇī Piyūṣa* op. cit. Varanasi: Vishvawidyalaya Prakashan, 1976, p.,73 (trans. author's)

237. ibid. p.,74. op. cit.

238. *bolī hamārī pūraba kī, hami lakhai na koi*
hamako to soi lakhai, dhura pūraba kā hoi

239. *A Weaver Named Kabir*. Oxford, 1993, p.,119.

240. ibid.

241. Dictionary of the Hindi language compiled Prof. R.C. Pathak. Benares: Bhargava Book Depot.

242. *tahāṁ moṁ garīb ko ko gudarābai, majlis dūri mahala ko pāvai*
sattari sahasa salāra hai jāke, savā lākh paigambara tāke
sekha ju kahiahīṁ koṭi aṭhāsī, chappana koṭi jāke khela khāsī
koṭi taitīsūṁ aru khilakhānāṁ , caurāsī lākh phirai divānā
kābā adama pai najari dilāī, una bhī bhisti ghanerī pāī
tuma dāte hama sadā bhikarī, deu jabāba hoi baja gārī
dāsa kabīra terī panaha samāṁnā, bhisti najīki rakhi rahimānāṁ
(Dr Tiwari: quoted in Dr Jayadeva Singh and Dr Vasudeva Singh. *Kabīr Vāṇī Piyūṣa*. Varanasi: Vishvidyalaya Prakashan, 1976, p.,75).

243. H.W. Longfellow-*Flowers*.

244. *dhavaṇi dhavantī rahi gaī, bujhi gae angāra*
ahraṇi rahā thamūkaṙa jab uṭhi calā lohāra
(The examples have been given in *Kabīr Vāṇī Piyuṣa* where they are meant to illustrate the expressiveness of the metaphors).

245. *Kabīr Granthāvali. ed.* Dr Prasanatha Tiwari. Allahabad: Hindi Parishad, 1961.

246. R. Verma. *Sant Kabīr*. Allahabad: Sahitya Bhawan Ltd., 1947.

247. *kabīra sansā dūri karu, kāgad deu bahāi*
bāvan akhara sodhi kai, hari caranī citu lāi

248. *bidiyā na parauṁ badu nahīṁ nānuṁ*
hari guna kathana sunana baurāno

249. ('Keep calling out "Keśava" all the time, don't keep sleeping. If you keep calling night and day, maybe you'll be heard some time'.)

250. Dr Mataprasada Gupta. *Kabīr Granthāvalī*. Allahabad: Sahitya Bhawan Pvt Ltd. 1985, p.,9.

251. C. Vaudeville. *A Weaver Named Kabīr* Oxford, p.,18.

252. Ramakumara Verma. *Sant Kabīr*. pp.,38-39 op. cit. (see also the points about this Tract brought forth by Dr Ramajilal 'Sahayak', a little later).

253. Elliot and Dowson. *The History of India as Told by its Own Historians.* Trübner 1871, vol.-IV, p.,447.
254. *The History and Culture of the Indian People.* Baratiya Vidya Bhavan. Vol.-6, p.,147.
255. *dekhi kai prabhāva pheri upajau abhāu dvija āyau pātasāha so sikandar su nāṁva hai— Bhaktamala.*
256. Dr Ramajilal 'Sahayak' *Kabīr Darshan.* Lucknow Visvavidyalaya (Hindi Department) 1962, p.,8.
257. *1. kāsī nagara rahai puni soī, nīrū nama julāhā hoī*
nīmā nāma nāri kara bhāī, nāri-puruṣa hī mila puni āī
2. nīrū nāma julāhā gamana liye ghara jāye
tāsu nāri baṙa bhaginī jala meṁ bālaka pāye
258. *caudāha sau pacapana sāla gaye, candravāra eka ṭhāṭa thaye*
jeṭha sudī barasāyata ko, pūraṇamāsī pragaṭa bhaye
259. *jugana jugana līnhā avatāra, rahauṁ nirantara pragaṭa pasārā*
satayuga sat sukṛta kaha ṭerā, tretā nāma munendahiṁ merā
dopara meṁ karunāma kahāye, kaliyuga nāma kabīra rakhāye
cāroṁ juga meṁ cāroṁ nāuṁ, māyā rahita rahai tihi ṭhāuṁ
(Quoted in Ramakumara Varma. *Sant Kabīr.* Allahabad: Sahitya Bhawan, p., 33fn.).
260. However, this point is taken up later in more detail. See Life—The controversy about Kabīr's mortal remains.
261. *(hamare kula kaune rāma kahyau*
jaba kī mālā lai nipūte taba te sukha na bhayo
sunahu jiṭhānī sunahu dirānī acaraja eka bhayo
sāta sūta ina muṁḍiyo khoye ihu muṁḍiyā kyūṁ na bhuyo)
262. *kabīra duniyāṁ bhāṁḍā dukha ka, bharī mahāṁuha bhūṣa*
adayā alaha rāma kī, kurahai ūṁṇī kūṣa
Sākhī 12.47.
263. *Ancient India as Described by Kiesias and Kuidian* pp.,17-18.
264. *1.bhujā bāṁdhi milā kari ḍārio*
hasatī krodhi munḍa mahi māriyo
hasati bhāgi kai āsā mārai
iā mūrati kai haḍa balihārai
āhi mere ṭhākur tumarā oru
kājī bakibo hasti toru(1)
re mahāvat tyjhu ḍarau kāṭi
hasahi turāvahu ghalahu khāṭi
hasati na torai dharai dhianu
vake ridhai basai bhagavanu(2)
kiā apāradhu santa hai kīnhā
bamdhi poti kuncara kau dīnā
kuncaru poṭa lai lai namaskarai
būjhi nahiṁ kājī amdhi aṁdhiāre(3)

tīna bāra patiya bhari līnā
mana kaṭhoru ajahu na patinā
kaha kabīra hamārā gobinda
cauthe pada mahi unakā jindu(4)
2. ganga gusāini gahari gambhīra
janīra bāṁdhi kari khare kabīra
manu na ḍigai tana kāhe kau ḍarai
carana kamala cita rahio samāi
gangā ki lahari merī ṭūṭī janjīra
mrigachālā para baiṭhe kabīra
kahi kabīra koū saṅga na sātha
jala thala rakhana hai raghunātha

265. The view finds place in Dr Ramajilal Sahayak *Kabīr-Darshan* The relevant verses quoted by him are:
1. purab janama hama tumhare sevak, ab to miṭyā na āi
tere dvāre dhuni sahaja kī mathai mere dagāi
2. purab janama hama bāṁmhana hote, oche karama tapa hīnāṁ
rāmadeva kī sevā cūkā, pakari julāhā kīnhāṁ
3. mānuṣa tana julahā kula dīna, dou sanjoga bahuri bidhi kīnā
kāsī nagara rahe pubi soī, nīrū nāma julāhā hoī
nīmā nāma nāri kara bhāī, nāri puruṣa hī mila puni āī
4. māya turakanī bāpa julāhā, beṭā bhakta bhaye

266. *jāke īdi bakarīdi kula gaū re badha karahi, māṁ ahi seṣa sahīda pīrā*
jāke bāpi vaisī karī pūta aisī karī, tihure loka parasidha kabīrā
Dr Ramajilal 'Sahayak'. *Kabīr-Darshana*. op. cit. pp.,19-20.

267. *garība goda liyā mukha cūma kari hemarūpa jhalakanta*
jagara magara kayā karai damakai padama ananta

268. *koi koi āi nīrū se kahaī, suta tumhara baṛa vādī ahaī*

269. *nīrū nīmā dou mili binibeṁ tahi bahūta*
saba gunāh mohiṁ bakasau jore bigārā pūta

270. *pāpī pūjā vaisī kari, bhakaiṁ mānsa mada doi*
tini kī daṣyā mukati nahiṁ, koṭi narak phala hoi

271. *kahahi kabīra hama uhāṁ na jāhiṁ, tuma abhaccha āneu ghāra māhīṁ*

272. *sakati se neha pakari kari sunati, yahu na bandu re bhāī*
aura ṣudāi turaka mohi karatā, tau āpai kaṭi kina jāī
hau tau turaka kiyā kari sunati, aurati sauṁ kā kahiye
pakarī ṭeka kabīr bhagati kī, kājī rahe jhaṣa bhaṛi

273. *tānā bānā kachū na sūjhai, hari hari rasa lapaṭyo*

274. *musi musi rovai kabīra ki māī*

275. *kahai kabīra yaha dukha kāsina kahiye*
apane tana ko apa hi sahiye

276. *hauṁ bārī mukha keri piyāre, karavaṭ de mokauṁ kahe kau māre*
jauṁ tana cīrahIṁ anga na morau, pinḍa parai tau prīti na torauṁ

hama tuma bīca bhayo nahim̄ koī, tumahi sukanta nāri maim loī
kahata kabīra sunahu re loī, aba tumarī paratiti na hoī

277. *Ramana Maharshi*. Prem Lata, New Delhi: Sumit Publications, 1986, p.,14.

278. Ramakumara Verma. *Sant Kabīr* Allahabad: Sahitya Bhawan Ltd., 1947, p.,72.
(*Sant-saṅgati ke hone se inhe*, (i.e., Kabīr's children) *anna-kaṣṭa rahtā thā*- 'his children were starved of food').

279. *rāmānanda ka siṣa kabīrā, mati kāsāṁcā bhagati kā dhīrā*

280. 1. *bhaktī drāviṙa ūpajī, lāe rāmānanda*
Kabīra ne paragaṭa karī, sāta dīpa navakhanḍa
2. *kabīra rāmānanda ka, satagura mile sahai*
jaga meṁ jugati anūpahai, soī daī batai

281. *saca sādhu ju rāmānanda*
jako sevaka kabīra dhīri ati sumati sura surānanda
Radhakrishna. *Sūṙadāsa* p.,23.
Dr Ramajilal 'Sahayak' *Kabīr-Darshan* op. cit. p.,33.

282. Dr Ramajilal 'Sahayak'. *Kabīr Darshan* ed. Dr Dinadayala Gupta, Lucknow University. Hindi Department 1968. Others, however, like Charlotte Vaudeville. *A Weaver Named Kabīr*, Oxford University Press, 1993 doubts this. Vaudeville says 'Western scholars have been inclined to doubt that Kabīr was actually Rāmānanda's disciple', p.,54 op. cit.

283. *nānā nāṁca nacāyekai, nācai naṭa ke bheṣa*
ghaṭa ghaṭa avināsī ahai, sunahu takī tuma śekha

284. 1. *śekha takī taba kahe risāī, hai koi bāṁdha kabīrā bhāī*
2. *śekha takī taba mīṁjai hāthā, sūkhe muṁha nahiṁ āvai bātā*

285. *haja hamārī gomati tīra, jahāṁ basahiṁ pītāmbara pīra*

286. Dr Jayadeva Singh. *Kabīr Vāṇī Piyuṣha* Vishvavidyalaya Varanasi p.,9.

287. Dr P. Chaturvedi. *Uttara Bhārata kī Sant Paramparā* p.,560.

288. *haja kābai hvai hvai gayā, ketī bāra kabīra*
mīrāṁ mujhameṁ kyā khatā, mukhāṁ na bolai pīra

289. C. Vaudeville. *A Weaver Named Kabīr*. Oxford, 1993 pp.,233 and 244. (Not quoted as appearing in it).

290. *prema na barī ūpaje, prema na hāṭa bikāya*
rājā parijā jehi ruce, sīsa dehi lai jāi

291. *sākhī āṁkhī jñāni kī, samujhi dekhi mana māhiṁ*
bina sākhī sanasara ka jhagṙā chūṭati nāhiṁ

292. Charlotte Vaudeville. *A Weaver Named Kabīr*. Oxford, 1993. pp.112-113 op. cit.

293. *Rāmacaritamānasa. Bālakāṇḍa* 8.6 *Gītā* Press.

294. *pāsā pakaṙyā prema kā, sārī kiyā sarīra*
sataguru daum̐ batāiyā, khelai dāsa kabīra
295. *kasaṇī de kancana kiyā, tāhi liyā tatasāra*
296. *kahai kabīra guru jñāni thaim̐ eka ādha ubaranti*
297. *bhaniti bicitra sukabi kṛta joū, rāma nāma binu soha na soū*
bidhubadanī saba bhām̐ti sam̐varī, soha na basana binā bara nārī
saba guna rahita kukabi kṛta bānī, rāma nāma jasa ankita jānī
sadara kahahim̐ sunahim̐ budha tāhī, madhukara sarisa santa gunagrāhīm̐
Rāmacaritamānasa. Bālakāṇḍa 9. 2-3. Gītā Press.
298. *Bhagavadgītā*. 3. 8.
299. *bhukhe bhagati na kījai, yaha mālā apanī lījai*
300. *dui sera mām̐gau cūna, pāu ghiyu saṅgi lūna*
adha sera mm̐gau dāle, mokau donau vakhata jivāle
khāṭa mām̐gau caupāī, sirhānā avara tulāī
ūpara kau magau khīdhā, terī bhagati karai anu bīdhā
maim̐ nāhī kītā labo, ika nāu terā mai phabo
kahi kabīra manu māniā, manu māniyā tau hari jāniā
301. *Bhagavadgītā* 6. 40.
302. *hama tuma mām̐hai ekai lohū*
ekai prāna jīvana hai mohū
ekahi vāsa rahe dasa māsā
sūtaga pātaga ek ai āsā
eka hī jananī, janyām̐ sansārā
kauna jñāna thaim̐ bhaye ninārā
303. *sīsa carana kara kampana lāge, naina nīra asa rāle*
bahay jibhyā bacana sūdha nahīm̐ nikasai
304. *1. sambata pandraha sau aura pām̐ca bhau magahara kiyo gauna*
agahana sudi ekādasi, ralo pauna mem̐ pauna
2. sambat pandraha sau pachattara, kiyo magahara kau gauna
māgha sudī ekādasī, ralo pauna mem̐ pauna
3. pandraha sau unacāsa mem̐, magahara kīnhom̐ gauna
agahana sudī ekādasī, milau pauna mem̐ pauna
4. sambat pandraha sau unhattarā rahāī
sataguru cale uṭhi hansā jyāī
Dharmadāsādvādasa Pantha
305. *maraṇa ke misi līlā ṭhani ṭhī*
sodhi laī magahara kī pāṭī
306. *sagala janama sivapurī gavāiā*
maratī bara magahara uṭhi dhāiā
bahuta barisa tapu kīyā kāsī
maranu bhaiā magahara ko vāsī
307. *magahara marai so gadahā hoye (Bījak)*

308. *jau tana kāsī tajahī kabīrā rāmahi kahā nihorā*
kahu kabīra sunahu re loī, bharama na bhūlahu koī
kyā kāsī kyā ūsara magahara, rāma hiradaya jo hoī

309. *1. vai kahai gāroṁ, vai kahai jarauṁ*
apanī apanī dharama vicāroṁ
duhu ora tai deṣana āvai, sejahi phūla kabīra pāvai
2. magahara meṁ eka līlā kīnhī, hindū-turuka bratadharī
kabara ṣadāi ke paracā dīnhī, miṭi gayo jhagarā bhārī

310. *Selections From the Sacred Writings of the Sikhs* George Allen & Unwin, 1960.

311. Charlotte Vaudeville. *A Weaver Named Kabīr*. Oxford, 1993, p.,227.

312. *Ramacaritamānasa.* Araṇyakāṇḍa 30. 5.

313. *jorata kaīka su gherata saba gaṛha, karataba jhelī jhelā*
jori kaṭaka gaṛha tori patisaha, kheli calao eka khelā

314. Harsh Narain. *Jizyah and the Spread of Islam.* New Delhi: Voice of India, 1990. pp., 26-27. (Quoting As-Sarkasī, *kitāb-al-Mabsūṭ* X. p.,77 cited in Khadduri, p., 177 & Khaddurī p., 177)

315. Bacon. *Of Vanity in Religion.*

316. *The History of India as Told by its Own Historians* Trübner 1871, vol.3, p.,427.

317. id.

318. Elliot and Dowson, p.,433.

319. id., p.,436.

320. id.

321. id., p.,461.

322. J.C. Powell-Price. *A History of India*, Nelson, 1955, p.,189.

323. *1. aho mere govyanda tumhārā ora, kājī bakiya hastī tora*
bāṁdhi bhujā bhalaiṁ kari ḍalyau, hastī kopi mūṁḍa maiṁ bhājyau
bhāgyau hastī cīṁsā mārī, vā mūrati kī maiṁ balihārī
mahavat tākūṁ māryauṁ sāṭī, isahi marāūṁ ghālauṁ kāṭī
2. ati athāha jala gahara gaṁbhīra, bāṁdhi janjīra jala bore hai kabīra
jali kī taranga uṭhi kaṭiaiṁ jaṁjīra, hari sumirana taṭa baiṭhe haṁ kabīra

324. Elliot and Dowson vol.4, p.,475.

325. id. p.,440.

326. id. p,.447.

327. Translation of the Holy Quran. Trans. Muhammad Ali Lahore: Ahmadiyya Anjuman-I-Ishaat-I-Islam 1928, chapter 9: 5.

328. id. 30:30.

329. Elliot and Dowson, 1871, vol.4, p.,448.

330. W.H. Moreland. *From Akbar to Aurangzeb*. London: MacMillan, 1923, pp.,304-305.
331. *The History and Culture of the Indian People*. Bharatiya Vidya Bhavan, 1960. vol.6, p.,24.
332. As stated in Dr Jayadeva Singh & Dr Vasudeva Singh. *Kabīr Vāṇī Piyūṣa* Varanasi: Vishvidyalaya Prakashan 1976, p.,4. *bahuta sī jātiyoṁ ne svaichā islam ko svikāra kara liyā.*
333. *The History and culture of the Indian People*. (ed. R.C. Majumdar). Bhavan. vol.V. p.,498.
334. S.R. Sharma. *Studies in Medieval History*. pp.,57,61 and 29.
335. Trans. Muhammad Ali. Lahore: Ahmadiyya Anjuman-I-Ishhat-Islam, 1928, p.,CXVI 24:30-31. The translator adds, 'There is also a saying of the Holy Prophet that when a woman reaches the age of puberty she should cover her body *except the face and the hands*'.
336. *be pardā nazarāīṁ kala jo canda bībāṁ*
'akbar' zamīṁ meṁ gairat-i-qaumī se gaṙa gayā
pūṁchā jo unase, āpa kā parādā kahāṁ gayā
kahane lagīṁ kī akla pai mardoṁ ke paṙa gayā
337. *jīva vilambyā jīva sauṁ, alaṣa na lakhiā jāi*
338. *mora tora kī jebaṙī, bali bandhyā sansāra*
kā sikaḍūṁ bāsuta kalita, dajhaṇa bārambāra
339. *viṣai karma kī kunkulī, pahira huā nara nāga*
sira phoṙai nahīṁ, ko āgilā abhāga
340. *sāta sūtu inu muṁḍiyo khoye, ihu muṁdiā kyoṁ na muyo*
341. *niradhana ādara koi na deī, lākh jatana karai houcita na gharehī*
jau niradhna saradhana kai jāī, āge baiṭhā pīṭha phirāī
342. P.D. Gupta. *Medieval India*. p.,141.
343. *ika paṙhahi pāṭha ika bhramaiṁ udāoa, ika nagana nirantara rahaim nivasa*
ika joga jugati tana hūiṁ khīna, aise rāma nāma sangi rahaiṁ līna
ika hūṁhi dīna ika dehi dāni, ika karaiṁ kalāyī surāpāna
ika tanta manta oṣadha jāna, ika sakala sidha rākhaiṁ-ayāṁa
ika tīrtha brata kari kāyā jīti, aisaiṁ rāma nāma sūṁ karaiṁ na prīti
ika dhauma ghoṁta tana hūiṁ syāma, yūṁ mukati nahīṁ bina rāma nāma
344. 1. *sakala varaṇa ikatra hvai, sakati pūtri mili khahiṁ*
2. *pāpī pūjā bhaṣaiṁ kari, bhaṣaiṁ mānsa mada doi*
3. *pāhaṇa kerā pūtalā, kari pūjaiṁ karatāra*
ihi bharose je rahe, te būṙe kālī dhāra
345. *Hindi Sāhitya ki Bhumikā*, p.,28.
346. *Hindi Kāvya meṁ Nirguṇa Sampradaya* p.,2 (Both quoted by Dr Jaydeva Singh in Kabīr Vānī Piyūsa, p.5.)

347. *astuti vidyā āsā chāṁṙai, tajai māna apamānā*
lohā kancana sami kara dekhe, te mūrati bhagavānā
348. Dr Ramajilal 'Shayak' *Kabīr-Darśana*, 1962, p.,29.
349. *jñana galī meṁ khabara mili gayī, hameṁ milī piyā kī pātī*
vā pātī meṁ agama saṁdesā, aḅa hama marane ko na ḍaratī
kahata kabīra suno bhāī pyāre, bara pāye avinasī
350. *isa tana ka dīvā karauṁ, bātī melauṁ jīva*
lahī sīmcoṁ tela jyoṁ, taba mukha dekhoṁ pīva
351. *māyā kī jhala jaga jalyā, kanaka kamiṇīṁ lāgi*
kahu dhauṁ kihi bidhi rākhiye, rui paleṭī āgī
352. *Tulsīdāsa. Rāmacaritamānasa Ayodhyā-kāṇḍa*
353. *Śrimad Bhagavadgītā.* chapter 6 vv.34-35.
354. *bāgīgara kā bāndarā, aisā jiu mana sātha*
nānaṁ nāca nacāya kari, rācai āpane hāth
355. *prema bhagati aisī kījiye, mukhi amṛta bariṣai canda re*
āpa hī āpa vicāriye, taba ketā hoi ananda re
356. *Sākhī. Ras kau anga.*2.
357. *jisu maraneṁ se jaga ḍarai, sau mere ānanda*
kaba marihoṁ kaba bheṭihoṁ pūrana paramānanda
358. William Shakespeare. Sonnets. 116.
359. *hridaya kapata mukh jñānī, jhuṭhe kahā bilobasi pānī*
kayā mānjisa kauna guṇāṁ, jau ghaṭa bhītara hai malanā
lauṭhi āṭha sati tīratha nhāī, kaurāpana taū na jāī
kahi kabīra nicārī, bhaya sāgara tāri murārī
360. *santa na bāṁdhe gaṭhaṙī peṭa, samāta lei*
sāṁī sūṁ manamukha rahai, jahaṁ māṁge tahaṁ dei

SELECTED VERSES

nīce loina kari rahau,
le sājana ghaṭa māhi,
sabā rasa khelau pia sau,
kisī lakhāvau nāhi.

KABĪR

THE RAMAINĪS

adbuda rūpa jāti kī bānī
upajī prīti ramainī ṭhānī

('Impelled by maya, the embodied soul sought its satisfaction in pleasures of the senses')

KABĪR

THE RAMAINĪS

1

barancahuṁ kauna rūpa aura rekhā, dosara kauna āhi jo dekhā
au oṁkāra ādi nahiṁ vedā; tākara kahahu kauna kula bhedā
nahiṁ tārāgana nahiṁ rabi candā, nahiṁ kachu hota pitā ke bindā
nahiṁ jala nahiṁ thala nahiṁ thira pauṁnā, ko dhare nāma hukuma kobaranā
nahiṁ kachu hota divasa au rāti, tākara kahahu kauna kula jātī

Sākhī— *Sunna sahaja mana sumirata, pragaṭa bhaī ika joti*
balihāri tā puruṣa kī, nirālamba jo hoti

ON BRAHMAN

How can *Brahman's* form and shape be described when none has seen him?
He cannot be comprehended
Even by the *Vedas* that spring from the Supreme,
Nor can his lineage ever be known.

There are no stars there, nor the sun nor moon,
No seed gave him birth, for he's unborn;
There is no land there, no waters, no firmament;
No day dawns there, nor is there night's darkness.

He has no overlord: who dare command him?
He is beyond all relationships and bonds.

I adore that person
Who leans on no support
In whose mind there shines
The light of the Soul.

2

alakha niranjana lakhai na koī, jehi baṁdhe baṁdhā saba koī
jehi jhūṭe baṁdhāya ayāyā, jhuṭhī bāta sāṁca kai jānā
dhandhā bandhā kīnha bevahārā,
karama bibarajita basai niārā
ṣaṭa āśrama ṣaṭa darasana kīnhā,
ṣaṭa rasa vāsa ṣaṭa vastuhiṁ cīnhā
cāri vṛkṣa chatra bakānai,
vidyā aganita ganai na jānai
avaro āgama karai bicārā,
te nahiṁ sūjhai vāra na pārā
japa tīratha vrata kījai pūjā,
dāna punya kijai bahu dūjā.

Sākhī— *mandira tau hai neha kā*
mata koi paiṭhe dhāya
jo koi paiṭhe dhayake,
binu sira seṁtihi jāya

THE NOOSE OF DELUSION

Death comes unseen
Catching everyone in its noose;
Deluded by it, the ignorant
Mistaking falseness for truth,
Consider works that shackle to be right effort
and shun those which are vital and virtuous.

Because death comes, the pundits beguile men
With the six *āśramas* and the Six Systems:[1]
And the six kinds of food allure men's minds.[2]
There are the four *Vedas* and the six *Vedāngas*[3]

Sacrifices and oblations in the fire,
And various discourses in the Shastras,
Prayer, worship, fasts, pilgrimages and gifts of charity;
Yet the Real cannot be known by these.

In the mind's temple
Dwell attachment and craving
He who rushes into it
Speeds to his own destruction.

3

asa jolahā ka maram na jānā,
jina jaga āya pasārinhi tānā
mahi akāsa dui gāṛha khaṁdāyā,
cāṁda suruja dui narī banāyā
sahasa tāra lai pūrina pūrī,
ajahuṁ binava kathina hai dūrī
kahahiṁ kabīra karama so jori,
sūta-kusūta binai bhala korī

GOD THE GREAT WEAVER

Who can fathom the ways of that Creator
Who like the weaver's woven cloth
Has spread out the fabric of the universe?

As the weaver digs two pits to fix his loom
The Lord has made the earth and sky to hold the world.
His shuttles are the sun and the moon
By whose light men engage in their tasks
The myriad strings are the stars of the heavens

As the weaver at his loom
The Lord forever works the warp and woof of existence
Some strings are strong; from them come virtuous beings
And the weak ones he leaves for the vile.[4]

4

apaṇḍita bhūle paṛhi guni vedā,
āpu apanāpau jana na bhedā
sanjhā tarapana au ṣaṭa karmā,
ī bahu rūpa karahiṁ asa dharamā
gayatrī juga cāri paṛhāī,

pūchahu jaya mukti kina pāī
aura ke chue leta hau soṁncā,
tumte kahata kauna hai nīcā
ye guna garva karahu adhikāī,
adhikai garva na hoya bhalāī
jasu nāma hai garva prahārī
so kasa garvahi sakai sahārī

Sākhī — *kula marajādā khoya kai*
khojini pada nirvāni
ankura bīja nasai kai
bhae videhī thāna

VAIN OBSERVANCES

The learned pundits are unlearned
Even though they have studied well the *Vedas*,
The soul's unknown to them; they can't discern it.

They worship three times a day[5]
And make the water-offerings to the manes,[6]
Say their prayers and chant the holy name,
Make oblations in the fire and bathe

Thus carrying out their dharma in many ways.
They keep repeating the *gāyatrī* all their lives[7]
But has it given *mokṣa* to any of them?[8]
They think a low-caste man's touch defiles
And go off to bathe to be pure again!
How low they've fallen! their great vanity
Will do them no good, for the Lord
Is the destroyer of arrogance;
And he can never overlook such self-conceit.[9]

He who has not allowed
Vanity and desire to sprout,
Who, rising above high and low
Seeks to attain *mokṣa*:
He in this very life
Has attained it.[10]

5

jina kalamā kaḷi māṁha paṙhāyā,
kudarata khoji tinahu nanim pāyā
karma te karma karai karatūtī,
veda kiteba bhayī saba rītī
karma to so jo bhava avatariā
karma to so nimāja ko dhariyā
karma te sunnati aura janeū,
hindū turaka na jānai bheū

Sākhī — *pānī pauna saṁjoya ke, raciyā yaha utapāta*
sunnahi surati samāiyā, kāsoṁ kahie jāta

GOD HAS NO RELIGION

Those who believed that in this Kali-age[11]
The *Kalimā* would bring one near to the divine[12]
Could themselves not know God though they essayed!
Self-centred, they did only works that bind
The *Vedas* and Quran also speak[13]
Of works that lead to repeated births and deaths:
Nor by the *namāz* is the soul revealed[14]
And do you think the Hindu's sacred thread[15]
Or the circumcision of the Turk
Can by themselves know race or religion?[16]
It's only the man who can diligently search
Inside his own Self, who can have God-vision.

The same Soul dwells in beings everywhere,
How can it ever be affected by caste
Or by the accursed body formed of water and air?[17]
For the Soul is immortal and the body does not last.

6

tehi sāhab ke lāgahu sāthā,
dui dukha meṭike rahahu sanāthā
dasaratha kula avatari nahīṁ āyā,
nahiṁ lankā ke rāva satāyā
nahīṁ devakī ke garbhaiṁ āyā,
nahīṁ jasodai goda khelāyā
prithimī ravanadavana nahiṁ kariyā,
paiṭhi patāla nahīṁ bali chaliyā
nahiṁ baliraja se māṁṙī rāṙī,
nahiṁ harināukusa badhaka pachārī
hoye barāha dharani nahiṁ dhariā,
chatrī māri nichatra na kariā
nahiṁ gobaradhana kara gahi dhariā,
nahiṁ gvālana saṅga bana bana phiriā
gaṇḍaka sāligarāma na sīlā,
maccha kaccha hoya jala nahīṁ hīlā
dvarāvatī sarīra na chāṙā,
lai jaganatha piṇḍa rahiṁ gāṙā

Sākhī — *kahaiṁ kabīra pukāra kai,*
vohi panthai mati bhūla
jehi rākhehu anumāna kai,
so thūla nahīṁ asthūla

GOD IS FORMLESS HE DOES NOT INCARNATE

Adore the Formles, that way alone
Can you free yourself
From the rounds of births and deaths.
God has no shape or form,
He was not born in Dashrath's clan,
He did not oppress Lankā's king
Or take birth from Devakī's womb,
He did not play in Yashodā's lap
He did not slay evildoers
Or sport on the earth,
He did not deceitfully send
Bali to the netherworld;

Nor did he slay Bāli or Hiraṇyakashipu.
He did not incarnate as Varāh
To retrieve the earth,
Nor descend to end the kshatriya race.
He did not lift Goverdhana hill,
He did not wander in the woods
With cowherd-maids.
He did not lie on the bed of the Gaṇdaka
As a Shaligrāma.
He did not incarnate
As the Tortoise or the Fish.
He did not relinquish the human form
At Dvārakā; nor at Puri
Did he cause his image to be installed.[18]

Kabīr proclaims from the housetops
Do not be misled
Into conjuring up a form for God
Who's really formless.

7

dara kī bāta kahau darabesā,
pātasāha hai kaune bhesā
kahāṁ kūca kahaṁ kārai mukāmā,
kavana surati ke karahu salāmā
maiṁ tohiṁ pūchoṁ mūsalamānā,
lāla jarada kī nānā bānā
kājī kāja karahu tuma kaisā,
ghara-ghara jabaha karāvahu bhaisā
bakarī muragā kina faramāyā,
kisake hukuma tuma churī calāyā
darada na jānahu pīra kahāvahu,
baitā parṙhi jaga bharamāhu
kahahiṁ kabīra eka saiyada kahāvai,
āpu sarīkhe jaga kabulāvai

Sākhī — *dina ko rojā rahatu hau,*
rāta hanata ho gāya
yaha to khūna vaha bandagī,
kyoṁ kara khusī khodāya

THE HYPOCRISY OF MOSLEMS

Where is your God's abode, O hermit say?
Where will you go to seek him? Where does he stay?
What is his shape, O Moslems? I ask you
Is he red, or yellow, or of some other hue?

O *qāzī*, what is it that makes you go
From house to house sacrificing buffaloes?
By whose command do you keep knifing
Poor innocent hens and cocks and goats?[19]
You pose as a saint yet know not what pain is
And keep beguiling people with sermons every day;
Though you call yourself a Syed, you do not shun violence,[20]
And still expect others to follow what you say.

> You keep the Ramadan fast all day
> Yet slaughter cows at night.[21]
> Shedding blood with one hand, praying with the other;
> What hypocrisy! Can God be pleased thus, brother?

8

joṁ tohiṁ karatā barana bicārā,
janmata tīni daṇḍa anurāsā
janmata sūdra bhue puni sūdrā,
kṛtama janeu ḍāri jaga mudrā
jauṁ tuha brāhamaṇa bamhanī ke āyā,
aura rāha te kāhe na āyā
jau tuha turaka turukinī āyā,
peṭe kāhe na sunati karāyā
kārī piyarī duhahū gāī,
tākara dūdha dehu bilagagāī
chaṙu kapaṭa nara adhika sayānī,
kahahiṁ kabīra bhaju sāraṅgapānī.

ALL HUMAN BEINGS ARE ONE

You think much of caste, both high and low,
What spoofery! all have to undergo
The three sorrows.[22] From dirt came all men
And to dirt will they return again.[23]

None's a brahmin by birth, these four-flushers put on
The sacred thread and think they're higher-up,
They bum-steer folk that they're twice-born
Why did they come then as others take birth?[24]

O Turk, if your Turkish origin you can tell
Merely by the circumcision rite,[25]
While lying in your mother womb itself,
Before being born, why weren't you circumcised?
One cow is black, another yellowish
But is not the milk of both the same
Says Kabīr, abandoning deception and deceit,
Find your peace in chanting Vishnu's name.[26]

9

calī jāta dekhī eka nārī,
tara gāgari ūpara panihārī
calī jāta vaha bāṭahiṁ bātā,
sovanahāra ke ūpara khāṭā
jāṙana marai sapedī saurī,
khasama na cīnhai gharani bhau baurī
vāhī ke saṅga nisu dina rācī,
piya se bāta kahai nahiṁ sāṁcī
sovata chāṁṙi calī piya apanā,
ī duḥkha aba dahuṁ kahaba kaisanā

Sākhī— *apanī jāṁghi ughāri kai,*
apanī kahī na jāya
kī cita jānai āpanā
kī mero jana gāya

JANUS-FACED MEN

I saw a woman go to fetch water
But strangely enough she was above her pot!
And I do no know what fancy caught her
That she slept on the ground beneath her cot!

She has a warm quilt, spotlessly white
Yet she shivers as though in a freeze!
And deserting her man that wanton wife
Aflame with lust to her lover speeds.

She's with her paramour all day and night
And to herself her secret keeps
Thinking her husband's asleep, she leaves his side,
Ah me! to whom shall I speak out my grief?

No one can speak himself of his failings
They are known to him alone
Or to someone who's close to him.[27]

THE RAMAINĪS

NOTES

1. Hinduism conceives life as consisting of four stages—*bramhacarya* (the celibate or student). *gṛhastya* (the householder), the *vānaprastha* (forest dwellen) and the *sannyāsī* (wandering hermit). Kabīr panthīs however add two more—*hansa* and *paramahansa*. The Six Systems are the six branches of Hindu philosophy—Nyāya, Vaiśeṣika, Sāṁkhya, Yoga, Mīmāṁsā and Vedānta.
2. The six kinds of food are those sweet, saltish, bitter, sour, pungent and acidic.
3. The four *Vedas* are the *Ṛg*, *Yajura*, *Sāma* and *Atharva*. Hindus believe them to be of divine origin. The *Vedāngas* are *Śikṣā*, *Kalpa*, *Nirukta*, *Chanda*, *Jyotiṣa* and *Vyākaraṇa*. Here the four trees (*cāra vṛikṣa*) and six branches (*chatra sākh*) Kabīr's decrying of the *Vedas* and its six branches and the Shastras, the Six Systems and the Hindu *āśramas*, is not in good taste, particulary as, being practically illiterate, he could't know what was in them. He often shows such contempt about matters of which obviously he could know nothing.
4. The entire vese is allegorical and as the weaver weaves his cloth, the Divine Weaver, i.e., God brings forth his creation. Another interpretation is in terms of the Tantra symbolism. According to Tantra there are six centres or *cakras* along the spinal column-1. *mūlādhāra* (the region of the earth). 2. *svadhishṭhāna* (above the previous one, and the region of water). 3. *maṇipura* (at the navel, the region of fire). 4. *anāhata* (air). 5. *viśuddha* (at the base of the throat, ether). and 6. *ājña* (between the eyebrows, the psychic centre). The piercing of these *cakras* is a mystic rite meant only to be practised under expert guidance. This results in the waking *kuṇḍalini*. Then there are believed to be canals within the body called *nāṛīs*, the *iḍa* and the *pingalā*. Thus the sun and the moon could stand for the two *nāṛīs* and the earth and sky, the *mūlādhara* and the *ajña cakras* (*narī*, the weaver's shuttle being equivalent to the *nāṛīs*)
5. *sandhyā* is prayers which are prescribed by the Śhastras, to be carried out three times in the day.

ṣaṭa karma—*ṣaṭa* (six); thus the six observances—bathing, prayes three times a day, worship, *tarpaṇa* (i.e., water-offering to ancestors), chanting God's name and offering oblations.

6. *tarapaṇa* (*tarapana* in Kabīr's diction) means the water-offering of customarily made to their dead ancestors (known as *pitṛs*). The *pitṛs* are said to be 1. The manes of the departed forefathers to whom *piṇḍas* (balls of rice and flour) and water and offered at stated periods. 2. The ten Prajāpatīs or mythical progenitors of the human race. and 3. The first *pitṛs* who were sons of the gods. The gods having offended Brahmā (the Creator) by neglecting to worship him were cursed to become fools but the curse was modified to the extent that they should apply to their sons for instruction. The sons taught them the rites of expiation and penance and so they (the sons were addressed as fathers). The sons of the gods thus became the first *pitṛs*. The *pitṛs* of brahmins are known as Sompas (Sukālins according to the *Harivaṁsa*), of the kastriyas, the Havishmata, of the vaisyas. Ājyapas, and of the sudras, the Su-kālins (the Sompas according to the *Harivaṁsa*).
7. The *gāyatrī* is the most sacred verse of the *Ṛg Veda* which it is the duty of all brahmins to repeat mentally in their morning and evening prayers. It is addressed to the Sun. It is considered so holy that copyists often refrain from transcribing it. Catebrooke's version of it is 'Earth, sky, heaven. Let us meditate on (these, and on) the most excellent light and power of that generous, sportive and resplendent sun (praying that) it may guide our intellect' (*A Classical Dictionary of Hindu Mythology* etc John Dowson, Trübner, 1961).
8. *mokṣa* or *mukti* means 'emancipation' or 'liberation'. According to Hindu belief there is rebirth. But when *mokṣa* is attained the soul becomes merged in *Brahman* (God) and there is no more rebirth.
9. According to Kabīr scriptural observances are useless and only a show. But in the *Gītā* 18.5-6 the Lord says in reply to Arjuna that these observances should not be given up but should be practised without expecting their fruit and desirelessly:-

yajña-dāna-tapaḥ karma na tyājyam kāryameva tat
yajña-danaḥ tapaśyava pāvanāni maniṣiṇam
etā na api tu karmaṇi saṅga tyaktvā phalāni ca
kartvyānīti me pārtha niṣeitaṁ matamuttamam

Apparently Kabīr had not gone deep enough into the matter. Also, since no one has come back after *mokṣa* how can one say how really *mokṣa* is attained? So Kabīr's presumption that those who regularly chant the *gāyatrī* have not achieved *mokṣa* is merely a shot in the dark.

10. There are two views about *mokṣa*. One is that it is attained on death, as Krishna says in the *Gītā, antākāle ca māmeva smaranmuktva kalevaram* (Chapter 8, v.5) and the other is in this very life when one is no more effected by the worldly maya, as in the case of sages like Caitanya and Rāmakrishna. The former is known as *jīvana-mukti* (*jīvana*-'life'; *mukti*-'*mokṣa*' or 'emancipation'). The *mokṣa* attained on death is called *videha-mukti (vi*-'shorn of'; *deha*-'the body').

11. Kali-age or kaliyuga-*yuga* means an age of the world. There are four *yugas* according to Hindu cosmogony, namely the Krita. Tretā, Dvāpara and Kali (the one in which we are living). These are respectively of 1,728,000), 1,296,000, 864,000 and 432,000 years. This forms a period of Mahāyuga or a whopping, 640,000,000 years make a Kalpa or a night and day of Brahmā. Righteousness steadily declines from one *yuga* to the next, being least in the Kaliyuga.

12. *Kalimā*-a sacred mantra for Moslems, namely *la ilāha illillāh Muhammadur rasūlillah* (None is so worthy of reverence except the Prophet Muhammad sent (by God)').

13. *kitāb* means literally 'a book'. Here it means the Holy Quran. In it there is frequent reference to the 'Book' and the 'believers' or Moslems are called 'the people of the Book'.

14. The Moslems pray (offering *namāz*) five times a day. The *namāz* on Friday is of particular importance. The *namāz* is obligatory for pious Moslems and they sit facing towards Mecca for it.

15. The sacred thread (*yajñopavīta*) is an essential ceremony for Hindus, particularly for brahmins and for the higher castes generally. But not for the sudras. it consists of wearing a thick thread round the shoulder and across the body.

16. Circumcision is obligatory for Mohammedans (and Christians). A part of the foreskin of the penis is cut off with ceremonial observances. Some critics interpret '*hindū turaka na jānai bheū*' as 'neither the Hindus nor the Moslems know what in reality karma is'. But as Kabīr has meant this verse to be a kind of satire on both Hindu and Moslem customs the sense has been taken as 'the *janeū* or the act of circumcision can't by themselves reveal if the person undergoing

it is Hindu or Moslem. It is *we* who associate the person with the rite calling one a Hindu and the other a Moslem'. This interpretation is also borne out by Kabīr's *Padas* in which he says 'If God wanted me to be a Turk wouldn't he circumcise me himself', and 'If circumcision makes a Turk why don't you do it to your women too? Are they not Turks too?'

17. The words in the *Sākhī* are *pānī* and *pauna* (Hindi *pavana*). The words mean respectively 'water' and 'air'. Symbolically, however they should be taken to mean the *panca bhūtas* or 'five elements (air, water, fire, earth and ether) which, according to Hindu belief, consititute the body.

18. This verse contains a number of references to the various avatars of Viṣṇu, and in it Kabīr tries to show the they are all mythical. First we briefly explain the references as follows:-

1.Dashrath was king of Ayodhyā. Rāma, his eldest son was the seventh incarnation of Lord Viṣṇu appearing at the end of the Tratā or second *yuga*. The Rāma story is told in detail in the *Rāmāyaṇa*.

2. Rāvaṇa was the demon-king of Lankā having ten heads. He carried off Sitā, Rāma's wife in consequence of which Hanumāna, the god of the Wind and devotee of Rāma, burnt up Lankā and later on Rāma killed Rāvaṇa and rescued Sītā.

3. Devakī, wife of Vasudeva was cousin of Kaṁsa, the tyrant usurper of the throne of Mathura. She was the mother of Krishna who was also an avatar of Viṣṇu. Devakī's eighth child, he was born in prison as according to a prophecy. The eighth child would kill Kaṁsa. So Kaṁsa had imprisoned both Devakī and Vasudeva, in order to kill the newborns instantly after birth. But when Krishna was born the locks of the prison opened of themselves and Vasudeva was directed by the divine voice to take the child to Gokul and bring Yashoda's daughter also newborn. Vasudeva, urged by Nanda, Yashoda's husband switched babies while Yashoda was still asleep. So Yashoda became Krishna's foster mother. Krishna used to be in the company of the cowherd girls when he grew up and their sports are narrated in the *Bhāgavata Purāṇa*. Destroying the wicked has reference to the *Gītā* in which Krishna says that God takes human form as an avatar to protect the good and destroy evildoers—*paritrāṇāya sādhunām vināśāya ca duṣkṛtāma*

4.Bali—was a good and virtuous *daitya* king He defeated

Indra, humbled the gods and extended his authority over the three worlds. The gods appealed to Viṣṇu for protection. Viṣṇu took the form of a dwarf (the Vāmana avatar) and came and asked Bali the gift of land equal to three steps of his. Having got the boon, he stepped over heaven and earth in two strides, but due to Bali's goodness and the virtue of Prahalāda, his grandson he left him Pātala, the infernal regions.

5. Bāli—(distinct from Bali) was the monkey-king of Kishkindhyā who was slain by Rāma because he (Bāli) had usurped Sugrīva's (his brother's) kingdom and also carried away Sugrīva's wife. He was supposed to be a son of Indra and born from the hair (*bāla*) of his mother, hence his name, Bāli.

6. Hiraṇyakashipu-was a *daitya* who had obtained from Shiva the sovereignty of the three worlds for a million years. He tortured his son Prahalāda, even trying to kill the boy, for showing devotion to Viṣṇu. Viṣṇu took the form of half-man-and-half-lion (the Narasiṁha avatar) because Hriaṇyakshipu had obtained the boon of security from the gods, men and beast. Issuing from a pillar, Viṣṇu in the form of Narasiṁha, killed Hiraṇyakashipu.

7. Shāligrāma or Shālagrāma is a smooth oval stone found chiefly in the river-bed of the Gaṇdaka river. It has spirals round it and is revered as a representation of Lord Viṣṇu by devout Vaiṣṇavas.

8. The Kūrma or Tortoise avatar finds mention in the *Śatapatha Brāhmaṇa*: 'Prajāpati having taken the form of a tortoise (*Kūrma*) created offspring That which he created he made (*akarot*); hence the word *kūrma*' (John Dowson. A Classical Dictionary of Hindu Mythology etc. Trübner, 1961). As regards the Matsya or Fish avatar, its earliest mention is also in the *Śatapatha Brāhmaṇa.* Manu found in the water brought for his bath, a small fish which began to speak and said that soon there would be a flood which would destroy all creatures, but he (Manu) would be saved. The Fish told him to build a ship and come to him. Then the Fish became large and entered the ocean. The deluge and flood came and the Fish secured the ship to his horn and Manu was saved. The *Mahābharata* relates this story also though somewhat differently.

9. It is believed Krishna gave up his human form at Dvarakā where he lay down in the forest and let a hunter, who mistook him for a deer, pierce the sole of his foot with an arrow.

10. Paraṣurāma, considered as one of the Hindu avatars, took a vow to kill all kshatriyas as a king, Kārta-vīrya, who was of that caste stealthily carried away the scrificial-calf of the Brahmin sage, Jamadagni. Kārta-vīrya's sons killed the sage and in revenge Paraṣurāma cleared the earth thrice seven times of all kshatriyas and with their blood filled five large lakes of Samanta-pancaka'.

11. About Jagannātha Puri there is a legend in the *Purāṇas* according to which king Indradyumna of Avanti coveted a sapphire image of Viṣṇu which was with the aborginals of Savaras. He sent an army of woodcutters to get it, but God made the image disappear. The king performed a thousand Asvamedha *yajñas* (horse-secrifices). Then God appeared to him, not as the blue image, but as log of wood that came floating from the sea. This was installed with great rejoicing, but when the wood was shaped into an image every chisel that worked on it broke. Then God appeared in the form of a carpenter who offered to chisel the wood into an image in 21 days. He worked on it, but the impatient king wanted it done earlier and when he entered the room where the carpenter was working, he found nothing but three incomplete images. After much prayer and supplication, however, Brahmā came and the image was made.

Kabīr was against avatars and did not believe that God could be born in a human shape or take human or any other form. The Hindu avatars are, however, not born in the ordinary way as the *Gītā* says (7:24):

avaktaṁ vyaktim āpannaṁ manyante mām abuddhayaḥ , paraṁ bhāvam ajānanto mamā 'vyayam anuttamam, ('Unaware of my supreme eternal and changeless nature, ignorant persons think me who am the Formless to be a man'). Besides, Kabīr himself frequently mentioned Krishna, as Govinda, in his verses. Sometimes it becomes difficult to reconcile his contrary utterances.

19. Moslems sacrifice animals, cows, buffaloes, goats, hens etc on the festival of Bakr'īd in the early morning as a religious observance.

20. A Syed is a particulary pious Moslem and commands a great deal of respect.

21. The Ramzān (or Ramadan) month is the ninth month of the Moslem year when the Holy Quran was given to the Prophet Mohammed. hence the month is considered very sacred by Moslems and they observe a complete fast from sunrise to sunset. But eating food is permitted in the night.

22. The three sorrows (*trividha duḥkha*) are mentioned in the *Sāṁkhya-sūtras* the opening aphorism of which is: *atha trividha duḥkha atyanta nivrittiḥ atyanta puruṣārthāḥ* ('The supreme purpose of life is the prevention of the three kinds of pain'). These three pains are 1. *ādhyātmika*-originating from the sufferer himself, so called because this pain arises from one's own self (*ātmā*). This consists of sorrows from diseases and mental suffering. 2. *ādibhautika*—(from *bhūtas*, or 'created beings'). These include pain caused by living creatures to man, e.g., by beasts, birds and so forth, 3. *ādhidaivika*—(from *devas* 'the gods'). These are sorrows caused by things (like the influence of stars and planets) which are of divine origin. Kabīr says that what is universal among human beings is that all persons, whether high or low, of whatever caste or community, have to suffer these three kinds of pain. It is not rites and customs that matter. These (the rites etc.), are mere vain outward show, *āḍambara*.

23. The words of the text, namely, *janmata sūdra bhue puni sūdrā* should not be taken literally. Here *sūdra* means not the caste but 'dirt'. The sense is that birth involves uncleanliness (women who gave birth to a baby were deemed unclean and segregated for some period to prevent their being infected, as in those day there were no antibiotics etc.). And so was it on death. Those who went to cremate the body at the burning-*ghāṭ* had to bathe and change clothes on coming back home. Kabīr says in this sense everyone is a '*sūdra*' irrespective of his caste.

24. A brahmin is, according to tradition, the chief of all created beings. His person is inviolate; he is entitled to all honour and enjoys many rights and privileges. The *Śatapatha Brāhmaṇa* declares 'there are two kinds of gods; first the gods then those who are brahmins and have learnt the *Veda* and repeat it: they are the human gods'. Kabīr means to bring out that one is not a brahmin by birth or by wearing the sacred thread etc. Nor can he claim any superiority or divinity. All castes and sects are manmade. What is important is the pursuit of virtue and devotion to God.

25. Just as Kabīr decries Hindu rites such as the *janeū* (wearing the sacred thread), he also considers Moslem customs such as circumcision, of no consequence. His reasoning may be risqué and odd but the spirit behind it is quite logical and appealing. He is satirical and those orthodox might consider him offensive. but he believed in the brotherhood of mankind and his attitude is commendable

26. The word in the text is *sāraṅgapāṇī* 'Sāranga' is the name of the bow of Lord Viṣṇu and *sārangapāṇī* (*pāṇi*-'the hand') means 'one in whose hand there is the 'Sāraṅga' bow, i.e., Viṣṇu. Here again we see the Vaiṣṇava influence on Kabīr. Though he strongly repudiates avatars, he urges the chanting of Viṣṇu's name. We see here one of the many contradictions in Kabīr.

27. The entire verse is meant to have an allegorical meaning, although the translation follows the literal sense. The verse depicts the two tendencies of the human mind, one towards good the other towards evil. When the mind is turned inwards towards virtue it is attuned to God, but the evil mind seeks worldly pleasures and is lost in sensual enjoyment. That is why the two contrary and opposed meanings have been incorporated—the pitcher below and the woman carrying it, above; the cot (charpoy) above and the woman lying below it; forsaking her husband for her lover, and so forth.

    The other allegorical symbolism is that of the *Tantra* (see note to verse 3, *asa jolaha kā marama na jānā* etc.) When the 'woman' the *kuṇḍalini* looks upward it rises beyond the *mūlādhāra cakra*, the lowest one representing the earth. In ordinary persons the coiled power (*kuṇḍalini*) rests dormant two and a half spans above the *mūlādhāra cakra*. Kabīr calls this the *sovanahāra* state. But in those who rise above worldly attachment it rises higher by degrees till it pierces the six centres (*cakras*) along the spine *suṣumnā* reaching the *sahastrāra* centre above the forehead. This is the significance of *sovanahāra ke ūpara khāṭā* in the text. The 'warm quilt' is the tendency to the spiritual. Having been endowed with this, still man shivers in the 'cold' or worldly entanglements. The lustful woman represents the quest of sensual enjoyment and her husband whom she sbandons is virtue. Thus the mind entangled in the world, abandons virtue. The *antaḥkaraṇa* ('power to discriminate between good and evil', or 'conscience') is ever awake but the truant mind thinks it is asleep, just as the woman thinks her husband to be asleep and leaves him. The hypocritical mind appears outwardly pious, but inwardly keeps dwelling on sense-pleasures.

PADAS OF KABĪR

samajhi vicāri jīva jaba dekhā
yahu sansāra supani kari rekhā

('When I meditated on the Soul and realized its nature, I saw that this world is an ephemeral dream')

KABĪR

jete patra banaspati,
aura gangā kī raina
paṇḍita bicārā kyā kahe,
kabīra kahī mukha baina

KABĪR

('The verses coming from Kabīr's mouth are as fruit-laden trees or as the waters of the Gangā. Pundits can't reach such excellence')

THE PADAS OF KABĪR

A. RĀGA GAUṘĪ

1

kȧuna marai kauna janamaiṁ āī
śranga nraka kaune gati pāī
pancata abigati thaiṁ utapanāṁ, ekai kiyā nivāsā
bichure tata phiri sahaja samanaiṁ, rekha rahī nahīṁ āsā
jala meṁ kumbha, kumbha maiṁ jala hai, bāhari bhītara pānī
phūṭā kumbha jala jalahi samānaṁ, yahu tata kathau giānī
ādaiṁ gaganā antai gaganā, madhe gaganā bhāī
kahai kabīra karama kisa lāgai, jhuṭhī sanka upāī

KARMA AND THE SOUL

No one dies here, none is reborn,
No heaven to enjoy, no hell in which one burns;
The five elements are contained in the One,[1]
They rise from it and to it again return
Leaving not a trace behind.

The jar is in the water and in the water too the jar is,
The one water mingles with the other when the jar breaks
Muse over this well in your minds, O pundits,
The soul remains formless in all the three states
Before birth, in life and after death.
How then, can karma have any effect upon it?

2

kauna marai kahu paṇḍita janā
so samajhāi kahau hama sanā
māṭi māṭi rahī samāi pavanai pavana liyā saṅgi lāi
kahai kabīra suni paṇḍita gunī rūpa bhuvā saba dekhai dunī

THE BODY DIES, NOT THE SOUL

O wise men, ponder carefully
Who is it that dies, and then tell me.

Dust unto dust this body is,
And with the wind the soul flies;
O pundits, all the world knows this
Says Kabīr, that only the body dies.

3

niraguṇa rāma niraguṇa rāma japahu re bhāī
abigati kī gati lakhī na jāī
cāri beda jākai sumṛta purānā nau byākaranā marama na jānā
sesa nāga jākai garaḍa samānā carana kamala kaṁvalā nahīṁ jānā
kahai kabīra jāki bhedai nāhīṁ nija jana baiṭhe hari ki chahīṁ

PRAY TO THE FORMLESS RĀMA

O brother, worship the Formless Rāma
No one has seen his shape or form
Neither the *Smṛtis* nor the *Purāṇas*[2]
Can know him; nor the nine branches of grammar.[3]
Shesha and Garuṛa wait on him[4]
And even Shrī who presses his lotus feet
Can't relate his infinite glory,[5]
For he is beyond compare;
Only he who truly loves him, say Kabīr,
Can obtain his grace.

4

rāma mohi tāri kahāṁ lai jaihau
'so baikunṭha kahau dhauṁ kaisā',
kari pasāva mohi daihau
'je mere jīva doi jānata ho'
tau mohi mukati batāo
ekameka rami rahyā sabani maiṁ,

tau kāhe bharamāvau
tāraṇa tiraṇa jabai laga kahiye,
taba laga tata no jānā
eka rāma dekhyā sabahina maiṁ,
kahai kabīra mana mānā

MOKṢA

If you free me from the uncrossable sea
Of births and deaths, O Rāma, pray
Tell me where you will then take me,
Of what sort will that heaven be,
To which I'll go by your kindness, say?
And if you consider you and me as separate
Tell me the way to be with you always.

But if your abode is in every Soul,
Why do you mislead me? For then I need not
Strive to obtain what I've already got!

All talk of redemption is vain
Till there remain redeemer and redeemed;
Says Kabīr, in my mind's eye I have seen
The same Rāma in the Soul of everyone.

5

are bhaī doi kahāṁ so mohi batāvo
bici hī bharama kā bheda lagāvo
joni upāi racī hai dharanīṁ
dīna eka bīci bhaī karanīṁ
rāma rahīma japata sudhi gaī
uni mālā uni tasabī laī
kahai kabīra cetahu re bhauṁdū।
bolanahārā turaka na hindū

THE SOUL IS NEITHER HINDU NOR MOSLEM

You believe in dualism, O brother
From where has this delusion sprung?
That which you conceive as two is really One
Is the birth of one man different from another's?
One says Rahīm, another Rāma,

But in reality both are confused;
The Hindu takes a rosary, the Musalmān
A talisman, Says Kabīr, O you fools![6]
Is a Turk's soul any different from a Hindu's?

6

mulā kahāṁ pukārai dūri
rāma rahīma rahyā bharapūri
yahu tau alaha gūṁgā nāhīṁ
dekhai khalaka dunīṁ dila māhīṁ
hari guna gāi banga maiṁ dīnhāṁ
kāma krodha doū bisamala kīnhāṁ
kahai kabīra yahu mulanāṁ jhūṭā
rāma rahīma sabani maiṁ dīṭhā

GOD IS IN EVERYONE'S SOUL

O mullah, why call from afar,
Rāma-Rahīm is everywhere;
Allah is not dumb, he'll answer your prayer,
See him in the universe and in your heart.

I sang Hari's praise and called to him
Anger and craving both I've foresworn
Says Kabīr, the mullah is lying,
In everyone I've seen Rahīm and Rāma.

7

mana thira rahai na ghara hvai merā
ina mana ghara jāre bahuterā
ghara taji bana bāhira kīyau bāsa
ghara bana dekhauṁ doū nirāsa
jahāṁ jāūṁ tahāṁ soga santāpa
jarā marana kau adhika biyāpa
kahai kabīra carana tohi bandā
ghara maiṁ ghara de paramāndā

THE MIND'S RESTLESSNESS

My mind does not know
A moment's rest,

Therefore it had to find
Life after life
A home in different bodies.

Wherever I stay,
At home or in the forest,
Grief and distress
Always haunt me;
And old age and death torment me.

I'm your slave, says Kabīr,
Lord; let me find rest
In yourself.

8

kā sidha sādhi karauṁ kucha nāhīṁ
rāma rasāina merī rasanā māhīṁ
nahīṁ kucha jñāna dhyāna sidhi joga
tātheṁ upajaiṁ nānā roga
kā bana maiṁ basi bhaye udāsa
je mana nahīṁ chārai āsā-pāsa
saba kṛta kāca harī hita sāra
kahai kabīra taji jaga byauhāra

LEAVE WORLDLINESS AND SEEK GOD

The *siddhīs* are useless[7]
I wish to drink
The nectar of Rāma's name
Meditation and learning.
The *siddhīs* and yoga
Are mere troubles—nothing.

What is the use of going away to the woods
If the mind remains ensnared in desire
Says Kabīr, karma will bring no good
Leave the world and seek the love of Hari.

9

saba dunīṁ sayānīṁ maiṁ maiṁ baurā
hama bigare bigarau jini aurā
maiṁ nahīṁ baurā rāma kīyo baurā
satagura jāri gayau bhrama morā
bidyā na paṛhūṁ bāda nahīm jānūṁ
hari guna kathata sunata baurānūṁ
kāma krodha doū bhaye bikārā
āpahiṁ āpa jarai sansārā
mīṭhā kahā jāhi jo bhāvai
dāsa kabīra rāma guna gāvai

DIVINE MADNESS

You are all sane folk, only I am filled
With a divine madness, but let not others
Be affected by it; it was instilled
In me by Rāma himself, O brothers.
My doubts were removed by the guru's grace
I have no learning, nor the gift of the gab,
But when I heard and sang Hari's praise
Love for the Lord made me mad.

The whole world of itself is burning
In the holocaust of rage and passion;
And if you ask me 'what is that thing
In which joy lies?' I'd say 'That which gives one satisfaction'.
God's slave, Kabīr, sings of Rāma's deeds,
Because to him that alone brings peace.

(B) RĀGA RĀMAKALĪ

1

akatha kahāṇī prema kī, kachu kahi na jāī
gūṁge kerī sarakarā, baiṭhe musakāī
bhomi binā aru bīja bina, tarabara eka bhāī
ananta phala prakāsiyạ, gura diyā batāī
mana thira baisi bicariyā, rāmahi layau lāī
jhūṭhi anabhai bistarī, saba thothī bāī
kahai kabīra sakati kachu nāhīṁ, gura bhayā sahāī
āvaranā jāṇī miṭi gaī, mana manahi samāī

THE GURU'S GRACE

Love can never be told
It's like a dumb man who sits
Eating sugar, sovouring it and smiling.

There is a tree with foliage
With no ground to grow on and sprouted from no seed,
But it gives fruit endlessly—
The fruit of soul-knowledge,
As my guru told me.

I made my mind calm
And supplicated Rāma;
All false perceptions vanished
As chaff before the wind.

It wasn't me, says Kabīr,
Who could gain this state:
'Twas by the guru's grace that I escaped
The murky sea of births and deaths
And my soul found eternal rest.

2

hai koī jagata-gura gyānī ulaṭi beda būjhai
pāṇi meṁ agani jarai, aṁdhere kauṁ sūjhai
ekani dādura khāye, panca bhavangā

gāi nāhara khayau, kāṭi kāṭi anga
bakarī bighāra khayau, harani khāyau cītā
kāgi lagara phāndiyā, baṭairaiṁ bāja jītā
mūsai manjāra khayau, syāli khayau svānāṁ
ādi kauṁ ādaesa karata, kahai kabīra gyānā

BODY AND SOUL

Who is the wise man in this world
Who can understand such contrariety:
The water was aflame, the blind had sight,
One toad ate up five female snakes,
The goat ate up the wolf, the deer the leopard.
The crow escaped the trap set for it
And the partridge outwitted the falcon.
The mouse ate the cat, the buffalo the dog:-
So says Kabīr, with salutations to the Lord.[8]

3

rāma rāi abigata bigati na jāna,
kahi kima tohi rūpa bakhāna
prathameṁ gagana ki puhami prathami prabhū,
prathameṁ pavana ki pānīṁ
prathameṁ canda ka sūra prathami prabhū,
prathameṁ kauna binānī
prathameṁ prāna ki pyanḍa prathami prabhū,
prathameṁ rakata ki reta
prathameṁ puriṣa ki nāri prathami prabhū,
prathameṁ bīja ki kheta
prathameṁ divasa ki raiṇi prathami prabhū,
prathameṁ pāpa ki punya
kahai kabīra jahāṁ basahu niranjana,
tahāṁ kachūāhi ki sunya

THE SONG OF CREATION

How shall I sing
Of your glory, O Eternal Being,
For you have no shape or form.
Tell me, O Maker, was there the earth first or the sky?

Was there water first or the wind?
O All-knower, was there the moon first or the sun?
Was there the soul first, or the body?
Was there the ovum first or the sperm?
O All-wise, was there man first or woman?
Was there the field first or the seed?
O Creator, was there day first or night?
Was there sin first or rectitude?
O Absolute Being, says Kabīr,
Is there something where you are,
Or only a void?

4

hari nāmaiṁ dina jāi re jākau
soī dina lekhai lāi re tākau
hari nāmaiṁ jana jāgai
tākai gobyanda sāthī āgai
dīpaka eka abhangā
tāmaiṁ sura nara paṛai patangā
ūṁca nīca samasariyā
tāthaiṁ jana kabīra nisatariyā

THE CASTE DIVIDE

Only that day will be
Entered in your book of life
On which you chant the name of Hari—.[9]
Of such a man God is a friend indeed.
There ever burns the One Eternal Light
To which gods and men, like moths, speed
And perish. Kabīr has removed the divide
Between high and low; therefore he has crossed
The uncrossable sea of existence, and found God.

5

jaba thaiṁ ātama tata bicārā
taba nirabaira bhayā sabahina thaiṁ,
kāma krodha gahi ḍārā
byāpaka brahma sabani maiṁ ekai,

ko paṇḍita ko jogī
rāṇāṁranka kavana sūṁ kahiye
kavana baida ko rogī
inamaiṁ āpa āpa sabahina maiṁ,
āpa āpasūṁ khelai
nānāṁ bhāṁti ghaṙe saba bhāṁḍe
rūpa dhare dhari melai
soci vicāri sabai jaga dekhyā,
nirguṇa koī na batāvai
kahai kabīra guṇī aru paṇḍita,
mili līlā jasa gāvai

DUAL AND NON-DUAL

When I meditate
On the Soul
I throw overboard
All hatred, desire and rage.

The same Soul abides
In all beings everywhere,
Who is a pundit, who's a yogi?
Who is a beggar, who is a king?
Who is the physician who the patient?

The World Soul is in everyone
Sporting with the soul inside: it creates
various forms and shapes.

I have pondered. I have questioned, but none
Could tell me about the formless *Brahma*
Says Kabīr, ever lost in duality's maze
It is the God with form that pundits praise.

6

jaga sūṁ prīti na kījiye, samajhi mana merā
svāda heta lapaṭāie, ko nikasai surā
eka kanaka aru kāminī, jaga meṁ doi phandā
inapai jo na bandhāvaī tākā maiṁ bandā
deha dhareṁ in maiṁ bāsa, kahu kaisaiṁ chūṭai
sīva bhaye te ūbare, jīva te lūṭe

eka eka sūṁ mili rahyā, tinahīṁ sacu pāyā
prema magana lai līna mana, so bahuri na āyā
kahai kabīra nihacala bhayā, nirabhai pada pāyā
sansā ta dina kā gayā, sataguri samajhāyā

SHUN WEALTH AND LUST

Love not the world, O mind,
Who has fared well on coming in its hold?
Wealth and passion are the two bonds that bind,
One who escapes these, him do I adore.

Humans, with all the body's weaknesses,
Find themselves helpless before lust and gold,
But those filled with divine bliss escape their clutches,
He finds eternal joy whose soul dwells in the World Soul.

And he who is drunk with love, who with God is one,

To this world of suffering never comes.
Says Kabīr, I have shed all fear and found peace
Ever since the guru blessed me all my doubts ceased.

(C) RĀGA ĀSĀVARĪ

1

bābā jogī eka akelā
jāke tīrtha brata na melā
jholī patra bibhūti na baṭavā
anahada baina bajāvai
māṁgi na khāi na bhūkhā sovai,
ghara angnāṁ phiri āvai
pāṁca janāṁ ki jamāti calāvai
tāsa gurū maiṁ celā
kahai kabīra uni desa sidhāye,
bahuri na ihiṁ jugi melā

THE TRUE YOGI

Listen, O revered ones,
The true yogi keeps aloof;
He does not go on pilgrimages,
Nor fasts, nor visits holy fairs,
He has no sacred books, nor any bag,
Nor smears himself with ashes.
He does not beg for food, nor yet sleep hungry:
He has got over the five impediments[10]
And ever hears the *anāhata* sound:[11]
Of such a yogi I am a disciple:
Says Kabīr, he goes
To that sphere from which there's no return
To this world of repeated rebirths.

2

hai koī rāma nāma batāvai
basta agocara mohi lakāvai
rāma nāma saba koi bakhānaiṁ
rāma nāma kā marama na jānaiṁ
ūpara kī mohi bāta no bhāvai
dekhai gāvai tau sukha pāvai
kahai kabīra kachu kahata na āvai
paracai binā marama ko pāvai.

RĀMA IS FORMLESS

Can anyone tell me of Rāma.
Or show me that Rāma who's unseen,
To chant whose name all men are keen,
But whose true essence none has known?

To pay him lip-service is vain,
Experience only can disclose,
He finds delight who chant his name,
Says Kabīr, who knows him, *he* knows.

3

gobyande tūṁ niranjana, tūṁ niranjana rāyā
tere rūpa nahīṁ rekha, nahiṁ mudrā nahiṁ māyā
samada nāhīṁ sikhara nāhiṁ,
dharatī nahiṁ gaganāṁ
rabi sasi dou ekai nāhīṁ,
bahata nahiṁ pavanā
nāda nāhiṁ vyanda nāhīṁ,
kāla nahiṁ kāyā
jaba taiṁ jala byamba na hote,
taba tūṁ hīṁ rāma rāyā
japa nāhīṁ tapa nāhīṁ,
joga dhyāna nahiṁ pūjā
siva nāhīṁ sakati nāhīṁ,
deva nahiṁ dūjā
ruga na juga no syāma atharaban,
beda nahiṁ byākaranāṁ
terī gati tūṁhīṁ jānaiṁ,
kabīrā to saranāṁ

KABĪR'S LORD

You are without attachment, O Lord Govinda,[12]
You have no form nor shape
Nor any mark distinguishing
Nor any maya by which you create.
You're not in hill or earth, nor in the skies and seas,
Nor in the sun, nor in the moon,
Nor are you unsteady as the wind,

Nor are you known by the *nāda*[13] or *bindu*,[14]
You are neither the body nor are you death.
When nothing was reflected in the waters,
O Lord Rāma, you were there.
You are neither meditation, nor are you prayer
Nor worship, nor austerities, nor Shiva nor Shakti[15]
Nor are you the form of any god.
You are neither the *Rig*, *Sāma*, *Atharva* or *Yajura*,
Neither the *Veda* nor grammar know you;[16]
You alone know who you really are,
Kabīr seeks in you his refuge.

4

rāma kai nāi nīsāṇ bāgā,
tākā marama na jānaiṁ koī
bhūka trisā guna vākai nāhīṁ
ghaṭa ghaṭa antari soī
beda bibarjita bheda bibarjita
bibarjita pāpa ra punya
jñāna bibarjita dhyāna bibarjita,
bibarjita asthūla sunya
bheṣa bibarjita bhīka bibarjita
bibarjita dyambha ki rūpa
kahai kabīra tihūṁ loka bibarjita,
aisā tatta anūpa

RĀMA, THE LORD INCOMPARABLE

The kettledrum of Rāma's name
Is sounded, but who can tell
Its significance? Craving does not remain there;
He dwells in every soul.

He is beyond all differences, beyond the *Vedas*
Beyond knowledge, beyond sin and sinlessness
Beyond the void, beyond region and place,
Beyond meditation, beyond appearances.

He is beyond all acts of charity,
Boastfulness and deceit do not dwell there,

He is beyond the three worlds, says Kabīr:
Such is that great Lord Rāma beyond compare.

5

so mere rāma kabai ghari āvai
tā dekheṁ merā jīva sukha pāvai
biraha agini tana diyā jarāī
bina darasana kyūṁ hoi sirāī
jisa bāsura mana rahai udāsā
jaiseṁ catriga nīra piyāsā
kahai kabīra ati āturatāī
hamakauṁ begi milau rāma rāī

THE AGONY OF A DEVOTEE

When will my Rāma come home?
Only when I see him will my soul rejoice,
The fire of separation burns me
Only his coming can cool it.

I keep sorrowing night and day
As the *cātak* pining for the rain[17]
Says Kabīr, my mind knows no rest,
Come to me now, O Rāma, without delay.

6

maiṁ baṛa maiṁ baṛa maiṁ baṛa māṁtī
maṇa dasa nā jaṭ kā dasa gāṁṭhi
maiṁ bābā kā jodha kahāūṁ
apaṇī mārī gīṁda calāūṁ
ini ahankāra ghaṇe ghara ghāle
nācata kūdata jamapuri cāle
haika kabīra karata kī bājī
eka palaka maiṁ rāja birājī

VANITY AND ARROGANCE

'I am great! I am great! I am great!'
What foolishness for a man to utter such tripe
As though he was a crusher's pole of weight![18]
'I'm strong' he says, 'and I'll do as I like.'

By such arrogance countless homes are wrecked,
And dancing and prancing here gleefully
Men keep going to the abode of Death.
We are God's playthings, the Player he;
And all creation is merely his play.
He makes one mount the throne as king
And in one moment takes his realm away.

(D) RĀGA SORAṬHI

1

ab maiṁ pāyā rājā rāma sanehī
jā binu dukha pāvai merī dehī
beda purāni kahata jākī sākhī
tīratha brati na chūṭai jama kī pāsī
jāthaiṁ janama lahata nara āgaiṁ
pāpa punua doū bhrama lāgai
kahai kabīra soī tata jāgā
mana bhayā magana prema sara lāgā

LOVE OF RĀMA

Now I have attained Lord Rāma
Without whom my body aches,
Of whom speak *Veda* and *Purāṇa*:
Death's noose cannot be escaped
By pilgrimages and fasting,
I have known, says Kabīr,
Him who gives bliss everlasting,
Who makes men virtuous and sinless[19]
And in his love I'm ever basking.

2

rāma rāi ko aisā bairāgī
hari bhaji magana rahai viṣa tyāgī
brahmā eka jīni sisṭi upāī,
nāuṁ kulāla dharāyā
bahu bidhi bhāṁḍai unahiṁ ghaṙiye,
prabhū kā pāra na pāyā
taravara eka nānā bidhi phaliyā
tākai mūla no sākhā
bhau jali mūli rahyau re prāṇī
sau phala kade na cākhā
kahai kabīra guru becana heta kari,
aura na duniāṁ āthī
māṭī kā tana māṁṭi milihai
sabada gurū kā sāthī

THE GURU'S GRACE

O Lord Rāma where is the man who has negated
Sense-pleasures, and drunk of the love of Hari?
There is Brahmā who has created[20]
All beings on this earth, yet even he
Cannot fathom, O Lord, your greatness.

There is here a fruit-laden tree with no roots
Nor any branches: being with the world too much
You have never tasted of its fruit.
Says Kabīr, give heed to the words of the guru
Because the world has no reality
Dust is your body and dust it shall be
Only the guru's blessings will go with you.

3

kabīra bigaryā rāma duhāī
tuma jini bigarau mere bhāī
candana kai ḍhiga birakha ju bhailā
bigari bigari so candana hvailā
pārasa kauṁ je loha chuvaigā
bigari bigari so kancana hvailā
gangā maiṁ je nīra milaigā
bigari bigari gangodika hvailā
kahai kabīra je rāma kahaigā
bigari bigari so ramahiṁ hvailā

CHANTING THE NAME OF RĀMA

I swear by Rāma I've changed, say Kabīr,
But you need not be, O my brothers;
The tree growing near a sandalwood tree
Will acquire the perfume of sandal, what other?

If iron is touched by the *pārasa* stone[21]
It will acquire the quality of gold
And whatever water in the Gangā flows
From elsewhere will be part of the Gangā too.
Says Kabīr, he who takes the name of Rāma
Will doubtlessly go to Rāma's abode.

4

kāyā manjasi kauna gunā
ghaṭa bhītari hai malanā
jau tūṁ hiradai sudha mana jñānī
tauṁ kahā birolai pānī
tumbī aṭhasaṭhi tīratha nhāī
kaṙavapana taū na jāī
kahai kabīra bicārī
bhavasāgara tāri murārī

SAVIOUR KRISHNA

What's the use of having a wash
When all the dirt is inside you?
If you're not pure in mind and heart
What will the sacred waters do?

The bitter gourd will be bitter still
Even if eighty-eight times it may be
Washed in the holy waters.[22] Says Kabīr,
O Krishna, take me across the uncrossable sea.[23]

5

rāma rāi ihi sevā bhala mānaiṁ
jau koī rāma nāma tata jānaiṁ
re nara kahā paṣālai kāyā
so tata cīnhi jahāṃ thaiṁ āyā
kaha bibhūti jaṭa paṭa bāṁdhai
kā jala paisī hutāsana sāṁdhai
rarā mamā doi ākhira sārā
kahai kabīra tihūṁ loka piārā

THE TWO LETTERS OF RĀMA'S NAME

He is the favoured one of Rāma
Who knows the nature of Rāma's name;
What is the use of washing your body?
Know that from which you came.

It's no use smearing your body with ash
Or wandering with matted hair

Bathing in rivers, or keeping the sacred fires lit:[24]
Says Kabīr, all that matters is
The two letters *rā* and *mā*[25]
Which are loved by all the world.

6

jana kī pīra ko rājā rāma bhala janaiṁ
kahaūṁ kāhi ko mānaiṁ
nainana kā dukha baina jānai,
baina kā dukha śravanā
pyaṇḍa kā dukha prāṇa jānai,
prāna kā dukha maranā
āsa ka dukha pyāsa jānai,
pyāsa kā dukha nīra
bhagati kā dukha rāma jānai,
kahai dūsa kabīra

RAMA, THE ALL-KNOWING

Rāma knows well the grief of beings
How shall *I* tell? Who'll believe?
The eyes tell grief which is beyond speech,
The ears are grieved by the words that hurt,
The soul knows the grief the body feels
And death relieves the suffering soul:
Greed knows the grief of cheated hope,
Water knows the grief of thirst:
Rāma knows the devotee's grief—
Thus says the the slave of Rāma, Kabīr.

7

takoṁ re kahā kījai bhaī
taji amṛta bisa lauṁ lāī
viṣa sangrahi kahā sukha pāyā
rancaka sukha kūṁ janama gaṁvāyā
mana barajaiṁ cita kahyau na karaī
sakati saneha dīpaka maiṁ paraī
kahata kabīra mohi bhagata umāhā
kṛta karaṇī jāti bhayā julāhā

THE NOOSE OF WORLDLINESS

What can one say of him who refrains
From the nectar of devotion, O brother,
And wallows in sense-pleasures?
What has he gained
By heaping worldly cravings one on another?

He wastes his life for a little joy
And even though he has determined to spurn
All worldly pleasures, his wayward mind
To relish them returns
Again and yet again[26]
As a moth speeding
To burn itself in a lamp's flame.

Says Kabīr, though by my past karmas
A weaver's caste is mine,
I have seen the light
Of devotion shine.

8

vai kyūṁ kāsī tajaiṁ murārī
terī seva cora bhaye banavārī
jogī jātī tapī sanyāsī
maṭha devala basi parasauṁ kāsī
tīna bāra je nita prati nhāvaiṁ
kāyā bhītari khabari na pāvaiṁ
devala devala pherī dehīṁ
nāva niranjana kabahuṁ na lehīṁ
carana birada kāsī kūṁ na daihuṁ
kahai kabīra bhala narakahiṁ jaihuṁ

THE HYPOCRISY OF HOLY MEN

Why should they leave Kashi
E'en though, O Krishna, for you to they do not care
Those yogis, ascetics, recluses and *sannyāsīs*
Who throng in temples, just to be there?

They bathe three times a day
But do not look within their Selves

Round all temples they circumambulate
But of the Absolute they cannot tell.

I will not associate Kashi
With your glory, Krishna, says Kabīr,
Even if I go to hell![27]

(E) RĀGA KEDĀRĀ

1

merī aṁkhiyāṁ jāna sujāna bhaiṁ
devara bharama sasura saṅga taji kari
hari pīva tahāṁ gaiṁ
bālapanai ke krama hamāre,
kāṭe jāni daī
bāṁha pakari kari kṛpā kīnhīṁ,
āpa samīpa laī
pānī kī būnda thaiṁ pyāṇḍa sājyā,
tā saṅgi adhilka raī
dāsa kabīra pala prema na ghaṭaī
dina dina prīti naī

LOVE FOR HARI

I have seen with wisdom's eye:
Leaving volition and repose[28]
In Hari's love now I abide,
His benevolence has drawn me close.

By his grace my ignorance is riven;
To him who creates by a semen's drop
My love I have given,
No more in the world tempest-tossed.

Says Kabīr, Hari's humble slave,
'My love for him can never cease
E'en a moment, day by day
More and more does it increase'.

2

vālhā āva hamare greha re,
tumha bina dukhiā deha re.
saba ko kahai tumhārī nārī,
mokauṁ ihai andeha re.
ekameka hvai seja na sovai,
taba laga kaisā neha re
jāna na bhāvai nīṁda na āvai,

griha bana dharai na dhīra re
jyūṁ kāmī kauṁ kāma piyārā,
jyūṁ pyāse kūṁ nīra re
hai koi aisā paraupagārī,
hari sū kahai sunāī re
jaise hāla kabīra bhaye haiṁ
bina dekhai jīva jāi re

PANGS OF PARTING

Lover, come home,
Without you I am restless.
People say I am your beloved,
But you do not share my bed,
What kind of love is this?

Hunger and sleep have fled,
Neither my home can allay me, nor the woods:
As dalliance to the lustful man
And water to one thirsty,
So is my longing for you.

Is their anyone so obliging
As to go and tell Hari,
'Kabīr's condition is such
That without you he can no longer live'.

3

maiṁ jana bhulau tū samajhāi
cita cancala rahai na bhaṭakyau
viṣai bana kūṁ jāī
sansāra sāgara māṁhi bhūlyau,
thakyau karata upāī
mohiṇī māyā bāghaṇī thaiṁ
rākhi lai rāma rāī
gopāla suni eka bīnatī
sumati tana ṭharāī
kahai kabīra suni yahu kāma ripa hai,
mārai saba kūṁ ḍhāī

MAYA THE FOE

O Lord, remove my delusion
My restless mind fails to reach you,
It keeps taken up with worldly pleasures,
Save me from illusive maya's snare,
Give me devotion, I beseech you
Says Kabīr, desire is my foe
It slays all those who come in its way.

4

prāṇī lāla ausara calyau re bajāi
muṭhi yeka maṭiya, mūthi yeka khaṭiyā,
saṅga kāhu kai nā jāī
dehalī laga terī miharī sagī re
phalasa laga sāgī māī
mar̐ahaṭa lūṁ saba loga kuṭambī
hansa akelau jāī
kahāṁ vai loga kahāṁ pura pataṇa
bahuri na milabau āī
kahai kabīra jagnātha bhajau re,
janama akyāratha jāī

THE SOUL GOES ALONE

O man, after having played your tune
The time has come to bid the world goodbye
Neither the dust that is your body
Nor the ashes of your bones
Will go with you: your wife and mother
Will reach you to your doorstep,
And your relations to the cremation-ground,
The soul goes all alone.

Then where will you find those whom you have left?
Says Kabīr, chant the name of Jagannātha[29]
While there's still time, or else
This life of yours will be purposeless.

(F) RĀGA MĀRŪ

1

mana re rama sumira rāma sumira bhāī
rama nāma sumirani binā burata hai adhikāī
dārā suta greha, neha sampati adhikāī
yamai kachu nahīm terau, kāla avadhi āī
ajāmela gaja, ganikā, patiti karama kīnhā
tau utari pāri gaye, rāma nāma līnhāṁ
svāna sūkara kāga kīnhā taū lāja na āī
rāma nāma amṛta chari, kāhe viṣa khāī
taji bharama karama vidhi naṣeda, rāma nāma lehī
jana kabīra guru prasādi, rāma kari sanehī

CHANT RĀMA'S NAME

O mind, dwell on Rāma, dwell on Rāma,
O brother, chant Rāma's name
Because without it you will surely fall.
What are wife, sons, home and wealth
To you now that death comes?

Ajāmila, Gaja and Gaṇikā did evil karmas
Yet they got salvation by taking Rāma's name[30]
You could not shed attachment, so you were cast
In lower wombs, then too you weren't ashamed.
You'd rather have the poison of sense-pleasures
Than the nectar of Rāma-devotion;
Do not be deluded, abandon evil deeds,
Take the blessings of the guru, says Kabīr.

2

rāma nāma hiradaya dhari
niramolika hīrā
sobhā tihūṁ loka timara,
jaya tribadhi pīrā
trisanā nai lobha lahari, kāma krodha nīrā
mada manchara kacha macha, hariṣa soka tīrā
kāmani aru kanaka bhuvara, boye bahu bīrā
jana kabīra navakā hari, khevaṭa guru kīrā

THE GURU TAKES ONE ACROSS

The name of Rāma is a priceless gem
Treasure it in your heart
So that you may earn merit
In the three worlds;
Move out of the darkness of existence
And escape the three sorrows.[31]

In the river of life
Craving and greed are the waves,
Passion and rage
Its waters;
Arrogance and envy
The creatures in it,
Joy and grief
Its two banks
And lust and opulence
The whirlpools.

Many have been drowned in this river;
Says Kabīr, to get across it
Hari is the boat
And the oarsman is the guru.

3

cali merī sakhī ho bolagana rāma rāyā
jaba taba kāla bināsailau kāyā
jaba laga lobha moha kī dāsī
tīratha brati na chūṭai jama kī pāsī
jāvaiṁge jama ke ghālaiṁge bāṁṭī
yahu tana gāri bāri hoigau māṭī
kahai kabīra je jana hari raṅga rātā
pāyo rājā rāmā parama pada dātā

BE IMERSED IN HARI'S LOVE

O soul, serve the Infinite Rāma
For death's ever dancing on your head
Till you are enslaved by greed and ignorance
You are being misled.

Fasts, pilgrimages and the like
Can't free you from the noose of Death
For Death's messengers will lay you low
And your body will be ashes.
Says Kabīr, those immersed in the love of Hari
Will attain *mokṣa*.

(G) RĀGA TORĪ

1

tūṁ pāka paramānande
pīra paikambara panaha tumhārī,
maiṁ garība kyā gande
tumba dariyā sabahī dila bhītari,
paramānanda piyāre
naiṁka najari hama ūpari nāhim,
kyā kamibakhata hamāre
hikamati karaiṁ halāla bicāraiṁ
āpa kahāvaiṁ moṭe
cākarī cora nivālai hājira,
sāṁiṁ setī khoṭe
dāṁima dūva karada bajāvaiṁ
maiṁ kyā karūṁ bhikāri
kahai kabīra maiṁ bandā terā,
khālika panaha tumhārī

PRETENDERS

O Lord, you are blissful ever;
Saints and prophets seek your refuge
Not to speak of me, a humble beggar?
You are a river of mercy that finds its way
Into every heart, O beloved Lord
What evil deeds are mine, that your gaze
Never falls on me? People devise
Many ways, observing what the scriptures declare,
And look on their accomplishments with pride,
But they do not do their duty quite
Although in every religious rite they're there.

But for you, O Lord, they do not care;
They seek your blessings, but in their hands
They hold a knife to slaughter and behead;
I, a humble suppliant, am powerless
To stop them. Says Kabīr, I'm your slave,
O World Creator, bless me with your grace.

2

aba hama jagata gauṁhana taiṁ bhāge
jaga kī dekhi ju gati rāmahi ḍhuri lāge
āyānapanai thaiṁ bahu baurānem
samajhi parī taba phiri pachitānem
loga kahai jāke jo mani bhāvai
lahaiṁ bhavangama kauṁna dasāvaiṁ
kabīra bicāri ihai ḍara ḍariye
kahaiṁ kā ho ihāṁ naiṁ mariye

WORLDLY BONDAGE

Now I have azzled out of the world,
Seeing its ways, I've turned to Rāma:
Ignorance had clouded my mind,
But now I burn with remorse:
A man may say whatever he likes
But when a serpent comes his way
Will he let it bite?

What does it matter what men say
Says Kabīr, so long as you keep away
From worldly bondage?
It's of that you should be afraid.

(H) RĀGA BHAIRAU

1

anjana alapa niranjana sāra
ihai cīnhi nara karahu vicāra
anjana utapati baratani loī
binā niranjana mukati na hoī
anjana āvai anjana jāi
niranjana saba ghaṭi rahyau samāi
joga dhyāna tapa sabai bikāra
kahai kabīra mere rāma adhāra

ETERNAL *BRAHMAN*

The three *guṇas* are ephemeral[32]
While *Brahman* is eternal[33]
O man, consider well

The *guṇas* are of the world
But without *Brahman* there's no *mokṣa*
The *guṇas* are changeful, they come and go,
While *Brahman* is in every soul.

Yoga, meditation, austerities and so forth
Are transient; says Kabīr, Rāma is my support.

2

eka niranjana alaha merā
hindū turaka duhūṁ nahiṁ nerā
rākhūṁ barata na māha ramajāna
tisahī sumirauṁ go rahai nidāna
pūjā karauṁ na nimāja gujārauṁ
eka nirākāra hiradai namasakarauṁ
nā haja jāūṁ na tīratha pūjā
kahai kabīra bharama saba bhāgā
eka niranjana sūṁ mana lāgā

HINDU AND MOSLEM

My Allah is one, the Absolute Being
Neither the Hindu nor the Turk knows him.

I do not keep the *rozā*, nor believe in fasting,[34]
I adore him who is everlasting,
I do not worship, nor observe *namāz*,[35]
I salute the Infinite Lord with all my heart.
I do not undertake pilgrimages or the *haj* voyage:[36]
Knowing the One, duality has ceased
And all my delusion is destroyed;
Says Kabīr, in him I've found eternal peace.

3

harijana hansa dasā līyaiṁ ḍolai
niramala nāva cavai jasa bolai
māna sarovara tata ke vāsī
rāma carana cita jāna udāsī
muktāhala bina canca na lāvai
mauni gahai kai hari guna gāvai
kaūvā kubadhi nikaṭa nahiṁ āvai
so hansā nija darasana pāvai
kahai kabīra soī jana terā
khīra nīra kā karai naberā

THE LOVERS OF HARI

The lovers of Hari are as the royal swan[37]
They chant his name and sing his praises
Though the worldly Mansarovara is their haunt
In Rāma's holy feet their minds repose
And they are indifferent to all else.

Their only purpose is to achieve *mokṣa*[38]
They do not speak except to chant the name of Hari;
Says Kabīr, consider only that man your friend
Who is untouched by depravity,
Who by his wisdom can dispel your ignorance.

4

Santani eka aherā lādhā
mṛgani kheta sabani kā sādhā
yā jangala maiṁ pam̐cau mṛgā
eī kheta sabani kā cari gā

pāradhīpanoṁ je sādhai koī
adha sādhā sā rākhai soī
kahai kabīra jo pancauṁ mārai
āpa tirai aura kūṁ tārai

THE FIVE EVILS

The saints have gone on a hunt,
They have killed the five deer
Who grazed away the fields of everyone—
Desire, envy, greed, arrogance and wrath—
Only an expert hunter can slay
These deer and save the fields from further loss.
Says Kabīr, he who gets rid of these five evils
Redeems himself and others as well.

5

āsaṇa pavaṇa kiyaiṁ dirha rahure
mana kā maila chāṁri dai baure
kyā sīngī mudrā camakāyaiṁ
so hindū so musalamāna
jisakā durasa rahai īmāna
so brahmā jo kathai brahma giyāna
kājī so jānai rahimāna
kahai kabīra kachu āna na kījai
rāma nāma japi lāhā lījai

WHAT MAKES A HINDU, WHAT A MOSLEM

O goof! control the five breaths within[39]
And remove the evil from your mind,
What's the use of polishing a horn or a coin,
Or putting ashes on your limbs?
He's a Hindu, he is a Moslem
Who is straightforward and of conscience clear,
He's a brahmin who has knowledge of *Brahman*
He's a Moslem who holds God dear.
Says Kabīr, chant the name of Rāma
That's all that's needed here.

6

bāpa rāma suni bīnatī merī
tumha sūṁ pragaṭa logani sūṁ corī
pahalai kāma mugadha mati kīyā
tā bhai kaṁpai merā jīyā
rāma rāi merā kahyā sunijai
pahle bakasi aba lekhā lījai
kahai kabīra bāpa rāma rāyā
aba hūṁ sarani tumhārī āyā

FATHER RĀMA

Listen to my prayer, O Father Rāma,
You know what's not clear to others,
At first passion spurred me on
But now my heart trembles with fear.

O Lord Rāma, hear me;
First forgiveness, then the reckoning.
'O Father Rāma', says Kabīr,
''Tis your shelter that I seek'.

7

ajahūṁ bīca kaise darasana torā
bina darasana mana mānaiṁ kyūṁ morā
hamahi kusevaga kyā tumahi ajānāṁ
duha maiṁ dosa kahau kina rāmāṁ
tumha kahiyata tribhavana pati rājā
manabanchita saba puravana kājā
kahai kabīra hari darasi dikhāvau
hamahi bulāvau kai tumha cali āvau

SEPARATION

Even today you remain away
How shall I live on then, say?
You don't heed, or maybe I don't deserve
Why don't you say that both are wanting?
They say you are the Lord of the universe
And you grant your devotees everything.
'Come to me, O Hari', says Kabīr,
'Either call me to you, or come yourself'.[40]

8

kāhe kūṁ bhīti banāuṁ tāṭī
kā jānūṁ kahāṁ parihai māṭī
kāhe kūṁ mandira mahal ciṇāūṁ
mūvāṁ pīchaiṁ gharī eka rahana na pāūṁ
kahe kūṁ chāūṁ ūṁca uṁcerā
sāṛhe tīni hātha ghara merā
kahai kabīra nara garaba na kījai
jetā tana tetī bhui lījai

THE HOUSE OF DUST

Why should I surround myself with walls?
When this earth shall mingle with that earth
Where I shall lie? Why erect at all
Lofty mansions, when after death
I can't stay a moment in these?

O foolish one, leave tall houses alone,
Three and a half cubits of land is all you'll need;
Shed your vanity, says Kabīr,
And mind that house of dust which will be your home.

(I) RĀGA BILĀVALA

1

rāma bhajai so jāṇiye jāke ātura nāhiṁ
sata santoṣa liyai rahai, dhīraja mana māhiṁ
jana kauṁ kāma krodha vyāpai nahīṁ,
triśnāṁ na jarāvai
prafulita ānanda maiṁ,
gobyanda guṇa gāvai
jana kauṁ para nindyā bhāvai nahīṁ
aru asati na bhāṣai
kāla kalapanā meṭi kari,
caranūṁ cita rākai
jana samadriṣṭā sītala sadā
dubidhā nahīṁ jānai
kahai kabīra tā dāsa sūṁ
merā mana mānai

THE IDEAL DEVOTEE

Consider him to be a devotee of Rāma
Whose mind is never perplexed,
Who is contented, truthful and calm,
And whom desire and rage don't vex.

Who keeps craving away from his mind,
And who joyfully sings Govinda's praise,
Who does not like to hear others maligned,
Whose utterances are truthful in all ways.

Who does not waste precious time in trifles,
Who surrenders himself to Hari's feet,
Who's free from doubt, unruffled and
same-sighted—
Such a one serves Hari, says Kabīr.

2

mana banajārā jāgi na soī
lāhe kārani mūla na khoī
lāhā dekhi kahā garabānā

garaba na kījai mūrikha ayānā
jini dhana sancyā so pachitānā
sāthi cali gaye hama bhī jānā
nisi andhiyārī jagahu bande
chiṭakana lāge sabahī sandhe
kisakā bandhu kisakī joī
calyā akelā saṅgi na koī
ḍhari gaye mandira ṭūṭe baṅsā
sūkhe saravara uṛa gaye haṅsā
panca padāratha bharihaiṁ khehā
jari bari jaigī kancana dehā
kahata kabīra sunahu re loī
rāma nāma bina aura na koī

EVANESCENT EXISTENCE

Awake! awake! O wandering mind,
Do not lose the Real for worldly gain;
O ignorant fool, do not be vain
Whoever gathered wealth, repined.

All whom I knew, now lie in graves
And soon will be my turn to leave
In this dark night, O Hari's slave,
Awake; for all ties will cease:
Who's whose relation, who whose wife here,
The Soul goes alone.
Palaces will be dust, clans disappear,
The full lake will be dry
And from it the swan-shaped Soul will fly
To its heavenly home.
All will return to the five elements,[41]
This prized body will burn on the pyre
Says Kabīr, O Loī nothing remains
In this world save Rāma's name.

3

mana patanga cete nahīṁ jala anjurī samāna
viṣiyā lāgi bigūciye, dājhiye nidana
kāhai naina anandiyai, sūjhata nahīṁ āgi

janama amolika khoiyai, sāpani saṁgi lāgi
kahai kabīra cita cancalā, guri kahyau samajhāi
bhagati hīṁna jaraī jarai, bhāvai lahāṁ jāi

RESTLESS MIND

O mind, you are like a moth
Yet you do not understand
This little life is short
As water in cupped hands.

You don't tire of sense-pleasures
You pursue them with delight,
They'll ruin you: realize,
O mind, you're trifling with fire.
With maya's serpent playing
You waste this precious life;
The mind's restless, never staying
At one place, always straying—
The guru told me so.
Says Kabīr, without devotion
It keeps burning, burning,
And goes where it likes to go.

4

svādi patanga jarai jari jāi
anahada sauṁ merau cita na rahāi
māyā kai madi ceti na dekhyā
dubidhyā māṁhi eka nahīṁ pekhyā
bheṣa aneka kiyā bahu kīnhāṁ
akala purisa eka nahīṁ cinhāṁ
kete eka muye marahige kete
ketaka mugadha ajahu nahīṁ cete
tantra mantra saba oṣada māyā
kevala rāma kabīra diḍhāyā

MAYA THE STUMBLING BLOCK

As the moth flies to the flame and burns
So my mind rushes to taste sense-pleasures,
To spiritual thoughts it never turns

The world's delight is all it treasures.

Swayed by the delusive power of maya
The One Absolute eluded me,
I pursued pleasures in many forms and shapes,
But could not see the Imperishable Supreme.

How many people have lived and died,
And many more will come and go away,
But countless are the fools that shut their eyes
To the Infinite Being even today.

Tantra, *mantra*, herbs—all, are maya says Kabīr,
Therefore in Rāma's name I have sought peace.

(J) RĀGA LALITA

1

rāma jaisau hī jāni japauṁ naraharī
mādhava madasūdana banavārī
anadina gyāna kathaiṁ ghariyāra
dhūvāṁ dhauhara hai sansāra
jaisai nadī nāva kara saṅga
jaisau hīm māta pitā suta aṅga
savahi nala dulamala phala kīra
jala budabudā aiso āhi sarīra
jibhyā rāma nāma abhyāsa
kahata kabīra taja garabhai bāsa

THE BUBBLE OF LIFE

I chant Rāma's name,
Who's also known as Banawārī, Narahari
Mādhava and Madhusūdana.
The morning gong proclaims
That this life is like smoke; soon gone:

Mother, father, son and all
Relations; are only for a while,
As a hired boat plies on the river,
Or as a ripe fruit soon devoured[42]
By a hungry parrot; or as bubble blown—

So chanting the name of Rāma, Kabīr
Has turned away his mind from thoughts of home.

2

rasanāṁ rāma guna rami rami pījai
guna atīta niramolika lījai
niraguna brahma kathau re bhāī
jā sumirata sudhi budhi mati pāī
biṣa taji rāma na japasi abhāge
kā būṛe lālaca ke lāge
te saba tire rāma rasa svādī
kahai kabīra būṛe bakavādī

RĀMA IS *BRAHMAN*

O tongue, relish the nectar of Rāma's name
Priceless and beyond the *guṇas*,
That formless *Brahman* should be attained
Which gives purity, wisdom and understanding.

O wretched man, you stick to your desires
And refrain from chanting Rāma's name:
Why are you bogged down in avarice's mire
And drowned in the waters of worldliness?

Says Kabīr, those who remember Rāma will be saved
And they'll be lost who only prate and prate.

(K) RĀGA BASANTA

1

hari boli sūvā bāra bāra
terī ḍhinga mīnīṁ kachu kari pukāra
anjana manjana taji bikāra
sataguru samajhāyau tatta sāra
sādha saṅgati mili kari basanta
bhau bandha na chūṭaiṁ juga juganta
kahai kabīra mana bhayā ananda
anata kalā bheṭe gobyanda

DEATH IS AT THE DOOR

O man, chant 'Hari' again and again
For death is at your door,[43]
Abandon outward show,
Do that which the guru has explained.

Seek the company of sages
Or else age after age
You'll be bound
To this ephemeral world of sorrows and sins.
Says Kabīr, I have found
Endless bliss at the feet of Govinda.

2

banamāli jānai bana kī ādi
rāma nāma bina janama bādi
phūla ju phūle ruti basanta
jāmaiṁ mohi rahe saba jīva janta
phūlani maiṁ jaisaiṁ rahata bāsa
yūṁ ghaṭi gobyanda hari nivāsa
kahai kabīra mana bhayā ananda
jagajīvana miliyau paramānanda

HARI, LIFES GARDENER

Hari knows life's secret;
Without chanting Rāma name

Existence is meaningless.
As flowers bloom in spring
Each filled with fragrance
Even so Hari-Govinda
Is in every soul
Says Kabīr, I've found God
And now know endless bliss.

3

mādhau dārana dukha sahyau na jāi
merī capala budhi tātaiṁ kahā basāi
tana mana bhītari basai madana cora
jini jñāna ratana hari linha mora
maiṁ anātha prabhū kahūṁ kāhi
aneka bigūce maiṁ ko āhi
sanaka sanandana siva sukādi
āpaṇa kavalāpati bhaye brahmādi
jogī jangama jatī jaṭādhāra
apanaiṁ ausari saba gaye haiṁ hāri
kahai kabīra rahu saṅga sātha
abhiantari hari sūṁ kahau bāta
mana jñāna jāni kaiṁ kari bicāra
rāma ramata bhau tiribau pāra

THE LURE OF LUST

O Mādhava, I can't stand this grief,
My uncontrollable mind is unsteady,
Lust, lurking inside me as a thief,
Has stolen the gem of wisdom from me.

I have none in whom I can confide
Save you, O Lord. All, all, have failed
To conquer passion; yogis, anchorites,
Sanaka, Sunandana, Shiva, Brahmā Shukadeva;[44]
Much less I. Says Kabīr, drive away
Ignorance from your mind; ever be
With Hari; tell him your faults when you may,
He will take you across the uncrossable sea.

4

aiso dekhi carita mana mohyau mora
tāthaiṁ nisa bāsuri guna ramauṁ tora
ika paṙhahiṁ pāṭha ika bhamaiṁ udāsa
ika nagina nirantara rahaiṁ nivāsa
ika joga jugati ṯana hūṁhiṁ khīna
aisaiṁ rāma nāma saṅgi rahaiṁ na līna
ika hūṁhi dīna ika dehiṁ dāna
ika karaiṁ kalāpi surā pāna
ika tanta manta oṣada bāna
ika sakala sidha rākaiṁ apāna
ika tīrtha brata kari kāyā jīti
aisaiṁ rāma nāma sūṁ karaiṁ na prīti
ika dhoma ghoṭi tana hūṁhi syāma
Yūṁ mukati nahīṁ bina rāma nāma
sataguri tata kahyau bicāra
mūla gahau anabhai bistāra
jurā maraṇa thaiṁ bhaye dhīra
rāma kṛpā bhaī kahi kabīra

VAIN RITUALS

It vexes me to see men perform
Various vain rites,
So I keep chanting your name, Rāma,
Day and night.

One pours on holy books,
One stares with a vacant look;
One discards his clothes,
One wears out his body with yoga:
But Rāma is not in their thoughts.

One pretends humility
One prides on charity;
One flaunts a peacock's tail
One's in his cups always
One practises Tantra, one utters *mantras*,
One puts his trust in herbs;
One has faith in breath-control

Or holy pilgrimage,
Yet they love not Rāma's name.
To darken their limbs, some expose
Them to the sun; but without Rāma
One cannot attain *mokṣa*

Says Kabīr, the guru said the truth
Is the One Cosmic Absolute,
I followed in his steps.
And by Rāma's grace I escaped
The rounds of births and deaths.

(L) RĀGA MĀLĪGAUḌĀ

1

panditā mana ranjitā,
bhagati heta layau lāi re
prema prīti gopāla bhaji nara,
aura kāraṇa jāi re
dāma chai paṇi kāma nāhiṁ,
jñāna chai paṇi dhandha re
śravaṇa chai paṇi surati nāhīṁ,
naina chai paṇi andha re
jākai nābhi padama suṁ udita brahmā,
carana ganga taranga re
kahai kabīra hari bhagati bāṁchūṁ,
jagata gura gobyanda re

HARI, MASTER OF THE UNIVERSE

O pundit, your mind is swayed by desire
Let devotion alone be your salvation,
Chant Govinda's name, there is no other way.

You have wealth, but of what use will it be?
You have knowledge, yet your doubts do not clear,
You'll not hear the truth, though you have ears,
You have eyes, yet you can't see the reality

Says Kabīr, I long for the love of Hari
From the lotus of whose navel Brahmā took birth
From whose feet the sacred Gangā flowed,
Hari, the Master of the universe.[45]

2

bhaji nāradādi sukādi bandita,
carana pankaja bhāminīṁ
bhaji bhajisi bhūṣana pīya manohara,
deva deva sirovanīṁ
budhī nābhi canadina caracitā,
tana ridā mandira bhītarā
rāma rājisi naina bānīṁ,

sujāna sundara sundarā
bahu pāpa parabata chedanā,
bhau tāpa durita nibā raṇā
kahai kabīra gobyanda bhaji,
parimānanda bandita kāraṇā

THE LORD OF THE LORDS

O soul, be at the feet of Nārada and Shuka,[46]
Make the Lord of lords, gentle and beloved,
The Formless Rāma, your refuge.

Imbibe wisdom precious as sandalwood
Let your tongue sing the Lord's praise
And your eyes ever look towards him,
Treasure him in your heart always,
The Lord, lovelier than the loveliest
Who forgives even the mightiest sin.
Says Kabir, worship Govinda
In whom all creation rests.

(M) RĀGA KALYĀNA

1

jaisaiṁ mana lāī lai rāma sanāṁ
kapaṭa bhagati kījai kauna gunāṁ
jyaūṁ mṛga nādaiṁ bedhyau āī
pyanḍa parai vākau dhyāna na jāī
jaūṁ jala mīna heta kari jāni
prāna tajai bisarai nahīṁ bāni
bhṛiṅgī kīṭa rahai lyau lāi
hvai lai līna bhriṅga hvai jāī
rāma nāma nija amṛta sāra
muhaṙai bādhyā marai gaṁvāra
kahai kabīra dāsani kau dāsa
aba nahīṁ chāṙauṁ carana nivāsa

SINCERE DEVOTION

Love Rāma with sincere love
Mere pretence is of no use
As a deer stands rooted to the ground
On hearing a sound
Even though it loses its life;
As the fish does not part with the water
Even though it gets caught on the hook;
As the *bhriṅgī* maggot brings a worm
And transforms it just by its looks
Into a *bhriṅgī*[47]
So should your love for Rāma be.
O fool! you'll not give your heart to him,
And die, with your wealth
Lying in coffers.
I'm a humble slave of Rāma, says Kabīr,
And I will ever worship his holy feet.

(N) RĀGA SĀRAṄGA

1

yahu ṭhaga ṭhagata jaga ḍolai
gavana karai taba mukhahu na bolai
tūṁ merau puriṣā hauṁ terī nārī
tumha calataiṁ pāthara thaiṁ bhārī
bālāpanā ke mīta hamāre
chāṛi kata cale ho nināre
hama sūṁ prīti na kari rī baurī
tumha se kete lāye ḍhaurī
hama kāhu saṅgi gaye na āye
tumha se gaṛha hama bahuta basāye
māṭī kī dehī pavana sarīrā
tā ṭhaga sūṁ jana ḍarai kabīrā

THE THUG *JĪVA*

The deceiver *jīva* keeps cheating everyone
And he does it insidiously:
I'm your spouse, says he, yet I'll go
I'll leave you, for I go alone.
Do not shower your love on me,
Be not infatuated with me, for none
Is mine, though many are my friends
I never come or go with anyone.

Says Kabīr, him I fear whose body is mere earth
And who's fashioned from the five elements.[48]

(O) RĀGA MALHĀRA

1

jatana bina mṛgani kheta ujāre
ṭāre ṭarata nahīṁ nisa bāsuri
biḍarata nahīṁ biḍāre
apaneṁ apaneṁ rasa ke lobhī,
karataba nyāre nyāre
ati abhimāna badata nahīṁ kāhū
bahuta loga paci hāre
budhi merī kiraṣī gura merau bijhukā,
akhira hoi rakhavāre
kahai kabīra aba khāna na daihūṁ
bariyāṁ bhalī saṁbhāre

OBSTINATE VICES

If you do not resolutely strive
To drive out deer-shaped desire, lust and rage,
They will devastate your field-shaped life.

Though I keep chasing them out night and day,
They are still there; however much I try,
These deer-shaped evils still will stay
On the delights of the senses bent,
Hunting for them in many ways.

Arrogant; for they have contempt for everyone:
Many are those who have tried
To keep them out: but all in vain:
When they all have failed, say, what chance have I?

As a scarecrow keeps the birds away,
Seeing the guru, evils take flight,
And the two letters of Rāma's name
Are the watchmen of my field-shaped life.
Says Kabīr, now evils are on the run
For I have taken timely measures
To cast them all out, one by one;
No longer shall I be a victim to pleasures.[49]

2

hari guna sumari re nara prāṇī
jatana karata patana hvai jaihai
bhāvaiṁ jāṇa ma jāṇī
chīlari nīra rahai dhūṁ kaisaiṁ
ko supinaiṁ saca pāvai
sūkika pāna parata tarabara thaiṁ
ulaṭi na taravari āvai
jala thala jīva ḍahake ina māyā
koī jana ubara na pāvai
rāma adhāra kahata haiṁ jugi jugi,
dāsa kabīrā gāvai

RĀMA, THE ONLY REFUGE

Brother, chant Rāma's name,
You may, or may not, heed;
But other ways are vain
And will not succeed.

Can water be contained
In a narrow lake,
Or dreams turn out real
When the dreamer wakes?[50]
Can the dry leaf that breaks
From the branch, again
Find its former place?

Maya is the cheat
That has sucked everyone
In its deep whirlpool;
From its clutches none
Can escape.

One's refuge is only Rāma;
Only he can save men
Age after age,
Says Kabīr.

(P) RĀGA DHANĀŚRĪ

1

na kachū re na kachū rāma binā
sarīre dhare kī ihai parama gati,
sādha saṅgati rahanā
mandiya racata māsa dasa lāge,
binasata eka chinā
jhuṭhe sukha kai kārani prāṇī
parapanca karata ghanā
tāta māta suta loga kuṭumba maiṁ
phulyo phirata manā
kahai kabīra rāma bhaji baure,
chāṁri sakala bhramanā

THERE IS NOTHING WITHOUT RĀMA

Without Rāma there is nothing, nothing:
This life's end
Is to befriend
Sages.

The body which lies
Ten months in the womb
Takes a moment to die.
Even then for empty pleasures
Men practise a thousand wiles,
Wandering puffed up
With parents, sons, family and friends.

O fool! says Kabīr,
Do not be misled by these,
Chant the name of Rāma.

2

kahā nara garabasi thorī bāta
mana dasa nāja ṭakā dasa ganṭhiā
ṭeṛhau ṭeṛhau jāti
kahā lai āyau yahu dhana kaū
kahā koū lai jāta

divasa cāri kī hai patisāhī
jyūṁ bani hariyala pāta
rājā bhayau gāṁva sau pāye
ṭakā lākha dasa brāta
rāvana hota lanka kau chatrapati,
pala maiṁ gaī bihāta
mātā pitā loka suta banitā,
anti na cale saṅgāta
kahai kabīra rāma bhaji baure,
janama akyāratha jāta

VAIN CONCEIT

Just two maunds of grain in your sack,
Ten pice in your pocket!
Yet, O conceited man, you brag and brag!

Your wealth? has anyone ever brought it with him,
Or taken it with him when he goes from here?
This kingdom you prize so much is two shakes,
As the bare woods unlovely made
When the green leaf turns into the sear.

Rāvaṇa, Lankā's king, was deprived in a moment
Of his mighty kingdom; friend, no one—[51]
Companions, parents, son or wife—
Will go with you when death comes.

O fool! says Kabīr, chant Rāma's name, or else
This life of yours will remain purposeless.

THE PADAS OF KABĪR

NOTES

1. The five elements are earth, water, fire, air and ether *chita jala pāvaka gagana samīrā, panca racita yaha adhama sarīrā* (*Rāmacaritamānasa*)
2. *Smṛti* is literally 'What was heard', as distinguished from *Sruti* or direct revelation. It stands for what has been remembered and handed down by tradition (John Dowson *A Classical Dictionary of Hindu Mythology and Religion*) says: 'In its widest application the term includes the *Vedāngas*, the *Sutras*, the *Rāmāyaṇa*, the *Mahābhārata*, the *Purāṇas*, the *Dharma-śāstras* especially the works of Manu. Yājnavalkya and other inspired lawgivers, and the *Nīti-śāstras* or ethics, but the ordinary application is to the *Dharma-śastras*; as Manu says 'By *Śruti* is meant the Veda and by *Smṛti* the institution of law' ii.10.

   The *Purāṇas*, eighteen in number, and the same number of *Upa Purāṇas* form the scripture of Hinduism. Amara Sinha says the *Purāṇas* have five distinguishing topics; 1. The creation of the universe, 2. Its destruction and renovation, 3. The genealogy of gods and patriarchs, 4. The reigns of the Manus, forming the periods called Manwantaras, and 5. The history of the Solar and Lunar races of kings. However there are marked variations in the patherns. All of them are in verse in the form of a dialogue between an exponent and an inquirer interspersed with the dialogues and observations of other individuals. They vary greatly in length.
3. *vyākaraṇa* means grammar. The Sanskrit grammar is very elaborate and a science in itself, not as English grammar merely an adjunct to language. Pāṇini is the celebrated Sanskrit grammarian. It is believed it was an inspired work that he wrote, and he is classed as a *ṛṣī*. He was an indifferent student and was expelled from school, but the god Shiva favoured him and endowed him with knowledge. Professor Williams considers his work as the 'most originanal of all productions of the Hindu mind'. His work has eight chapters (Kabīr mentions nine in some other context) and so the book is known as *Aśṭādhyāyi*. He lived about four centuries before Christ. There have been many other grammarians, but none so distinguished as him.

4. Shesha is the king of the serpent race called Nāgas dwelling in Pātāla (the infernal regions). It is believed to have a thousand heads which is the couch and canopy of Viṣṇu. Sometimes it is depicted as supporting the earth. At the churning of the ocean the gods used Shesha as a great rope twisted round the Mandara mountain and so used it as a churn. He is represented as dressed in purple, wearing a white necklace and holding a plough in one hand and a pestle in the other.

   Garuṛa is a mythical vulture, half-man half-bird and the vehicle of Viṣṇu. He is the king of birds, believed to be a descendant of Kaśyapa and Vinatā one of the daughters of Dakṣa. He is represented as having the head, wings, talons and beak of an eagle and the body and limbs of a man. His face is white, wings red and body golden. Sampati is his son.

5. Viṣṇu is sometimes represented as recling on the serpent Shesha with Lakṣmī (also known as Kamalā or Śrī) beside him and massaging his feet.

   The verse is another example of Kabīr's many contradictions. He worships the formless Rāma, and is dead against avatars. yet he speaks in the same breath of Viṣṇu, one of the main gods and of the Hindu trinity. In fact Kabīr keeps hovering between monism and dualism, though his emphasis is on monism.

6. The woid *bhoṁdū*, meaning 'stupid' or foolish' conveys the sense all right, but it isn't the kind of word normally used in good poetry (*mūrkha*) would be immensely preferable. This is an example of the coarseness and roughness of Kabīr's verses, evident in many places.

7. *Siddhīs* are said to be a class of semi-divine beings of great purity and holiness who are believed to dwell in the region of the sky between the earth and the sun. The *siddhīs* are also identified with eight miraculous power which can be acquired by saints. These are, 1. *Mahimā*—the power of becoming infinitely light, 2. *Animā*—the power of becoming infinitely small, 3. *Garimā*—the power of becoming infinitely heavy., 4. *Laghumā*—the power of becoming infinitely light, 5. *Prāpti*—obtaining whatever one desires, 6. *Prākāmya* —doing whatever one wants to, 7. *Īśistva*—absolute supremacy and 8. *Vaśitva*—the power to subdue anyone.

8. The verse is allegorical. The fire is the *ātman* (soul), the water, the body; the body has eyes to see but it is the soul which give them the power of seeing; the toad is the *ātman*

and the five snakes the five obstructions to soul-knowledge, i.e., desire, anger, greed, attachment and arrogance. The cow is the *ātman* while the lion the body and the lion's limb which the 'cow' tears apart are its tendencies (*sanskāras*) So too the goat, the deer, the mouse and the buffalo are the *ātman* and the wolf, the leopard, the cat and the dog represent the body. The body represents the trap set for the soul (the crow), the partridge or pheasant is the *ātman*, the falcon the body.

9. Hari is another name for Viṣṇu.
10. The five impediments are, desire, anger, attachment, greed and arrogance.
11. The *anahāta* is the *nāda* sound heard by one practising Laya Yoga. Laya Yoga is one of the five different kinds of yoga, the others being Haṭha Yoga, Mantra Yoga, Tantra Yoga and Rāja Yoga. The three main practices of Laya Yoga are 1. Awakening the *kuṇḍalinī* 2. Seeing the light of the Self, and 3. Hearing the *nādi* sound. The *nādi* sound is heard when the yogi sits in the desired posture and concentrates. At first many loud sounds are heard resembling the roar of the ocean, the thundering of clouds, the sounding of a drum and so forth. Then the sound's intensity grows less and less. It is then like the tinkle of a bell, a flute's note, the sound of a lute and finally like the hum of a bee. The mind of the yogi gets lost in the sound and he forgets everything else. His mind mingles with the *nādi* sound as 'milk with water', i.e., it becomes one with it. When this happens another sound, never heard before, arises in the yogi's heart. The *nādi* sound is then merged in the Principle of Word (*śabda*).
12. Govinda is one of the names by which Krishna, Viṣṇu's avatar, is called.
13. For *nāda* see note to verse 1 (Rāga Āsāvarī) ante.

14-15. *bindu*, Śiva and Śakti— These are tāntrik terms. The Tantra concept of creation is unique it believes creation begins with sound. Shiva or Brahmā has two aspects, *nirguṇa* (attributeless) and *saguṇa* (with attributes). As the former he is disassociated from Śakti. From the union of Śiva and Śakti, sound (*nādi*) is born and from *nādi*, *bindu*. From *bindu* comes *śabda* (word) and from *śabda* the ethereal region, from touch air, from colour fire, from taste water, from smell earth. Thus the process of creation gradually unfolds the gross from the subtle. When this is reversed in dissolution, the gross disappears into the subtle.

16. *Veda* is from the root *vid* 'know'. The *Vedas* are the sacred books which are the foundation of Hindu religion. They are believed to be hymns that emanated like breath from Brahmā, and are therefore *Śruti*, i.e., 'what was revealed, or heard'. There are for *Vedas, Ṛg. Yajur, Sāma* and *Atharva,* the earliest being the *Ṛg Veda*. Each *Veda* has two parts, the *mantra* and the *brāhmaṇa*. The *mantra* consists of prayer and praise and is in metrical hymns. The *brāhmaṇas* are prose treatises containing liturgical and ritualistic glosses, and applications of the hymns illustrated by numerous legends. To the *brāhmaṇas* are added the *Āraṇyakas* and *upaniṣads.* The two divisions are also the *jñāna-kāṇḍa* (the division of knowledge) and the karma-*kāṇḍa* (division of works). For grammar (*vyākaraṇa*) see notes to verse 3, *Rāga Gaurī ante.*
17. *cātak* is the pied-crested cuckoo who according to poetic belief drinks only the rain drops which fall on the full moon's night in October when rainfall is rare in India. Hence it is used by Hindi poets to symbolize deep devotion.
18. The word *jaṭ* refers to the central solid iron pole of in a *kolhū* which is a kind of crude device used in villages for crushing sugar-cane and making jaggery from its juice-*dasa gāṁṭhi* (*dasa*-ten, *gāṁthi*-knot) denotes that the pole has ten grooves i.e., is very long and would therefore be very weighty. Kabīr's observation is satirical.
19. The text says, *pāpa punya doū bhrama lāga.* Interpreted literally, as some commentators have done, it would mean 'Who frees a man from both virtue and sin'. But how can this be, for virtue is not a fault but an accomplishment? So the sense has been taken to mean that God removes all sins.
20. Brahmā, one of the three gods of the Hindu, trinity (the other two being Viṣṇu, the Preserver and Śiva, the Destroyer) is believed, according to Hinduism to be the Creator of all beings on earth. The analogy of the tree without branches or roots bears resemblance to the tree with roots above and branches growing below in the *Bhagavadgītā* chapter 15, verse 1. *ūrdhava mūlamadhah śākham śvattham pnahurvyayam* ('The bunyan tree with roots above and branches growing below)
21. The *pārasa* stone is a legendary stone which is attributed with the power of turning iron into gold when the iron is touched by it.
22. Making a pilgrimage eighty-eight times is considered to be very meritorious, and each time the pilgrim bathes in a holy river like the Gangā or Yamunā.

23. The word 'Murārī in the text is another name for Krishna (*muralī*'a pipe' or 'flute'). Krishna is usually shown as piping, hence the name.
bhavasāgara (*bhū-* 'the world', *sāgara-* 'the sea') thus the word stands for the sea of worldly existence. Crossing it implies being emancipated (getting *mokṣa*) when the soul becomes one with God and has no more rebirth in a body.
24. The sacred fires are the *pancāgnis* five fires known as 1. *anvāhārya*, 2. *garhapatya*, 3. *āhavanīya*, 4. *avastha*, and 5. *samya* According to another rite fires are burnt all round while one sits in the sun. It is a form of austerity (*tapa*).
25. The two letters *rā* and *mā* form '*Rāmā*'. The idea is that one should understand the true significance of Rāma, who according to Kabīr, means the One Formless Absolute (*Brahman*).
26. The idea expressed here by Kabīr resembles the teaching of Lord Krishna in the *Gītā*:
viṣayā vinivartante nirāhārā asya dehinaḥ
rasa-verjam raso 'pyasya paraṁ dṛṣṭvā nivartate
yatata by api kaunteya puruṣasya vipaścitaty
indriyāṇi pramāthīni haranti prasabhaṁ manaḥ
('Though the objects of the senses turn away from the soul of one who does not dwell upon them, the longing remains. But even this vanishes when he has seen the Supreme. However much a discerning man may strive to restrain his senses, O Arjuna, they are so impetuous that they will for certain carry away his mind by force').
Bhagavadgītā, chapter 2, vv.59-60.
27. The verse is autobiographical, as Kabīr, even though living in Kashi (Varanasi) for some time was mostly associated with Magahara. See Introduction.
28. The words in the text *devara* (brother-in-law) and *sasura* (father-in-law) are respectively symbolic of *pravṛtti* (action or attachment to worldly objects) and *nivṛthi* (withdrawal from the world, or detachment).
29. Jagannātha is Lord Viṣṇu. His idol at Puri in Orissa is given the name Jagannātha. See note to *Ramainīs*, verse 6.
30. Ajāmila was a brahmin of Kanauj who married a slave. Gaṇikā was a prostitute who had tamed a parrot. At the time of her death the parrot, who had been trained to say 'Rāma', took Rāma's name. So Gaṇikā was redeemed. All these persons were of bad karmas, but by chanting Rāma's name they got salvation.

31. The three sorrows are those given by one's own self, by other creatures and the third given by the gods or divine agency. See note to *Ramainī* verse 8.
32. The three *guṇas* are 1. The *sattva guṇa* implying purity. 2. The *rājasa guṇa* which stands for passion or activity and 3. The *tāmasa guṇa* which implies sloth or laziness, i.e., inactivity (*guṇa*-quality). According to the Sāṁkhya philosophy these *guṇas* are present in varying proportions in every being and the preponderance of a particular *guṇa* determines the nature of the individual.
33. *Brahman* is the formless Cosmic Absolute. When Kabīr refers to Rāma, he really means the formless *Brahman*.
34. *rozā* is the fast during the day which Moslems keep in the month of Ramzān during which the Moslems believe the Holy Quaran was revealed by Allah to Prophet Mohammed.
35. *namāz* is the prayers Moslems offer with their face toward Mecca, five times a day,
36. *haj* is the pilgrimage to Mecca every Moslem must make at least once in his lifetime. Kabīr clearly tell us in this verse that he does not go on the *haj* pilgrimage (*nā haja jāūṁ*), yet some commentators say he went. Here we have it from the horse's mouth. What further proof is needed that he didn't?
37. The royal swan (*rājahaṁsa*) is believed to be a mythical swan living in the Mansarovara lake in the Himalaya mountains. According to tradition it eats only pearls. The '*haṁsa*' also often stands for the soul, but here the former sense more appropriately suits the context.
38. *mokṣa* is emancipation when the soul is one with *Brahman* and there is no more rebirth for it.
39. The five breaths are, *prāṇa, apāna*, *samāna*, *udāna* and *vyāna*. Life is dependent on *prāṇa* which moves from the nose down to the chest. The other breaths have various other functions mentioned in the *Yoga-sutras* of Pātanjali (chapter 4. *sūtra* 38).
40. The verse is an *ulāhanā* ('taunt') to God, a device often used in Hindi devotional poetry.
41. The five elements are earth, water fire, the sky and ether.
42. The word *dulamula* in the text is rather vague. However it has been interpreted as a 'ripe or overripe' fruit.

Here again we see a departure from the belief of Rāma being the formless *Brahman* which critics attribute to Kabīr. The various names-Narahari, Banawārī, Mādhava and Madhusūdana are of Krishna, an avatar of Viṣṇu. Thus Kabīr's monism is not irrefutable.

43. The words *sūvā* (literally 'parrot') and *minīm-billī*, i.e., a 'cat') stand respectively for 'man' and 'death'. As the cat is ready to pounce on the parrot and eat it up, so too death is ready to carry the man away.

44. Sanaka—The four mind-born sons of Brahmā, the Creator. Sanananda was also one of them. Shukadeva was the son of Krishna Dwaiparya and the writer of the *Bhāgavata* and the *Purāṇas*.
The uncrossable ocean implies the sea of wordly existence which is crossed by achieving *mokṣa* (emancipation), i.e., being one with God.

45. We see again here the uncertainty hovering in Kabīr's mind about the nature of God. Here he sings of Viṣṇu (or Hari) in unmistakable terms, showing his positive adoration of a God having form. In fact Kabīr keeps veering bitween monism and dualism. And though a Moslem by birth, his inclination was mostly towards Hinduism.

46. Nārada was one of the seven great *ṛṣīs*. He is shown playing on the *vīṇā* (lute). He was also the writer of *Nāradīya-dharma-śāstra*. In some respects he resembles Orpheus and is known as the *rāja-ṛṣi* (royal sage).

47. It is traditionally believed the *bhriṅgī* (a kind of maggot) brings a worm to its nest. By merely being there the worm comes to imagine that it too is a *bhriṅgī*, and this belief becoms so strong that it actually turns from a worm to a *bhriṅgī*!

48. The verse is metaphorical. The wife or spouse stands for the body, the *jīva* (embodied soul) is the thug or cheat, which inhabits this body formed of the five elements—fire, water, earth, the sky and ether.

49. *kheta* (field) and *mṛga* ('deer') are not to be taken in their literal seen. The 'field' cannotes existence or life and the 'deer' the evils, chiefly craving, passion and anger.

50. Dr Mataprasada Gupta. *Kabīr Granthāvalī* Allahabad: Sahitya Bhavan 1985, p.380, interprets *saca* ('true') in the text as *sukha* meaning happiness, but this seems unecessary and in fact not appropriate to the context. So the word is taken to mean 'true'. Obviously dreams do not prove to be true or real on waking.

51. Rāvaṇa was the ten-headed powerful king to Lankā. He carried off Sītā, Rāma's wife. So Rāma defeated and killed him in a prolonged war, and gave his kingdom to his brother, Vibhiṣana. The story is told in the *Rāmāyaṇa*.

FROM THE GURU GRANTHA SAHIB

astuti nindā doū bibarajita
tajahi māna abhimānā
lohā kancana sami kari jānahi
te mūrati bhagavānā

KABĪR

PADAS FROM THE GURU GRANTHA SAHIB

1

usatati nindā doū bibarajita tajahu mānu abhimānā
lohā kancana sama kari jānahi, te mūrati bhagavānā
terā janu eka adhu koī
kāmu krodu lobhu mohu bibarajita, hari padu cīnhai soī
raja guṇa tama guṇa sata guṇa kahiai, eha terī sabha māiyā
cauthe pada kau jo naru cinhai, tina hī parama padu pāiyā
tīratha barata nema suci sanjama, sadā rahai nihakāmā
trisanā aru māiyā bhamu cūkā, citavata ātama rāmā
jiha mandira dīpaku paragāsiā andhakāru taha nāsā
nirabhau pūri rahe bhrama bhāgā, kahi kabīra jana dāsā

(rāga kedārā)

THE FORMLESS RĀMA (1)

The man who is indifferent to both praise and blame
Who is free from vanity and arrogance,
To whom iron and gold are the same
He is the very image of God.

He who is free from anger and desire
In whom there's no attachment or greed
That man, who's rare in this world, can aspire
Lord, to be your devotee indeed.

The three *guṇas* are your maya;
Only he who goes beyond them
Knows the Fourth:[1]
Only he achieves *mokṣa*.

The Formless Rāma cannot be known by fasts or pilgrimages
Nor by sacred rites, austerities and the like
Only he knows who has escaped maya's net
And has no craving for sensual delights.

Only from him in whom the lamp of wisdom shines
The blinding darkness of ignorance can flee,
Says Kabīra, 'I am the slave of the Lord Divine,
Now doubt and fear can no more vex me'.

2

kiyā japu kiyā tapu kiyā brata pūjā
jākai ridai bhāu hai dūjā
re jana manu mādhava siu lāīai
caturāī na caturabhuju pāīai
paraharu lobhu aru lokācāru
paraharu kāmu krodhu ahankāru
karama karata badhe ahammeva
mili pāthara kī karahi seva
kahū kabīra bhagati kari pāiyā
bhole bhāi mile raghurāiyā

(rāga gaurī)

THE FORMLESS RĀMA (2)

Worship, prayer
And austerities are of no use
If duality is there.
Let Mādhava be your refuge,[2]
Duplicity will take you nowhere.

Forsake
The world and its ways,
Vanity, desire and
Rage.

Deceived
By arrogance you are undone
And venerate a stone; says Kabīr,
Only humility will reveal
The Formless One.

3

upajai nipajai nipaji samāī
nainaha dekhata ihu jagu jāī

lāja na marahu kahahu gharu merā
anta kī bāra nahī kachu terā
anita jatana kari kāiā pālī
maratī bāra agani saṅgi jālī
coā candanu maradana aṅgā
so tanu jalai kāṭha kai saṅgā
kahu kabīra sunahu re gunīā
binasaigo rūpa dekhai sabha dunīā

(*rāga gauṛī*)

THE SOUL IS BRAHMAN

From *Brahma* this soul comes
And after being embodied
In various bodies
Returns to *Brahma.*[3]

Thus this world dissolves
Before one's very eyes
Aren't you ashamed
To call it yours?
When you die
Nothing will remain yours here.
You never tired
Of pampering your body in many ways
When you knew well that some day
It will be burnt on the funeral pyre.

That body of yours which you perfumed
With many scented pastes
Will soon be consumed
By blazing faggots.
O discerning one
Says Kabīr think what will become
Of your body when you're dead and gone;
While all the world looks on.

4

nā mai joga dhiānu citu lāiā
binu bairāga na chūṭasi māiā

kaise jīvanu hai hamārā
jaba na hai rāma nāma adhārā

kahu kabīra khojau asamāna
rāma samāna na dekhau āna

(*rāga gaurī*)

MERCIFUL RĀMA

I do not practise yoga
Or meditation,
Maya can't go
Except by renunciation.

Only Rāma's name
Is my support;
Without it life is vain.

Says Kabīr, I have searched
Both heaven and earth,
But found no one
As merciful as Rāma.

5

bāraha barasa bālapana bīte
bīsa barasa kachu tapu na kīo
tīsa barasa kachu deva na pūjā
phiri pachutānā biradi bhaio
merī merī karate janamu gaio
sāira sokhi bhunja balaio

sūke sarabari pāli bandhāvai
lūṇe kheti hatha vāri karai
āio coru turantaha le gaio
merī rākhata mugudha phirai
carana sīsu kara kampana lāgai
nainī nīru asāra bahai
jihavā bacanu sudhu nahī nikasai
taba re dharama kī āsa karai
hari jīu karipā karailiva lāvai
lāhā hari hari nāma lio

gura parasādī hari dhanu pāio
ante cala diā nāli calio
kahata kabīra sunahu re santahu
anu dhanu cachuai lai na gaio
āī talaba gopālarāi kī maiā
mandara choḍi calio

(rāga āsā)

WASTED LIFE

You spent twelve years in boyish play
For twenty kept away
From all austerities:
For thirty you did not pray
To any gods; now in old age
Remorse is all that's left to you.

Saying 'mine, mine' you spent
all your life,
And now the serpent death comes
With its poison-bite:
Fool you were, like one
Who raises a mud-fence
As though to protect
A field that's waterless!
Or like one who tends
His crop
After it's harvested!

O idiot! 'mine, mine' you keep repeating
Till Death comes suddenly
Robbing you of your life;
Your head, hands and feet shake;
Tears flow endlessly;
Your tongue falters, you can hardly speak;
Then, ah! too late;
You turn to God.

'Tis only by Hari's grace
You can obtain his love.
By my guru's kindness I could get

The gift of devotion and now
I can cheerfully face death.
Says Kabīr, everything remains here,
Wealth and all:
When God gives the call
You will have to go.

6

bahu parapanca kari paradhanu liāvai
suta dārā pahi āni luṭvai
mana mere bhūle kapaṭu na kījai
anti niberā tere jīa pahi lījai

chinu chinu tanu chīlai jarā banāvai
taba terī oka koī panīo na pāvai
kahatu kabīru koi nahī terā
hiradai rāmu kī na japahi saverā

(rāga soraṭhi)

ILL-GOTTEN WEALTH

By practising a thousand wiles
You deprived others of their wealth
For the sake of your son and wife;
Mistake not, you'll have to repay
This ill-gotten pelf

Each moment you grow week with age
You can no longer cup your hands
To give water to a thirsty man.

No one is yours here, says Kabīr,
So chant Rāma's name without delay.

7

jo janu bhāu bhagati kachu jānai
takau acaraju kāho
jiu jalu jala mahi paisi na nikasai
tiu ḍhuri milio julāho
hari ke logā mai tau mati kā bhorā

jau tanu kāsī tajahi kabīrā
ramaīai kahā nihorā

kahata kabīra sanahu re loī
bharami na bhūlahu koī
kiā kāsī kiā ūkharu magaharu
rāmu ridai jau hoī

(rāga dhanāśrī)

KASHI AND MAGAHAR

For one who has true devotion
Death is no deceiver,
As water with water is one,
So Kabīr, the weaver,
Has become one with *Brahma*.

Listen, O lovers of Hari,
I am a man of little understanding
But I ask you,
If Kashi can by itself confer *mokṣa*
To those who die there
What credit is it to Rāma?

Says Kabīr, O people, give heed,
Do not be deceived
If one has love of Rāma in his heart
What difference does it make
Whether he dies in Magahara or Kashi?[4]

8

dina te pahara te gharauāṁ
āva ghaṭai tana chijai
kālu aherī phirai badhika jiu
kahu kavana bidhi kījai
so binu āvana lāgā
māta pitā bhāī suta banitā
kahahu koū hai kā kā

jaba lagu joti kāiā mahi baratai
āpā pasū na būjhai

lālaca karai jīvana pada kārana
locana kachū na sūjhai

kahata kabīra sunahu re prānī
choḍau mana ke bharamā
kevala namu japahu re prānī
parahu eka kī saranāṁ

(rāga dhanāśrī)

EPHERMERAL LIFE

From a day to a *pahara*
From a *pahara* to a *gharī,*[5]
The years of life
Diminish steadily,
And the body becomes weak.

Death, like a huntsman,
Ever lies in wait,
Now it's very near
And there's no escape.

Parents, son, brother, wife,
None is yours,
Neither man nor beast
Know the soul;
To preserve life
Is their only goal:
Beyond that they cannot see.

Says Kabīr, quit deceit,
Chant the holy name
And seek your refuge in *Brahma*

9

sarīra sarocara bhītare āchai kamala anūpa
parama joti purakhotamo jā kai rekha na rūpa
re mana hari bhaju bhrama tajahu jagajīvana rāma

āvata kachū na dīsaī naha dīsai jāta
jaha upajai binasai nahīṁ jaise purivana pāta

mithiā kari māiā tajī sukha sahaja bīcāri
kahi kabīra sevā karahu mana māṁjhu murāri

(***rāga bilāvalu***)

THE LORD WITHIN

The thousand-petalled lotus
Within you
Is the abode
Of the Eternal Being
Who has no shape or form.

Therefore, O mind,
Drive out delusion
And chant the name of Hari and Rāma,

There is no coming or going;
As a lotus leaf renewing,
This world arises
And is destroyed.

Says Kabīr, I could happily meditate
On the Absolute
And remove maya's veil.
O brother, dive deep into your mind
And serve Krishna, the Lord Divine.[6]

10

mātā jūṭha pitā bhī juṭhā jūṭhā hī phala lāge
āvahi jūṭhe jāhi bhī jūṭhe jūṭhe marahi abhāge
kahu pundita sūcā kavanu ṭhāu
jahā baisi hau bhojanu khāu

jihabā jūṭhā bolata jūṭhā
karana netra sabha jūṭhe
indrau kī jūṭhi utarasi nāhī
brahama agani ke lūṭhe
agani bhī jūṭhī pānī jūṭhā
jūṭhi baisi pakāiyā
jūṭhī karachī parosana lāgā
jūṭhe hī baiṭhi khāiā

gobaru jūṭhā caukā jūṭhā jūṭhī dīnī kārā
kahi kabīra teī nara sūce sācī parī bicārā

(rāga basanta (hinḍola))

THIS IMPURE EXISTENCE

All are self-centred
Father and mother,
Those to whom they give birth
Those who come in the world
And those who go—
All these hapless beings that live and die.

O pundit, say,
Where is that place
Pure enough for me to sit
And have my meals?

The tongue speaks falsehoods
The ears hear them,
Even though all evils are burnt
In the fire,
The mind still returns
To impure thoughts.

Fire is impure and water too,
Impure the way one sits to cook
The cooking-place and the cow-dung
With which it's plastered;[7]
The ladle with which the food is served
And the people who eat.

Only he is pure, says Kabīr
Who has realized
The impurity of all of these.

PADAS FROM THE GURU GRANTHA SAHIB

NOTES

1. The Fourth state is known as the *turīya* in Vedānta. It is beyond the three states of waking, drcam and dreamless sleep, the state which includes all the other three. It is that which is ever awake and is therefore known as the Eternal Witness. Kabīr is here alluding to this Vedānta view of Gauḍapāda in his (Gauḍapāda's) *Kārikā* on the *Maṇḍukopaniṣad*.
2. Here we notice again the contrariness in Kabīr's thinking. he condemns duality and worship of idols, yet speaks of taking refuge in Mādhava (Krishna)!
3. *Brahma—Brahman* (the Formless Cosmic Absolute) which Kabīr often calls 'Ātmārāma'.
4. The verse is autobiographical. Dying in Kashi meant for those with blind faith, getting *mokṣa*. Kabīr belonged to Magahar and most probably died there. So he ridicules the idea of death in Kashi conferring *mokṣa*. See introduction-section on Kabīr's life.
5. A *pahara* is a period of time of three hours, while a *gharī* is twenty-four minutes.
6. For *sahaja* see introduction. It means generally that by which one can leave worldly pleasures and turn to God. We see here again Kabīr's wavering attitude between the Absolute (*Brahman*) and the God with form. 'Murarī' which occurs in the text is another name for Krishna. Kabīr frequently asserts that he does not believe in avatars, but then who else is Krishna except the avatar of Viṣṇu?
7. Hindus plaster the places which they wish to be clean or consider sacred, with the dung of cows. The cow is worshipped because of its association with Krishna. Many villagers use cow-dung or mud for plastering their houses. The verse is rather peculiar inasmuch as it is not quite evident what Kabīr means by *jūṭhā* (lit,. 'leftovers of food'). Some critics feel Kabīr implies impurity to these because they have existed from times of yore. But more appropriately it seems to mean the ephemerality of them all.

THE *SĀKHĪS*

hari jī yahai bicāriyā
sāṣī kahau kabīra
bhausāgara meṁ jīva haiṁ
je koi pakṙai tīra

('Harī commanded Kabīr
To compose *Sākhīs*,
So that the Souls
Trapped in the sea of births and deaths
May find the shore'.)

(1) REMEMBERING RĀMA

1

kabīra nirabhai rāma japu
jaba lagi dīvai bāti
tela ghaṭai bātī bujhai
taba sovaigā dina rāti

CHANT RĀMA'S NAME WHILE THERE'S TIME

Says Kabīr, chant Rāma's name without fear,
For when you become weak with age
And death's near,
'Twill be too late:
As when the oil in the lamp grows less
The wick flickers and fades away.

2

kabīra kahai maiṁ kathi gayā
kathi gaye brahma mahesa
rāma nāma tatasāra hai
saba kāhū upadesa

RĀMA'S NAME IS THE ONLY TRUTH

Says Kabīr Brahmā and Shiva[1]
Have taught everyone
Without distinction
That Rāma's name
Is the only truth
And I too say the same

3

jihi ghaṭi prīti na prema rasa
phuni rasanā nahiṁ rāma
te nara isa sansāra meṁ
upaji ṣaye bekāma

PURPOSELESS LIVING

The lives of those who are not immersed
In the love of Rāma,
Are futile and purposeless,
'Twas better they were not born.

4

kabīra prema na cāṣiyā
caṣi na līyā sāva
sūne ghara kā pahunāṁ
jyūṁ āyā tyūṁ jāva

THE NECTAR OF RĀMA'S NAME

He who has not tasted the nectar of Rāma's name,
Nor enjoyed its sweetness,
Is like a guest in an empty house
Who stays and goes away unattended.

5

pahilai burā kamāi kari
bāṁdhī viṣa kī poṭa
koṭi karama phili palaka maiṁ,
āyā hari kī oṭa

GOD FORGIVES ALL SINS

You carry on your head
The bundle of countless sins committed
In your previous lives;[2]
But if you seek Rāma's shelter
He'll kick away
That bundle in a trice.

6

lambā māraga dūri ghara,
bikaṭa pantha bahu māra
kahau santau kyoṁ pāie,
durlabha hari dīdāra

THE PATH OF DEVOTION IS HARD

As a wayfarer
Whose home is far away
And the rugged road
He has to take
Is full of marauding highwaymen:
So too is the way
Of Hari-devotion:
O sages, say,
How then can one
Have a sight of the Lord?

7

kabīra kaṭhināī kharī
sumiratāṁ hari nāma
sūlī ūpari naṭa vidyā
girai ta nāhīṁ ṭhāma

UNSWERVING DEVOTION

Says Kabīr, chanting Rāma's name
With unwavering faith
Is a task as arduous
As an acrobat's
Balancing himself
On a spear's blade,
One way this or that
And he falls
To his death.
So will be the fate
Of the devotee,
Should he deviate
Even a moment
From his quest.

8

kabīra rāma rijhāi lai
mukhi amṛta guṇa gāi
phūṭā naga jyoṁ joṛi mana
sandhihi sandhi milāi

BE ONE WITH RĀMA

Delight in Rāma's name
And sing his nectar-like praises.
As a split gem made whole again[3]
By skilfully joining the pieces each to each
So that it looks again like a perfect gem;
So become one with Rāma, says Kabir.

(2) SEPARATION

1

bāsuri sukha nāṁ raini sukha,
nā sukha supinai māṁha
kabīra bichuṙe rāma sauṁ
nau sukha dhūpa na chāṁha

NO BLISS WITHOUT RĀMA

Without Rāma
There's no happiness
Night or day;
Not even in a dream.

If Rāma is not with me,
Says Kabīr,
shade or sun.
Alike miserable seem.

2

mūvāṁ pīchaiṁ jini milai,
kahai kabīrā rāma
pāthara ghaṭā loha saba
pārasa kaune kāma

SEEING RĀMA IN LIFE ITSELF

What use Rāma
Coming to me
When I'm no more?

If iron becomes stone
How can *pārasa*[4]
Turn it to gold?

3

kabīra pīra pirāvanī
panjara pīra na jāi
eka ju pīra pirīta kī
rahī kaleje chāi

SWEET PAIN

All pain is torment
Says Kabīr.

But love's dart
That strikes the heart
Is both painful
And sweet.

4

saba raga tanta rabāba tana,
biraha bajāvai nitta
aura na koī suni sakai,
kai sāīṁ kai citta

THE SOUL'S LONGING FOR GOD

As the tune issuing from a *rabāba*[5]
Can be heard only by the listener
Or by the player who plays it;

So the anguish
Of the Soul parted from God
Can be known only to God himself
Or to the Soul that feels it.

5

nainā nījhara lāiyā.
rahaṭa bahai nisa ghāma
papihā jyauṁ piu piu karauṁ
kabare milahuge rāma

WHEN WILL YOU COME, RĀMA?

As a waterfall
My eyes shed tears continually.
Arising from the heart
And crowding in the eyes
They ever drop

As water pouring from the buckets
Of a Persian wheel.[6]

As the cuckoo calls
Plaintively 'pī ! pī !'
I pine for you, O Rāma,
When will you come to me?

6

jau roūṁ tau bala ghaṭai,
haṁsauṁ tau rāma risāi
manahi māṁhi bisūraṇāṁ,
jyuṁ ghuna kāṭhahīṁ khāi

WEEPING FOR RĀMA

If I weep
Sorrow will make me weak,
And if I make merry
And seek
Worldly pleasures,
Rāma will be displeased
Seeing that I treasure
What I should have abjured.

My hidden sorrow
Keep gnawing my heart
All the while,
As a woodworm eating
The wood inside.

7

biraha jalāi maiṁ jalauṁ
jalatī jalahari jāūṁ
mo dekhā jalahari jalai
santauṁ kahāṁ bujhāuṁ

PARTING'S FIRE

Burning with the fire of parting
I went to the lake to assuage it

But the lake caught fire too!
Tell me then, O sages,
Where can it be cooled?

8

rainā dūra bichohiyā
rahu re sankha ma jhūri
devali devali dāharī
desī ūge sūri

GOD AND THE SOUL

O conch,
In the night
The tide
Carries you away;
But do not despair,
As soon as it is day
The waves will cast you again
On the seashore
And your sound
Will resound in temples
Evermore.

Even so, O Soul,
When you emerge from the darkness of ignorance
You will turn to the divine,
And find
Your salvation in the Lord.

(3) WISDOM

1

āgi ju lāgī nīra mahiṁ
kāndau jariyā jhāro
itara dakhina ke paṇḍitā
mue bicāri bicāri

STRANGE FIRE

Ah! how strange,
The water of the lake is aflame,
But the greater surprise
Is that instead
Of the water, what burns
Is the mud in its bed!

Likewise
When the flames of wisdom arise
In a man who has gone astray,
It is the evil deep inside
That they burn away.
Pundits from everywhere
Kept turning the pages of their books
But they could not find there
Any solution to this mystery.

2

aherī dou lāiyā
miraga pukāre roi
jā bana meṁ krīlā karī
dājhata hai bana soi

WORLDLY PLEASURES

The huntsman has set the wood ablaze
To drive out the deer
So that they could be an easy prey;
But the deer are disconsolate
To leave the spot where they frolicked and played.

So too when worldly pleasures
Are snatched away
The heart is loath to leave them:
But when peace descends
On the passionless soul
It rejoices that the worldly wilderness
Is no more.

(4) INSIGHT

1

kautuka dīṭhā deha bina
ravi sasi binā ujāsa
sāhiba sevā māṁhi hai,
beparavāṁhī dāsa

THE FORMLESS (I)

How strange
He is seen
Yet remains
Formless!

That wonderful light
Is neither the moon's nor the sun's;
They derive
Their own light from that One.[7]

Serve the guru
He will bring you peace
And all your worldly cares
Will cease.

2

agama agocara gami nahīṁ
gahāṁ jagamagai joti
tahāṁ kabīrā bandagī
pāpa punni nahīṁ choti

THE FORMLESS (II)

Says Kabīr, I humbly bow
To what the mind can't reach
Nor the senses feel.

That Light divine
Of the Absolute[8]
Beyond bad and good,
I salute

3

antari kaṁvala prakāsiyā
brahma vāsa tahaṁ hoi
mana bhaṁvarā tahaṁ lubadhiā
jānaigā jana koi

THE FORMLESS (III)

The lotus-shaped space
Within the body
Is *Brahman's* abode

There the mind sports
Like a bumblebee
Eager to taste
Its nectar

Only some rare
Devotee
Can know
This mystery[9]

4

sāyara nāhīṁ sīpa nahiṁ
svāti būṁd bhī nāhiṁ
kabīra motī nīpajai
sunni sikhara gaṛha māṁhi

THE *SAHASTRĀRA*

There is no sea here
Nor the *svāti* raindrop
Nor an oyster
In which it falls
To make a pearl.[10]

Yet when the *kuṇḍalinī*[11]
Reaches the *sahastrāra*[12]
It is lit up
By a light that's seen
Neither in the heavens
Nor on the earth.

5

ṁana lāgā unmanna sauṁ
gagana pahūṁcā jāi
cāṁda bihūṁ cāndinā
alakha niranjana rāi

BEYOND THE *GUṆAS*

My mind no longer hassles
It has become one with Rāma
It has arrived
At the *sahastrāra*[13]

The moon does not shine there
Yet the light
Is as cool as the moon's

I have found the Formless I seek,
Beyond the *guṇas*,[14]
Where the senses cannot reach.

6

pānī hī taiṁ hima bhayā
hima hvai gayā bilāi
jo kachu thā soī bhayā,
aba kachu kahā na jāi

BRAHMAN AND THE SOUL

When ice melts it is
Limpid water, no longer ice.
So too the reflection of the Infinite
On the mind-stuff—the embodied soul[15]
Returns to the Infinite again
And the Whole is again the Whole.

What can one say when there's no change
What was still is, and will ever be the same.

7

pankhi uṙānī gagana kaum̐
piṇḍa rahā paradesa
pānī pīyā cancu binu
bhūli gayā yahu desa

THE SOUL'S BLISS

As a bird soars to the sky
On its wings,
The soul rises to the *sahastrāra*
Borne on the *kuṇḍalinī*,[16]
Tasting the bliss of *Brahman* there.

The body remains where it was,
But what was its home
Is now a land unknown,
For the soul no longer seeks
The pleasures of the world
Nor does it need
The senses to savour *Brahman's* endless bliss.

8

pankhi uṙām̐nī gagana kaum̐
uṙo caṙho asamāna
jihi sara manḍala bhediā
so sara lāgā kāna

THE *ANĀHATA* SOUND

The soul-shaped swan
Soaring on the wing-shaped *kuṇḍalinī*[17]
Reached the *sahastrāra*.

The *anāhata*-shaped dart[18]
From the heavens around
Made the ear its mark
And it heard the sound.

9

jaba maiṁ thā taba hari nahīṁ
aba hari haiṁ maiṁ nāhiṁ
prema galī ati sāṁkarī
yā meṁ do na samāṁhi

ABANDON DUALITY

God is not attained
Till the ego remains.
Though love is born between
God and the devotee,
Love is not love
Till there is duality

For lover and beloved
Are one and the same;
Two can't go abreast
In love's lane.

10

devala māṁhe dehurī
tila jetā bistāra
māṁhe pātī māṁhi jala
māṁhai pūjanahāra

THE WORSHIPPER AND GOD

In the body-shaped temple
With a finely curtained door
There is no need
To make offerings
Of water or leaves.

For the offerings and the worshipper
Are both within:
It is the mind
Which should be with God.

11

jākāse mukhi auṁdhā kuāṁ
pātāle panihāri
tākā jala koī hansā pīvai
biralā ādi bicāri

THE *KUṆḌALINI'S* PASSAGE

As a well upside-down
Opening above
While the woman who draws water
Is below:

So is this *tāntrik* yoga
In which the woman-shaped *kuṇḍalinī*
At the rock-bottom *mulādhāra*
Rises up through the *suṣumnā*
To the well-opening-shaped *sahastrāra*[19]

Where the pure soul
Dwelling in the *śūnya*
Can savour its nectar-like bliss.
Only some rare man
Can know this.[20]

(5) ON THE MIND

1

mana ke mate na cāliye
chāṁri jīva kī bāni
tākū kare sūta jyoṁ
unlaṭi anpūṭhā jāni

TAME THE MIND

O soul, do not heed
The promptings of the mind
To revel in sense-pleasures.

As a weaver unwinds
The twisted thread from the spindle
To wind it round the bobbin;
So turn back the mind
From worldly enjoyments
To the Divine.

2

kabīra serī sāṁkarī
cancala manuvā cora
guna gāvai laulīna hoi
kachu ika mana meṁ aura

MIND, THE THIEF

The path to God is narrow, says Kabīr,
And the mind restless;
It goes along it as a dissembling thief,
Never at one place;
Outwardly singing
The Lord's praises,
Inwardly clinging
To worldly pleasures:
Whom does it deceive
But itself?

3

mana jānai saba bāta
jānata hī auguna karai
kāhe ko kusalāta
kara dīpaka kūṁvaī paṙai

THE MIND SINS KNOWINGLY

The mind knows
What is good or bad
Yet it goes
The evil way.

If a man has a lamp
Yet falls in a well
Of such a man[21]
What can one say?

4

hiradā bhītari ārasī
mukha dekhā nahiṁ jāi
mukha tau tabahi dekhiye
mana kī duvidhā jāi

THE SOUL'S MIRROR

The soul is reflected
In the mirror of the heart
Only when the mind is at rest,
Dispassionate and pure.

5

kāgada kerī nāṁva rī
pānī kerī ganga
kahai kabīra kaise tirūṁ
panca kusangī saṅga

THE UNCROSSABLE SEA

For one thing it's a paper-boat
Quite unfit,

Then there are five rogues
Ready to rock it:
How can one cross
The flooded river?

So too is afloat
On the uncrossable sea[22]
This body fashioned
Of the five elements:[23]
And the five foes—
Desire, rage, delusion
Vanity and greed,
Which are lying in wait to drown it:
How can it get across then,
Says Kabīr?

6

karatā thā tau kyauṁ rahā
aba kari kyūṁ pachatāi
bovai peṙa babūla kā
āma kahāṁ taiṁ khāi

THE CONSEQUENCE OF EVIL DEEDS

When you did evil deeds
Weren't you aware
That you were doing evil?
What's the good of repenting now?

If you sow *babūla* seeds[24]
Can the tree yield
Mangoes?
You will reap
Only
What you sowed.

7

manā manoratha chāṙi de
terā kiyā na hoi
panī maiṁ ghī nikasai
tau rūkhā khāi na koī

VAIN WISHES

O mind,
Do not expect too much;
You can't get
All that you expect,
And some wishes are such
That they can never be;
For if ghee could be got
By churning water
No one would have to eat
Dry bread without ghee.[25]

(6) THE WAY TO GOD

1

kauna desa kaṁha āiyā
jānai koī nāṁhi
ohu māraga pāvai nahīṁ
bhūli pare ehi māṁhi

THE SOUL'S HEAVENLY HOME

Leaving its heavenly home
The embodied soul roams
The world,
Deceived into thinking
'My real home
Is this earth'.

It forgets
The subtle path by which it came
So that it cannot return to *Brahma*
Again.[26]

2

utataiṁ koi na āvaī
āsauṁ būjhaiṁ dhāi
itate saba koi jāta hai,
bhāra ladāi ladāi

THE MYSTERY OF THE OTHER WORLD

What the other world's like
No one knows,
For none ever returns
To tell.
But from here
Everyone goes
When he is dead,
Carrying with him the load
Of his karmas.[27]

3

sabakauṁ būjhata maiṁ phirauṁ
rahani kahai nahiṁ koya
prīti na joṛai rāma sauṁ
rahani kahāṁ tai hoya

THE PART AND THE WHOLE

To live in this world
Without knowing the Self
And That of which it is a part,
Is a life purposeless.

I ask and ask
Again and yet again,
'What is the bond that binds
The Soul to God?'—
But all in vain.

It is only by love
The Soul can be one
With That from which it has come
The Lord above

4

kabīra māraga kaṭhina hai
koī sakai nahiṁ jāī
gae te bahure nahīṁ
kusala kahai ko āi

BRAHMAN'S BLISS

The path of devotion
Is hard to tread[28]
It is not for everyone,
And he who reaches
The Eternal *Brahma*
Does not return:
So of that bliss
Who
Can tell?[29]

5

prāna pinḍa kau taji calai,
muvā kahai saba koi
jīva achata jāṁmaiṁ marai
sūṣima lakhai na koī

DEATH-IN-LIFE

When the Soul leaves the body
Everyone says, 'he is no more';
This physical death is known to everybody,
But no one knows
That death-in-life
Which comes even when one is alive
If evils such as delusion and desire
Tarnish the Soul.

(7) MAYA

1

māyā muī na mana muvā
mari mari gayā sarīra
āsā tṛṣṇāṁ nāṁ mui
yauṁ kahai dāsa kabīra

MAYA'S BOND

Men die and are reborn
And so the cycle of births and deaths
Keeps going on and on.

But maya makes the bond
Of wordliness
And craving so strong
That to escape it
Is like gathering grapes from thoms.

2

kabīra so dhana saṅcie,
jo āge ko hoi
sīsa caṛhāe poṭalī
le jāta na dekhā koi

REAL WEALTH

Gather the wealth
Of good deeds
Which will stand you in good stead,
And plead
For you in the other world.

I have never seen, says Kabīr,
Anyone carry on his head
His bundle of riches
When he is dead!

3

kabīra māyā pāpinī,
phanda le baiṭhī hāṭi
saba jaga tau phande parā
gayā kabīrā kāṭi

SINFUL MAYA

This maya, Kabīr says,
Which makes people sin,
Has spread her net
In the world,
As a cheat keeping shop
In the marketplace:

Everyone was caught in it
Only I could escape.[30]

4

kabīra māyā mohinī,
jaisī mīṭhī khāṁra
satagura kī kirapā bhaī,
nahiṁ tau karatī bhāṁra

MAYA'S SNARE

Says Kabīr, maya tastes
Sweet as jaggery
And so it makes
Everyone its prey:
It was only the guru's grace
That could save me.

5

kabīra māyā mohinī
mohe jāṁna sujāṁna
bhāgehū chūṭai nahīṁ,
bhari-bhari mārai bāṁna

MAYA'S ARROWS

Says Kabīr, maya captivates
Even the wisest of men.
They can't escape
For it sends
Bewitching arrow-like glances
After them
By which they're helplessly enslaved.

6

kabīrā māyā ḍākinī
saba kāhū kauṁ khāi
dāṁta uparūṁ pāpinī
je santoṁ niyare jāi

MAYA, THE DEMONESS

Maya is a demoness, says Kabīr,
Who tears everyone to pieces
With her teeth:

But if she approaches
A saint, I'll pull them out
And make her toothless!

7

kabīra guṇa kī bādalī
tītarabānīṁ chāṁhi
bāhiri rahe te ūbare,
bhīṁge mandira māṁhi

MAYA'S ILLUSIVE SHADE

Say Kabīr, as are the *guṇas*
So is maya's chequered shade—
Like a partridge's plume;
And the man who stays
In it, as one who seeks
Protection from the rain
In some sheltered place,

And yet finds it strange
That he alone gets wet!
So is the man who falls
In maya's illusive net;
Immersed in worldliness
He can never reach God.

(8) THE REMOVAL OF ILLUSION

1

kājala kerī koṭharī
masi ke karma kapāṭa
paṁhani boī pirathamī
panḍita pārī bāṭa

WILY PUNDITS

The world is like a room
Dark as lampblack
And the karma-shaped doors
Are also black.
There are stone images
All around,
And on the ground
Stones are strewn
Thus by the worship of idols
The pundits have brought ruin.[31]

2

japa tapa dīsai thotharā
tīratha brata besāsa
sūvai saiṁvala seviyā
yauṁ jaga calā nirāsa

VAIN RITES

Fasts and austerities,
Pilgrimages, prayer,
And all such beliefs,
Get you nowhere:

It's like a parrot pecking
At a cotton-pod
Mistaking it for
A juicy fruit.

All these pious acts
Are a hoax,
They can never
Get you *mokṣa*.

(9) BEYOND DIFFERENCES

1

kabīra haradī pīarī
cūnā ūjala bhāi
rāma sanehī yūṁ milai,
donauṁ barana gaṁvāi

THE GODMAN

Turmeric is yellow
Lime white-hued
But when they mix
They're so no more.
So when the devotee
Finds the Infinite,
He's neither a man
Nor a god,
He's a godman—
Between the two.

2

kābā phira kāsī bhayā
rāmahi bhayā rahīma
moṭa cūna maidā bhayā
baiṭhi kabīrā jīma

HUMANITY IS ONE

When fanaticism is abandoned
Kaabaa and Kashi are alike,
Leave differences aside
And see humanity as one.

Broadmindedness
Is as bread made from fine flour,
Dogma like coarse bread:
For me the former,
Says Kabīr,
The other one, I'll not eat.

(10) THE NATURE OF GOD

1

rahai nirālā māṁḍ taiṁ
sakala māṁḍ tihi māṁhi
kabira sevai tāsa kauṁ
dūjā koī nāhiṁ

GOD AND THE UNIVERSE

The universe is in God,
Yet he's beyond it;
He is both inside it
And outside.[32]

(11) ON LIFE AND DEATH

1

kabīra mana mirataka bhayā
durabala bhayā sarīra
pāchai lāgai hari phirai,
kahata kabīra kabīra

GOD SEEKS HIS DEVOTEE

Says Kabīr, when my mind was dead
To all sensual desires,
And my body emaciated
Because of being parted
From Hari:
Then saying, 'Kabīr, Kabīr!'
Hari came seeking for me
Of himself!

2

ghara jārai ghara ūbarai,
ghara rākheṁ ghara jāi
eka acambhā dekhiā,
muā kāla kauṁ khāi

THE 'DEATH' OF DEATH

If you slay the sensual-pleasures
That besiege your house of flesh,
You will save it: but if you treasure
Those cravings, you'll destroy yourself.

Death gobbles up one who is dead,
But, ah me! what a strange surprise,
He in whom sense-desires have died
Though living, he slays Death itself![33]

3

kharī kasauṭī rāma kī
khoṭa ṭikai na koi
rāma kasauṭī so ṭikaiṁ
jo jīvata mirataka hoi

THE TOUCHSTONE OF RĀMA-DEVOTION

The touchstone of Rāma-devotion
Can never fail
To distinguish the spiritual man
From the sensual.

Only he can pass its test
Who has forsaken worldliness;
Only that man in whom
All cravings are dead.

4

roṙā hvai rahu bāṭa kā,
taji pāṣaṁḍa abhimāna
aisā je jana hvai rahai,
tāhi milai bhagavāna

HUMILITY

Be humble and lowly
Like gravel on a path,
Only those who shed arrogance

and hypocrisy
Can hope to reach God.

5

kabīra jo ūgyā so āṁthavai,
phūlyā so kumilāi
jo ciṇiyāṁ so ḍhaho paṛai,
jo āyā so jāi

ALL FOR A WhILE

That will surely fall which has gone up,
That which has blossomed must fade
The mighty mansions will be dust
And all beings who come must go some day.[34]

(12) LASCIVIOUSNESS

1

kabīra eka kanaka aru kāmani
doū agani kī jhāla
dekhem̐ hī tana prajalai,
parasyām̐ hvai paimāla

LUST AND GOLD

Wealth and woman
Are two flames
Don't ever look at them
Or you'll be scorched;
And if you even touch them
You'll be done for.[35]

2

kabīra nāri parāī āpaṇī
bhugatyā narakahi jāi
āgi āgi saba eka hai,
tāmaim̐ hātha na bāhi

WOMAN, THE HINDRANCE

Necking with your wife
Or another woman,
Both are like
Playing with fire.

And what's the difference
Between one fire and another?
Therefore, says Kabīr,
Keep away from women
Altogether.[36]

3

kabīra nārī kunḍa naraka kā,
biralā thambhai bāga

koi sadhū jana ūbarai,
saba jaga mūvā lāga

WOMAN, HELL'S CESSPOOL

Says Kabīr, a woman
Is hell's cesspool,
Hardly anyone
Can put the kibosh on her.

She's like a mare
Hard to bridle;
Maybe some rare sage
Can wriggle
Out of her clutches;
The rest can't escape
And meet their nemesis.

THE SĀKHĪS

NOTES

1. In the *Ramāyaṇa* Tulsīdāsa says:
Umā kahauṁ maiṁ anubhava apanā
sata hari nāma jagata saba sapanā
('O Umā—(Parvatị) I tell you what I have felt—Rāma's name is the truth and the world is false as a dream') And again, *mahāmantra joi japata mahasū*
kāsīṁ mukuti hetu upadesū (*Bālakāṇḍa*)
(This is a great *mantra* (chanting of Rāma's name) which Shivā keeps ever chanting, and which through him has assumed the power of giving *mokṣa* to those who die in Kashi). Pārvatī (Shiva consort) was a Viṣṇu devotee, whose name she would chant a hundred times before her meals. Śhiva once called her when she was chanting Viṣṇu's name. She told the messenger that she would come after she had completed the chanting. Shiva sent the messenger back telling her that chanting Rāma's name once was equivalent to chanting Viṣṇu's name a hundred times, so she should say 'Rāma' once and come straightaway.
2. Hinduism believes in the karma doctrine, i.e., one suffers punishment for the evil actions of previous lives. Karma is of three kinds, 1. *prārabdha* which must bear fruit for works already done. it's like an arrow which has left the archer's bow and so can't be taken back So punishment for *prārabdha* can't be avoided. Then there is 2. *sañcita* karmas which are works accumulated from previous lives which will bear fruit when the time for their so doing comes Thirdly, 3. *kriyāmāṇa* karma which a person keeps performing in the present life. They will bear fruit either in that very life or later. By taking shelter in the Lord the second type of karma can be wiped out by his mercy and grace, and since the person begins to live a virtuous life devoted to God, he does not do evil and there are no bad *kriyamāṇa* karmas.
3. Saints often liken the Absolute to the thunderbolt and the mind to a gem. Thus the idea is that the mind which is split between the divine and the worldly should be made one with the divine.

4. *pārasa* is the legendary stone believed to turn iron into gold by its mere contact.
5. A *rabāba* is a kind of stringed musical instrument which was popular in India during the Moslems rule. It came to India from Iran, and was a cross between the *sārangī* and the *saroda*, being played sometimes by a bow and sometimes twanging it with the finger on which a triangular metal device was attached.
6. A *rahaṭa* or Persian wheel is meant to draw water from a well. It has several hollow bucket-shaped vessels attached to a strong belt which goes round emptying each bucket as it reaches the top.
7. *na tatra sūryo bhāti na candratārakana*
   nemā vidyuto bhanti kuto yamagniḥ
   tameva bhantimanubhāti sarvama
   tasya bhāsā sarvamidama vibhāti
   Kaṭha Upniṣad 5.15.
   ('Neither the sun, nor the moon, nor the stars shine there; nor these lightnings and much less this fire. When that (the Cosmic Absolute or *Brahman*) shines then everything shines afterwards. It is by Ḥis light that all this is lighted').
8. *yadā paśyaḥ paśyate rukmavarṇa*
   kartaramīśama puruṣa brahmayonim
   tadā vidvān puṇyapāpe vidhūya
   niranjana parama sāmyamupaiti
   Muṇḍaka Upniṣad 3.1.3.
   ('When the seer realizes the light that shines by itself, which is the master and creator of the universe, he shakes off both good and bad deeds and becomes pure and one with the Supreme')
   Dr Raymond Moody MD (*Life after Life* USA: Bantam Books, 1976 pp., 58-59) who made a detailed study of people declared dead, but who came back to life says the souls of such people meet with a being of Light. He says: 'Despite the light's unusual manifestation (an indescribable brilliance which does not dazzle), however, not one person has expressed any doubt whatsoever that it was a being, a being of Light. Not only that, it is a personal being. It has a very definite personality'.
9. According to the Tantra doctrine the 'thousand-petalled lotus' is on the upper part of the head. How then does Kabīr say *antari kaṁvala*, i.e., the lotus inside the body'? For this we find a parallel in the *Chāndogya Upaniṣad* (chapter 8, section1, vv., 1-5) as follows (only the translation in

English is given): 'There is a mansion in this city of *Brahman* of the shape of a small lotus with a subtle ether-like space (*ākāśa*). That which is inside this lotus should be sought.... This *ākaśa* within the heart comprises the sun, the moon, heaven and earth, fire and air, the lightning and stars; in brief whatever exists in the universe... This inner *ākāśa* does not age or die. It is the *Ātman* free from old age, death, sorrow, hunger and thirst, and its desire is only for the truth'.

Much the same thought is contained in the *Śrīmadbhāgavata* (10.87.18):

udaramupāsate ya ṛṣivartmasu kūrpadṛsaḥ
parisarapadhatima hṛdayamāruṇayo daharam

Thus Kabīr is referring here to the soul within. As the *Chāndogya Upaniṣad* 8.1.6 says: *ye iha ātmānam etan satyan kāmān cha anuvidya vrajanti teṣām sarveṣu lokeṣu kāmacāraḥ bhavati* ('They who die after having understood the Soul and who desire to know it here can have perfect freedom to do as they wish in the three worlds'). But such seekers of the Soul, says Kabīr, are rare, and only those who have learnt of it at the guru's feet can know it.

10. The ancient belief, now discarded, was that a drop of rain was received by the oyster as it rose to the sea's surface. This drop entered the two halves of the oyster-shell and formed a pearl. Kabīr refers to this traditional belief (though now we know that the pearl is formed by some irritant like a grain of sand entering into the oyster, and being unable to drive it out, it keeps covering it with layers of nacre (mother-of-pearl) which is inside its shell. This brilliant nacre gradually take the shape of a pearl.

    The *svāti* raindrop is believed to fall very rarely in the winter when rain is scarce.

11. The *sahastrāra* is the topmost of the six *cakras* believed to lie in the spinal column. This *cakra* is in the upper part of the head.

12. The *kuṇḍalinī*, spoken of by Sir John Woodroofe, the distinguished writer on Tantra yoga, as the 'serpent power', when woken by yoga pierces these *cakras* and when it reaches the *sahastrāra* the yogi experience the bliss of *Brahman*. See also note to *Padas-Rāga Āsāvarī*, *Pada* no.,1.

13. For *sahastrāra* see note to the previous verse

14. The *guṇas* are three—*sattva* (purity and goodness), *rajasa* (passion or activity) and *tamasa* (sloth).

15. The mind-stuff (*antaḥ-karaṇa*) is that power of the mind which enables it to discriminate between right and wrong

and follow the right path. The Infinite is the Cosmic Absolute.

16. For *kuṇḍalinī* and *sahastrāra* see note to verse 4 *ante* of *Sākhīs* (4) Insight.
17. For *sahastrāra* see note to v.4 *ante* of this section.
18. For *anāhata* and *śunya* see *Pada* no. 1 *Rāga Āsāvarī*.
19. For the *kuṇḍalinī, mulādhāra, sahastrāra* and *suṣumnā* see notes to v.,4 of this section and *Pada* 1 *Āsāvarī Rāga*.
20. According to another interpretation the drawer of the water from the well (*panihārini*) could be taken to be the tongue, the well the cavity in the head from which nectar keeps dripping, and the person who tastes the nectar's bliss, one who practises *khecarī*— a form of yogic rite in which the tongue is turned upward to touch the upper palate and the gaze fixed between the eyebrows. But this interpretation is not as suitable as the one contained in the translation. The word *śūnya* (lit., nothingness) is a *tāntrik* term denoting the state of perfect quietude of the mind when all thoughts are stilled.

    It is strange that in this and other *Sākhīs*, Kabīr shows such intimate knowledge of such an esoteic practice as Tantra, particulary when he was unlettered. Ironically he condemns Tantra, *mantra* etc., at some places, but in quite a few verses praises them! This depicts one of the many contradictions in him.
21. *Bhagavadgītā* (3.36-37) Arjuna asks Krishna 'what makes a man sin forcibly even when he doesn't want to?' And Krishna tells him that the culprits are desire and rage which are the foes of man and most evil and insatiable:

    atha kena prayukto ayam pāpama carati puruṣaḥ
    anicchannapi varṣneṁya balādiva niyojitaḥ
    kāma eva krodha eva rajoguṇasamudbhavaḥ
    mahāśano mahāpāpmā vidhayenamiha vairiṇam

    This couplet is a little diffevent from the usual ones which are *dohas*. This one is a *soraṭhā*, i.e., a *dohā* reversed.
22. The five elements are air, earth, water, fire and ether
23. The uncrossable sea—the world of repeated births and deaths 'crossed' by getting *mokṣa*.
24. A *babūla* tree is a thorny one bearing no fruit, resembling the acacia tree. Apart from Hinduism, other religions also believe in divine judgment. The Holy Quran says, 'He who has done an atom's weight of good shall see it.... And we will set up a just balance on the day of resurrection so no soul shall be dealt with unjustly in the least, and though

there be the weight of a grain of mustard seed, we will bring it and sufficient are we to take account'... 'And the measuring out on that day will be just; then as for those whose measure of good deeds is heavy, they shall be successful. And as for those whose measure of good deeds is light, these it is that have made their souls suffer loss'. (Trans. Muhammad Ali. Lahore: Ahmadiyya Anjuman-I-Ishaat-I-Islam. 1928. 99-7&8, 21-47 and 7-8&9). According to Buddhism too escape from the consequences of karma (*kamma*) is not possible:

'Not in the heights of heaven, nor in the depth of the sea
Not in the caves of the mountains, taking refuge there,
Nowhere at all may be found a single corner of the earth,
Where, taking footing, a man may be loosed from his evil deeds'.

Nonetheless the doctrine of karma and rebirth in accordance with it, was most positively asserted by Hinduism. The *Rāmāyaṇa* of Tulsīdāsa says:

karama pradhāna visva kari rākhā
jo jasa karai so tasa phala cākhā (*Ayodhākāṇḍa* 2.18.2).

25. cf. The *Gītā*'s famous verse, 2:47.
karmanevādhikāraste mā phaleṣu kadācana
mā karmaphaleturabhūra mā te sanogstava akaramaṇi
('You have a right to works but not to the fruits thereof. Therefore do not make the desire for fruit the motive of your works, nor be attached to inaction')
roṭī (chappati) means unleavened bread which Indians generally eat in their meals. These can be smeared with ghee for taste—as buttered slices in the West.

26. cf., *Ode, Intimations of Immortality*
'Our birth is but a sleep and a forgetting;
The Soul that rises with us our life's Star,
Hath had elsewhere its setting,
And cometh from afar:
Not in entire forgetfulness,
And not in utter nakedness,
But trailing clouds of glory do we come
From God who is our home'.
William Wordsworth

27. cf., 'Death is of such kind as is birth, a mystery of nature' Marcus Aurelius (quod sibi ipsi scripsit, iv.5.) and Euripides says in *Phoenix, Fragment* 12,
'Living we know, but ignorance of death

Makes all afraid to leave the light of day'. And Shakespeare says 'Ay, but to die, and go we know not where' *Measure for Measure* Act 3, scene 1.

In the Gospel of Shri Ramakrishna we are told, 'Suppose God came to you as a man and says "I am God" will you believe it then? After his death Lazarus said to Abraham "Let me go back to the earth and tell my friends and relations that hell and afterlife exist". Abraham replied "Do you think they will believe you? They will say it is a charlatan who is telling them such things"'.

Thus, as Kabīr says, what the other world is like, will ever remain unknown.

28. cf., *Kaṭha Upaniṣad* 3.14 'This path is hard to tread. It's much like walking on a blade as sharp as a razor's edge'—*kṣurasya dhārā niśitā durtyayā durgam pathastat kavayo vadanti*.

29. The sense is similar to the idea contained in *Sākhī* 2 *ante*.

30. We see here again an example of the many contradictions in Kabīr. He strongly condemns arrogance and egoism in many verses yet here he depicts it in himself! Commentators add 'by the grace of God', i.e., it was with divine help that he overcame maya, but the wordings of the verse do not read so.

31. Although here Kabīr expresses himself strongly against idol-worship, quite often he speaks of singing the praises of those very gods whose idols they are, such as Rāma, Krishna etc., for example in one of his *padas* (not translated) he says:

mānasarovara taṭa ke vāsī
rāma carana cita jāṁna udāsī
mukatahal binu canca na lāvai
mauni gahai kai hari guna gāvai

('As the royal swan of Manasarovara lake eats only pure pearls so too Rāma's devotees who are pure in heart chant his name and sing his praises'.)

This seems to be one of the many contradictions in Kabīr, and a major one too. Sometimes he repudialed idol-worship and at other times appears to be for it.

32. There are three kinds of beliefs about God and the universe:

1. Deism—God creates the universe and then remains outside it. There are two—the world and God.

2. Pantheism—God created the universe and then entered into it. Thus the whole universe is God, and outside it there is nothing. All is God.

3. God is both immanent as well as transcendent. Kabīr did not believe in pantheism. God, he believed, is in the universe and yet remains outside it also. This is what the *Sākhī* denotes.
cf., *Chāndogya Upaniṣad* (3.12.36)
pādo asya sarva bhūtāni tripādasyāmūtama divi. 'This entire universe is only a quarter of him. Three-fourths is the heavens and the rest'). The *Śvetāśvatara Upaniṣad* has also the same idea. 'God surrounds the universe from all the four sides, and is also ten cubits beyond it'—
sa bhūmiṁ viśvato vṛtvā atyatiṣthdda-śādgulam. (*Śveta. Upa.* 3.14).

34. cf.,
'The cloud capp'd towers, the gorgeous palaces
The solemn temples, the great globe itself,
Yes, all which it inherit, shall dissolve
And like this insubstantial pageant faded
Leave not a wrack behind. We are such stuff
As dreams are made on, and our little life
Is rounded with a sleep'.
Shakespeare. *The Tempest* iv.1.

35. The sage Shri Ramakrishna also frequent couples woman and gold as the two hindrance in the spiritual quest. Godl (*kanaka*) is symbolic of wealth. 'It is "woman" and "gold" that bind man and rob him of his freedom. It is woman that creates the need for gold. for woman one man becomes the slave of another, and so loses his freedom'. (*The Gospel of Shri Ramakrishna*, p., 99')

36. The 'salutary' advice Kabīr gives to others in this *Sākhī* was hardly followed by him. From the sources about his life we have, he is said to have two wives and children too. The counsel given here hardly befits one who wasn't contented with one wife, as the poet Bihārī says (the *Satasaī*):
paṭa pāmkhai bhakha kāṁkarai, sapara parei saṅga
sukhī parevā puhami maiṁ, ekai tutī bihanga
('To be contented one must leave lust—simple food plain clothes and one wife. See the homely pigeon whose dress is just his feathers, grit his food and who's happy with just one mate'). But poets have their contradictions too and so why should one blame Kabīr alone, for Bīharī also says:
ya bhava pāravāra hauṁ, ulaṁghi pāra ko jāi
tiya-chabi-chāyāgrahinī, grahati bīca hīṁ āi
('How can a man cross the sea of births and deaths when woman, the temptress lies ever in wait to pounce on him')

Such are the quirks of wise men. However, this adds to the many contradictions one notices in Kabīr. One of his wives was a shrew. Maybe this verse is a reflection of his disgust with her.

SĀKHĪS FROM THE GURU GRANTHA SAHIB

kabīrā eku acambhau dekhio
hīrā hāṭa bikāi
banajanahāre bāharā
kauḍī badalai jāi

('I have seen a wonder, says Kabīr,
The Hari-shaped diamond is going cheap as a cowrie
In the worldly-shaped bazaar,
Because the saints who know its worth
Are not among the buyers')

SĀKHĪS FROM THE GURU GRANTHA SAHIB

1

kabīra kāgada kī obarī, masu ke karama kapāṭa
pahana borī pirathamī, paṇḍita pāṛi bāṭa

THE HYPOCRISY OF PUNDITS

See what the pundits have done, says Kabīr:
Their books of learning are like a room
Whose doors are the works they advocate;

They have submerged the world
In the ocean
Of stone images.[1]

2

kabīra kanacana ke kuṇḍala bane, ūpari lāla jaṛāu
dīsahi dādhe kāna jiu, jina mani nāhi nāu

THE GEM OF RĀMA'S NAME

The ear-ornament of gold
Set with rubies
Is splendid to behold

But if the ears
Do not hear
The name of Rāma
Of what use are they?

Says Kabīr, such ears are
As though burnt away.

3

kabīra aisā eku ādhu jo jīvita mritaku hoi
nirabhai hoi kai guna ravai jata pekhau tata soi

THE FORMLESS *BRAHMAN*

Some rare person, Kabīr says,
Is able to restrain his senses
So that they are dead
To sense-pleasures;

Who, abandoning fear,
Is endeared
To the Formless One,
And sees him
Everywhere.

4

kabīra bāṁsu baḍāī būḍiā iu mata ḍūbahu koi
candana kai nikaṭe basai bāṁsu sugandhu na hoi

DO NOT BE VAIN

Do not ride the high horse
Says Kabīr:

See,
The bamboo grows tall
Yet remains deprived
Of the perfume of the sandalwood tree,
Even though it grows
By its side.

5

kabīra haja jaha hau phirio kautaka ṭhāo ṭhāi
ika rāma sanehī bāharā, ūjaru merai bhāṁi

LOVE OF RĀMA

Says Kabīr,
I have gone on *haj*[2]
Many times,
And visited numerous places;

But to my mind
One who is bereft

Of the love of Rāma
Will stay desolate.

6

kabīra sūkhu na enha juga karahi ju bahutai mīta
jo citu rākhai eka siu te sukhu pavahi nīta

HOW TO BE HAPPY

Friendships
However many,
Will not bring happiness.

Only he finds
Eternal bliss
Says Kabīr,
Whose mind
Rests
In the Formless *Brahma*.

7

kabīra mānasa janamu duralabhu hai hoi na bāraibāra
jiu bana phala pāke bhui girahi, bahuri na lāgahi dāra

HUMAN BIRTH IS DIFFICULT

Birth as a human being
Is difficult, says Kabīr,[3]
It can't be got repeatedly,

As when the ripe fruit is severed
From a tree in the woods
It can't ever
Be on it again.

8

kabīra jhankhu na jhankhiai, tumaro kahio na hoi
kāma karīma ju kari rahe, meṭi na sākai koi

WE ACT AS GOD WILLS

Says Kabīr, what's there to fret about,
Or rue?
Things will not work out
As you wish them to:
You will do
What the divine will has ordained for you.[4]

9

kabīra garabu na kījīai, ūcā dekhi avāsu
āju kāli bhui leṭaṇā, ūpari jāmai ghāsu

VANITY

Do not pride
Yourself upon you stately house,
For in the end you'll lie
Beneath the earth
And the grass'll grow over it.

10

kabīra mai jāniyo paṙibo bhalo, paṙibe siu blala jogu
bhagati na chaḍau rāma kī, bhāvai nindau logu

RĀMA-DEVOTION IS BEST

Learning is good
And yoga is better
As I conceive it:

But even more I prize
Devotion to Rāma;
Let men deride
But I'll not leave it.

11

hāḍa jare jiu lākarī, kesa jare jiu ghāsu
ihu jaga jaratā dekhi kai bhaio kabīra udāsu

THIS WORLD OF SUFFERING

Bones burn in the holocaust
Of funeral pyres
And as withered grass
Hairs are afire.

So too burns this world
With passion and grief
Today and tomorrow.
Seeing this, Kabīra
Was filled with sorrow.

12

kabīra gangā tīra ju gharu karahi, pīvahi niramala nīru
binu hari bhagati na mukati hoi iu kahi rame kabīra

DEVOTION ALONE BRINGS *MOKṢA*

He who lives on the Ganga's bank
Can drink water which is pure,
Or else he can't.

So too, says Kabīr
One cannot get *mokṣa*
Without devotion to Rāma:

Therefore I have made
My heart Rāma's abode.

13

kabīra haradī pīratanu harai, cūna cihanu na rahāi
balihārī iha prīta kau, jiha jāti baranu kulu jāi

FORGET CASTE AND CREED AND BE ONE

If you apply a paste
Of turmeric and lime
On a wound.
The turmeric will take away
The pain, and the lime leave
Not a scar behind:

Thus the two opposed
In every way,
Will still combine
To heal.

So too all men
Are one
Whatever the differences
Between them.

O how wonderful, says Kabīr,
Is that love which unites
Men of various colours castes and creeds;
It's such love that I prize.[5]

14

kabīra mukati duārā saṅkurā, rāī dasaeṁ bhāi
mana tau maigalu hoi rahao nikaso kiu kai jāi

NARROW IS THE WAY TO GOD

The entrance to *mokṣa*
Says Kabīr,
Is tiny as a tenth
Of a mustard seed,
And my uncontrollable mind
Is like a rogue elephant;
How can it get through?[6]

15

kabīra supanai hū barrāi kai jiha mukha nikasai rāmu
tāke paga kī pānahī mere taṇa ko cāmu

DEEP DEVOTION

Says Kabīr,
I would part with my skin
For making the shoes of him
Who even while mumbling in his sleep
Utters the name of Rāma.

16

kabīra māṭī ke hama pūtare, mānasu rākhiu nāu
cāra divasa ke pāhune, baḍa baḍa rūṁdhahi ṭhāu

THE SENSELESS QUEST FOR LAND

Says Kabīr,
We are puppets
Made
Of mud, called 'men';
Two shakes
And we'll be gone;
Yet we long
To possess
And to retain
Land without end:
How strange!

17

kabīra pāpī bhagati na bhāvaī, hari pūjā na suhāi
mākī candanu paraharai, jaha bigandha taha jāi

THE SINFUL MAN

Says Kabīr,
To a sinful man
Neither devotion
Appeals
Nor does worship of Hari
Please:

He is like a fly
Who does not alight
On sandalwood,
But delights
To sit on dirt.

18

kabīra baidu kahai hau hī bhalā, dārū merai vasi
iha tau basatu gupāla kī, jaba bhāvai lei khasi

DEATH WILL COME WHEN GOD WILLS

The physician says 'I'll cure you';
But he does not know
That the Soul is God's[7]
And when *he* calls for it
It will go.

19

kabīra sāta samundahi masu karau, kalama karau banarai
basudhā kāgadu jau karau, harijasu likhanu na jāi

THE GLORY OF HARI

Says Kabīr,
If all the world was my paper
And my ink the seven seas,
And all the forest-trees

My pen;
Even then
I could not write
With these
The glory of Lord Hari.

20

kabīra hari kā sumaranu chāḍi kai pālio bahutu kuṭambu
dhandhā karatā rahi gaiā bhāī rahiyā na bandhu

PUT YOUR TRUST IN GOD NOT IN MEN

Says Kabīr,
Your thoughts were not for Hari
But for your family;
Only they were on your chest.

But when the end came,
Neither your brother
Nor your relations
Came to your help.

21

kabīra sabhu jagu hau phirio mandalu kandha caḍhāi
koī kāhū ko nahī sabha dekhī ṭhoki bajāi

THIS SELF-SEEKING WORLD

Says Kabīr, I went around
Everywhere,
Probing into men
Looking inside their minds
Fathoming them

As I would test
The genuineness
Of a *ḍholak*[8]
Slung across my breast
By its sound.

But alas! I found
Everyone for himself,
Caring for no one else.

22

kabīra dekhi kai kiha kahau, kahe na ko patīāi
hari jaisā taisā uhī, rahau harakhi guna gāi

GOD'S FORM IS INDESCRIBABLE

I have seen Hari;
But if I tell people
What's he like
What can it profit them?
Who will believe me, say?[9]

He is as he is, says Kabīr,
He can't be described
So I'll keep him to myself
And sing his praise.

23

kabīra kāli karantā abahi kara aba marantā su itāla
pīche kachū na hoigā jau sira para āvai kālu

DO NOT PROCRASTINATE

Says Kabīr, do today
What you've thought of doing tomorrow,
And do now
What you intend to do today:

For time does not wait;
And when death comes
All you failed to do
Will remain undone.

24

kabīra kauḍī kauḍi jori kai jorai lākha karori
calatī bāra na kachu milio laī langoṭī tori

THE VANITY OF WEALTH

Cowrie by cowrie
You salted away
Lakhs and crores;

But when death came
And 'twas time to go,
You could take
Nothing with you,
Not even your loin-cloth!

24 to 26

24. *kabīra roṛā huā ta kiā bhaiā panthī kau dukhu dei*
aisā terā dāsu hai jiu dharanī mahi kheha
25. *kabīra kheha hūī tau kiā bhaiā jau uḍi lāgai anga*
harijanu aisa cahīai jiu pānī sarabanga
26. *kabīra pānī hūā ta kiā bhaiā sīrā tātā hoi*
harijanu aisā cāhiai jaisā hari hī hoi

WHAT SHOULD HARI'S DEVOTEE BE LIKE

If there's gravel on the path
The wayfarer
Will find the going tough,
So it'd be better if instead
There was dust.
Such indeed
Should be the nature of Hari's devotee,
Says Kabīr.

But if there's dust
It will fly about
And spread muck;
So Hari's devotee
Should be such
As is water.

But water
Can at times be hot
And at times cold,
So Hari's devotee
Should be constant and controlled,
Like Hari himself!

27

kabīra kāma pare hari simarīai aisā simarahu nita
amarāpura bāsā karahu hari gaiā ahoraī bita

PRAY SELFLESSLY

You pray to God when
You want some work done;
Though you may yet gain heaven
Even by such devotion,
Remember, self-seeking
Cannot
Bring you near to God:
Says Kabīr;
He can't be bought
At the marketplace.[10]

28

kabīra sansā dūri karu kāgada deha bihāi
bāvana akhara sohdi kai hari caranī citu lāi

THE WAY TO GOD IS NOT THROUGH KNOWLEDGE

Knowledge can't lead you to God;
The fifty-two letters of the alphabet
Are of no help,
They are best forgot.

There are only two
That are of consequence
For you—
Hā and *rī*.[11]

Abandon doubt, says Kabīr,
And let your mind dwell on Hari's feet.

29

kabīra mulāṁ munāre kiā caḍhuhi sāīṁ na baharā hoi
jā kārani tūṁ baṁga dehi dila hī bhītari joi

AZĀN

O mullah,
Why climb the minaret
To call on Allah?
He is not deaf!

Says Kabīr, he abides
Within yourself,
Seek him inside.

30

sekha sabūrī bāharā, kiā haj kabai jāi
kabīra jā kī dila sābati nahī, tākau kahāṁ khudāi

MECCA IS IN THE HEART

O Sheikh,
Why are you rarin' to go
On *haj* to Mecca?[12]
Kabīr says,
He whose heart is not pure
Can't find Ḳhudā.[13]

31

kabīra khūba khāna khīcarī jāmahi amrita lonu
herā roṭī kārane galā kaṭāvai kaunu

BE CONTENT WITH WHAT IS YOURS

Says Kabīr,
Your own *khicharī*[14]
Is food enough
And the salt in it
Is as though nectar.

Why should you spoil for food
That is another's
However delicious?

32

kabīra haj kābe hau jāi thā, āge miliā khudāi
sāīṁ mujha siu lari pariā tujhe kinhi phuramāī gāi

ḲHUDA DOES NOT PERMIT COW-SLAUGHTER

I was no my *haj* pilgrimage
To Kaabaa,[15]
When Khudā met me on the way
And questioning me, said,
'Who allowed
You
To slaughter cows?'

33

kabīra jīa ju mārahi joru kari kahate hahi ju halālu
daphataru daī jaba kāḍhi hai hoigā kaunu havālu

SLAUGHTER OF ANIMALS IS EVIL

You slaughter animals
Wilfully
And say

'It's sanctioned
By my faith'.[16]

But, says Kabīr,
When you are called
To account for your deeds
What answer will you give?

Will this be believed
To be reason enough
For your cruelty?

34

kabīra merā mujha mahi kichu nahī jo kichu hai so terā
terā tujha kau saupate kiā lāgai merā

RENDER UNTO GOD WHAT IS GOD'S

Says Kabīr
Whatever I have
Is yours, Lord,
Nothing is mine:

So what do I lose
By returning you
What is yours?

35

kabīra koṭhe maṇḍapa hetu kari kāhe marahu savāri
karaju sāḍhe tīni hātha ghanī ta paune cāri

HOW MUCH LAND DOES A MAN REQUIRE?

Says Kabīr,
Why frazzle yourself
Looking after mansions and shelters,
When all the land that'll be yours
In the end
Is three and a half cubits,
Or maybe
Three and three fourths?

36

cintā bhi āpi karāhasī acintu bhī āpe dei
nānaka so sālāhiai ji sabhanā sāra karei

BRAHMAN, LORD OF THE UNIVERSE

He who gives us worries
Also removes them

Says Nānaka,
Adore that *Brahma*
Lord of the universe,
By whose command
All that is here, works.

37

sunu sakhī pia mahi jīu basai jīa mahi basai ki pīu
jīu pīu būjhahu nahī ghaṭa mahi jīu ki pīu

PERFECT LOVE

Listen friend,
My heart is with my lover
And he is in my heart
So I can't ever
Know if the two are apart![17]

38

hari so hīrā chāṛi kai karahi āna kī āsa
te nara dojaka jāhige sati bhākai ravidāsa

HARI–DEVOTION IS BEST

The sage
Ravidāsa rightly says [18]
That hell is the place
For those who do not prize
The diamond of Hari-devotion
And instead, have faith
In other gods.

SĀKHĪS FROM THE GURU GRANTHA SAHIB

NOTES

1. The *Sākhī* is more or less the same as *Sākhī* 1 under head 'The Removal of Illusion'. However the first line of the two *Sākhīs* are slightly different.
2. The *haj* is a pilgrimage to Mecca, the holiest place for Moslems, who are expected to go there at least once in a lifetime. Though here Kabīr says he has gone on *haj*, but at another place he says such pilgrimage is fruitless. Most probably he means the going on *haj* metaphorically and not in reality.
3. cf., Śhankarāchārya. *Vivekachuḍamaṇi* 'Three things difficult to attain are, humanity, desire for emancipation and the favour of spiritually endowed men. These three are acquired only by the favour of the gods'. (*sūtra* 3).
4. The verse raises an interesting question. Are we free to do what we wish ('I am the captain of my soul') or is it all predestined and we merely work out our destinies? In other words free will or fate? Here Kabīr favours the latter idea—'The Moving Finger writes and having writ, moves on, and so forth 'There's a destiny which shapes our ends'.
5. This verse of Kabir is very appropriate at the present times when in Western nations hatred exists between the blacks and the whites (apartheid) and in India among Hindus who maintain still more narrow compartment diving society into upper castes, scheduled castes, *dalits*, backward castes, other backward castes, tribals and even between them split up into hundreds of castes and sub-castes. Colour consciousness exists even in India and complexion is an important factor in marriage negotiations! The verse is similar to *Sākhī* 1 under heading 'Beyond Differences'.
6. cf., 'It is easier for a camel to go through the eye of a needle than for a rich man to enter into the kingdom of God' (*St Mathew* 19.24).
7. Here again we see Kabīr's confused attitude towards the nature of God. The word for God in the text is Gupāla (Gopala) which is another name for Krishna. Yet he vehemntly

denied avatar and idol-worship. A similar idea is contained in a parable of Shri Ramakrishna: 'God laughs..... when the physician says to the mother weeping bitterly because of her child's desperate illness "Don't be afraid mother, I'll cure your child". The physician does not know that no one can cure the child if God wills that he should die' (*The Gospel of Shri Ramakrishna*).

8. A *ḍholak* is a small drum with two faces frequently sounded on festive occasions when Indian women come together. It has adjustable bits of round wooden stumps tied around it, which are moved too and fro to get the most melodious sound.
9. In the Holy Bible Moses asked God: 'And Moses said unto God, Behold, when I come unto the children of Israel, and shall say unto them, the God of your fathers hath sent me unto you; and they shall say to me, what is his name? What should I say unto them? And God said unto Moses, I AM That I am: and he said, Thus shalt thou say unto the children of Israel, I AM hath sent me unto you' (*Exodus* 3.13-14). In the same way Kabīr says *hari jaisā taisā* u*hī*—'Hari is as he is'.
10. cf., *Bhagavadgītā* 7: 16-17
catura-vidhā bhajante māṁ janāḥ sukṛtino rijuna
ārto jijñāsura arthārthī jñānī ca bharatarṣabha
teṣāṁ jñānī nitya-yukta eka-bhaktir viśiṣyate
priyo hi jñānino 'tyartham aham sa ca mama priyaḥ
('Four kinds of virtuous persons worship me, O Arjuna; those distressed, those hankering after worldly things, those seeking wisdom and those eager to know my true nature. Of these that man is best who ever dwells in me with unswerving devotion, for I am very dear to him and his is dear to me'.)
11. There are fifty-two letters of the alphabet in the Hindi language. Hari has two letters— *hā* and *rī* (*ra*).
12. Mecca, the holiest place for Moslems. *Haj* is the pilgrimage undertaken by devout Moslems to Mecca.
13. Khuda is the name given to God by Moslems, equivalent to Allah.
14. *Khicarī* is a very simple dish made by cooking together pulse and rice. It is the poor man's diet, or sometimes eaten after recovery from some illness when simple food is needed.
15. Kaabaa is the holy spot for Moslems at Mecca which they venerate on their visit to that place. The pilgrimage to Mecca is called *haj*.

16. *halāla* means slaughter of an animal as a religious rite. Moslems carry out such slaughter calling it *korbānī* on festivals like Idd. Kabīr was against killing animals and deprecated the practice.
17. By 'lover' Kabīr means of course God and the beloved is the devotee. So too in the *Rāmayaṇa* of Tulsī, Sītā narrating her love for Rāma says 'Only my heart knows my love for you and that heart is always with you. Know my love by this', (*jānata piā eka mana mora, so mana sadā rahata tihi paīṁ, janu prīti rasa itanahi mahīṁ*).
18. Ravidāsa, was a devotee of Hari, and also wrote verses.

BIBLIOGRAPHY

General Observations on Books on Kabịr

Kabīr is known worldwide and apart from books in Hindi and English on him and on his writings, his works have been translated in European language like French, German, Italian and also in Russian. There are translations in Indian regional language too— Bengali, Panjabi, Sindhi and Tamil. Charlotte Vaudeville (*A Weaver Named Kabir*) Delhi: Oxford University Press gives a very exhaustive list of these works. We give in this bibliography only some of the principal books in Hindi, English and foreign languages.

Hindi

Anant, L.B. *Kabīr Granthāvalī* ed. Delhi, 1968.

The *Bījak* of Kabīr (some edns. only given)

(a) Light Press, Benaras, 1886.

(b) Nawal Kishore Press, Lucknow, 1972.

(c) Venkateshvar Press, Bombay, 1906.

(d) Ganga Prasad Varma Press, Lucknow 1872 commentary by Purandasa.

(e) Baptist Mission Kanpur, 1914 ed. Ahmed Shah.

(f) *Kabīr kā pūrā bījak.* Prem Chand Calcutta, 1890.

(g) *Kabīr Sahib kā bījak.* Belvedere Press, Allahabad, 1926.

(h) *Kabīr Sahab kā bījak.* commentary V. Shastri, Allahabad 1926

(i) *Kabīr Sahab kā bījak* ed. H. Shastri and M.Prasad. Kabir Granth Prakashan Samiti, Barabanki, 1950.

Das, S.S. *Kabīr Vacanavalī.* Benares: Kashi Nagari Pracharani Sabha, 1925.

Das, S.S. *Kabīr Granthāvalī.* Benares: Nagari Pracharini Sabha, 1928.

Hari, Viyogi. *Sant-sudhā-sār* New Delhi, 1953.

Gupta, Dr Mataprasad. *Kabīr Granthavāli* Allahabad: Sahitya Bhawan, 1985.

Gupta, M.P. *Kabīr Granthāvalī*, Agra, 1969.

Lakhandas, Sadhu. *Kabīr Sahab kī barī aur choṭi sabdavali*, Benares. Kabīr chaura.

Ramjīlal 'Sahayak' Dr, *Kabīr-Darshan* Lucknow: University (Hindi Dept.), 1962.

Raghavadas, Maharaj. *Sadguru Kabīr Sahab kā saṭīka sākhī Granth.* Benares, 1950.

Shastri, V. Sadguru Kabīr Sahab kā *sākhī-sangraha.* Benares 1950.

Singh, P. *Kabīr Granthāvalī saṭīka*, Delhi, 1965.

Singh, Dr J. and Dr Vasudeva. Kabīr Vānī *Pīyūṣa.* Varanasi, 1976.

Tiwari, P.N. *Kabīr Granthāvalī.* Allahabad: Hindi Parishad, 1961

Tiwari, P.N. *Kabīr-saṅgraha* ed. Allahabad, 1954.

A. Upadhyay 'Hariaudh'. *Kabīr-vacnavalī* ed. Benares: Kashi Nagari Pracharanī Sabha, 1947.

Kabīr Sahab ki sabdāvalī (4pts.) Belvedere Press Allahabad, 1907. (Many Reprints).

Varma, R.K. *Kabīr Padāvalī* ed. Allahabad 1954.

Varma Ramakumar. *Sant Kabīr.* Allahabad: Sahitya Bhawan Ltd. 1947.

Yugalanand, Swami (2pts) ed. *Satya Kabīr Sahab kī sākhī.* Lucknow 1899. Bombay 1908 (Reprinted many times).

Indian Regional Language Editions

Bhattacharya, P. *Kabīr.* Calcutta 1890 (Bangalā).

Gyani, Nihal Singh. 243 *slokas* found in the Guru Grantha Sahib in Gurmukhi with Panjabi trans. and commentory. Lahore, 1986 (Punjabi)

Mukhopadhyay, U. *Dohāvalī. Galcutta*, 1901, (Bangalā)

Kabīr Sahib Jī kā ślok with Sindhi trans. Hyderabad (Sind) 1924 (Sindhi).

Sen, K.M. *Kabīr* (3pts.) Calcutta, 1910. *Kabīr ke pada* (3pts). Shantiniketan Series, 1920 (Bangalā)

Singh, Mohanram. Kabīr Kamāl dāsa kirta naigal. Kundur, 1897 (Tamil)

Yogendranath Sarkar. *Kabīr.* Calcutta, 1893. (Bangalā)

English

Chand, Prem. A translation of Kabīr's Complete *Bījak* into English. Calcutta, 1911.

Hess, Linda. *The Bījak of Kabīr* (English trans. San Fransisco. North Point Press, 1983.

Jhabwala, J.H. Translations of Hindi text into English, Bombay.

Lal, Lala Kanoo. *One Hundred and seventy-five Moral Sayings of Kabīr*. Madras, 1923.

Macauliffe, M.A. *The Sikh Religion* 1909, Delhi 1963 vol.-vi

Machve, Prabhakar. *Kabīr* New Delhi: Sahitya Academi 1968.

Shah, Ahmed. *The Bījak of Kabīr* Hamirpur, 1917.

Tagore, Rabindranath. *One Hundred Poems of Kabīr*. London, 1914.

Trumpp. E. The *Adi-Granth*. London, 1877.

Uniyal, J.P. *Kabīr*. New Delhi, 1968.

Vaudeville, Charlotte. *A Weaver Named Kabīr*. Delhi: Oxford University Press, 1991.

Wilson, H.H. *Religions Sects of the Hindus* (Extracts from the *Bījak*)

Foreign (Non-Indian) Languages

Glasenapp, H.Von, *Indische Geisteswelt*. Baden-baden, 1958, vol.1. (German)

Lipkin, S.L. *Lirika* Moscow, 1965. (Rusian)

Mirabaud-Thorens. *Cent Poèmes de Kabīr. traduits de I' anglais*, Paris, Gallimard 1922 (Tran. From Rabindranath Tagore's *One Hundred Poems of Kabīr*. (French)

Vaudeville, C. *Kabīr Granthāvalī Dohā* Institut Français d'Indologie Pondichery, 1957 (French)

Paroles De Kabīr UNESCO Collection Paris, Gallimard, 1959 (French)